INVERCLYDE L

D0719563

KILMAC(

27 FEB 2014	25 MAR 2014	10 OCT 2014
17 APR 2015	3 JUN 2016	17 JUN 2016
28 OCT 2016	22 JUN 2019	

INVERCLYDE LIBRARIES

This book is to be returned on or before
the last date above. It may be borrowed for
a further period if not in demand.

For enquiries and renewals Tel: (01475) 712323

Inverclyde Libraries

34106   003063778

The Bedside
Guardian 2013

The Bedside Guardian 2013

EDITED BY MARTIN WAINWRIGHT

guardianbooks

Published by Guardian Books 2013

2 4 6 8 10 9 7 5 3 1

Copyright © Guardian News and Media Ltd 2013
Foreword copyright © Carol Ann Duffy 2013

Martin Wainwright has asserted his right under the Copyright, Designs
and Patents Act 1988 to be identified as the editor of this work

This book is sold subject to the condition that it shall not,
by way of trade or otherwise, be lent, resold, hired out, or otherwise
circulated without the publisher's prior consent in any form of
binding or cover other than that in which it is published and
without a similar condition, including this condition,
being imposed on the subsequent purchaser.

First published in Great Britain in 2013 by
Guardian Books
Kings Place, 90 York Way
London N1 9GU

www.guardianbooks.co.uk

A CIP catalogue record for this book is available from the British Library

ISBN 978-1783-56003-5

Cover design by Two Associates
Typeset by seagulls.net

Printed in England by CPI (UK) Group Ltd, Croydon, CR0 4YY

Contents

WINTER

SUMMER

Foreword

CAROL ANN DUFFY

British newspapers can be imagined as a Hall of Mirrors, reflecting us back to ourselves in grotesque, hilarious, tragic or noble display; but there is one among them which tells us we are fairest of all. The *Guardian*, it seems to me, is the only of our newspapers truly loved by its readers. Founded in Manchester in 1821, in the aftermath of the Peterloo Massacre, its guiding principle was famously re-iterated by the great editor C. P. Scott on the *Guardian*'s first centenary: 'Comment is free but facts are sacred.' This independence and fairness, which the *Guardian* has protected and cherished for nearly 200 years, define the soul of this newspaper and, I would argue, have never seemed so nationally and internationally important. The *Guardian* is at the forefront of investigative journalism of the highest order (in recent times, the Bradley Manning, News International phone-hacking and Edward Snowden stories) but it will also give several pages to contemporary poetry or the visual arts. It is a civilised and civilising presence in our public life. In this year's selection for our bedsides, Martin Wainwright offers an educative, enthralling, entertaining celebration of the *Guardian* in 2013; from the appointment of the new Archbishop of Canterbury to butterflies on Wenlock Edge, by way of Michael Gove, the Bad Sex Award, J. K. Rowling and the Leveson enquiry. Also included here, at my request, is a contribution by Araucaria, the Reverend John Galbraith Graham, who used his crossword to announce his terminal illness to his readers. 'Araucaria has 18 down of the 19 which is being treated with 13 15.' The solutions were cancer, oesophagus, palliative and care. One could not point to a better example of the *Guardian*'s strengths – bravery, honesty, intelligence and pure class. As always, enjoy, love.

September 2013

Introduction

MARTIN WAINWRIGHT

It is exhilarating to be asked to do the impossible because there can be no very punishing criticism when you fail. Hence the cheerful spirit in which I accepted Alan Rusbridger's invitation to edit this year's *Bedside Guardian*, the 62nd in a venerable line.

Back in 1953, when the annual compilation began, it was the jealous monopoly of the literary editor. The then holder of that post, Ivor Brown, lamented that post-war paper rationing and tight budgets had 'cut down descriptive reporting in favour of the curt factual record'. He nonetheless found rich treasures in the 12- or occasionally 18-page daily papers which formed a manageable seam.

We cannot hope for such cosy work in 2013, although the 'bedside' notion is a comforting reminder of past times. The internet is none the worse for being taken with a mug of Ovaltine and the book is slim enough not to wake you up if you fall asleep with it propped on your duvet. But to choose the 'best' from the millions and millions of words and images now poured out by the *Guardian* online as well as in print, by readers and outside writers as well as the staff; I cannot claim such an achievement. This is more a 'representative' collection, a glimpse of our coverage of the year gone by.

It includes dashed-off blog chatter as well as crafted features which smell of the lamp, a neat paragraph of TV preview and a

Twitter stream. They combine to recall a year which saw momentous events to which the *Guardian* was central – the Leveson report and the Edward Snowden revelations – and others to which it applied its armoury of descriptive powers: Baroness Thatcher's death, the Egyptian crisis and the re-election of President Obama. Alongside these, there continued as vigorously as ever what Ivor Brown called 'grace, humanity and wit in lighter comment'. Nowadays a tweet can last as robustly as anything ever has in a profession whose very name – journalism – has the mayfly meaning 'of the day'.

Reassured by the thought of readers reaching for their tablets to widen my choice, I have imposed two rules: no more than one piece by any writer and roughly the same number of contributions by men and women. The second stems from my time as the first chair of the National Lottery Charities Board in Yorkshire and the Humber when our committee had to be half-and-half. Until such time as equality of opportunity is a reality, this is a powerful means to that end.

As the paper's northern editor for 18 years, I have also kept a watch for northern writers and matters, and for that reason it is doubly welcome that this year's foreword is by Carol Ann Duffy who lives and works in the *Guardian*'s native city of Manchester. She would be honoured were she to live at Charing Cross or even in Islington, an area once subjected to a news-ration by the paper at a time of unusual sensitivity about its metropolitan ways. But to have the poet laureate in Manchester is enormously important to the regions, especially the north, in the same way as Hockney in Bridlington, the BBC (and let us hope the new Press complaints body) in Salford or the debut of the test-tube baby at Oldham and the hip joint replacement at Wrightington near Burnley.

The *Guardian* has gone triumphantly global. Now for a similar tonic at its roots, the primary source of its radical, restless and distinctive place close to but apart from those who wield power.

Warmest thanks to Lindsay Davies of Guardian Books whose skill, speed and decisiveness while I havered ensured that this *Bedside* appeared on time. Roger Tooth, the *Guardian*'s head of photography, was similarly generous and the book owes a special debt to the many people who suggested entries and spotted pieces which I had missed. These included many of the *Guardian*'s readers who contribute to the paper and website more than ever before, from comments on threads to photographs on GuardianWitness to conventional letters such as David Larder's which is one of the most powerful pieces in this collection. Thanks too to Jonathan Baker for his typesetting skills and Sophie Lazar for her meticulous copy editing; I am old enough to light a candle for the days when the *Guardian* had an entire proof-reading department (even though it was unable to save us from *Private Eye*'s well-merited 'Grauniad' jokes). The only definite editorial advice I was given was to include something about cats on the grounds that they unfailingly 'generate traffic' on the internet. This I have done, with a mouse story added for balance.

September 2013

Autumn

Michael Gove – the next Tory leader?

DECCA AITKENHEAD

These are some of the things we know about the rising star of the Tory party. David Cameron's glittering understudy outshone the future PM at Oxford, where he was elected president of the union. During a distinguished career as a political journalist, he became the unlikely star of a satirical TV show, and continued to write a newspaper column after becoming an MP. Affectionately indulged across the Westminster spectrum on account of his charm, his personal appeal transcends party loyalty. Contrary to popular opinion, however, his name is not Boris Johnson.

'People keep talking about Boris becoming prime minster,' reflects an Oxford contemporary. 'But I think it's going to be Michael Gove.'

If you have never met the secretary of state for education, and do not vote Tory, you may well be of the view that Gove is a nasty little rightwinger with a reactionary vision to return Britain to the 1950s. If so, the description I hear from practically everyone who has ever crossed his path will sound unrecognisable.

'I have only nice things to say about him,' is the preface I hear time and again. Gove is, Chris Huhne says, 'The politest man in the House of Commons. Incredibly well-mannered. Much more so than people who come from grander backgrounds.' A senior Labour figure tells me, 'The truth is, he doesn't act like a Tory. He is far too decent. He's in politics for all the right reasons.' The political columnist Matthew d'Ancona agrees: 'He is just an

incredibly nice guy. A lot of people are very nice guys, "but" –
and with politicians that can have a very big capital B. But he
is an absolutely nice guy. He's not a fair-weather friend at all,
he's fundamentally loyal, he is a very empathetic character and
very solicitous of people's feelings. I'm yet to come away from
a gathering where he hasn't charmed everybody in the room.
Michael is very ironic and incredibly good at taking the piss out
of himself; he's one of those people you hope will be at dinner.'

From those who knew Gove as a young child, right through
to colleagues today, the unanimity of opinion is almost freakish.
George Allan was Gove's headmaster throughout secondary
school, 'And when I see Michael on the television now, I can still
see the 11-year-old boy. He didn't change his persona throughout
his school career. Consistency – that's the word, consistency. We
couldn't claim to be the authors of his remarkable civility. He
created his own image.'

If Cameron fails to deliver a second term – and a clear Tory
majority in 2015 is looking like a tall order – there will almost
certainly be a new party leader. With the question of succession
becoming a very real issue, the education secretary is a very real
contender.

In August 1967, a baby called Graham was born in Edinburgh
to a young unmarried mother, and became Michael Gove four
months later, the adopted son of a couple in Aberdeen. A younger
sister was adopted five years later, and the Labour-voting family
lived in a small ground-floor flat in a tidy if austere grey terrace,
until his father's fish-processing business became successful
enough for them to move into a three-bedroom semi.

Gove attended his local state primary until the age of 11, when
he passed the entrance exam to Aberdeen's most prestigious
private school for boys. Robert Gordon's College dominates the

city centre, a relatively short distance from Gove's childhood home but a significant cultural leap. Every day the teenage Gove would set off from his little semi with its neat vertical white blinds and symmetrical hanging baskets, to an imposing granite colossus resembling a Soviet-style Eton. But he made the journey with remarkable ease. He rode an ancient bicycle, carried an umbrella, was fond of wearing suits, and quickly established himself as one of the school's most precocious characters.

Mike Duncan taught Gove English and debating, and remembers a star debater and 'endlessly enquiring' boy who enjoyed testing his teacher by reciting the opening line of a novel and challenging Duncan to name the book. Well read and self-consciously clever, Gove and his friends were big fans of sci-fi role-play games such as *Wargame*, and another called *Nuclear War*, which involved building up stocks of weapons and occasionally firing them off. A poem penned in his final year, 'An Essay On Teaching (With Apologies To Alexander Pope)', may or may not make teachers smile today, and satirical entries about the senior boys in 1985 suggest he and his friends were already enthusiastic subscribers to *Private Eye*:

> Michael Gove: His eventual entrance to Oxfam University has finally confirmed his place among mere immortals. He now earns his money tutoring Mr Duncan in English. Naked without his tweeds, it is Colonel Fogey's ambition to be a listed building when he grows up.

When Gove was invited back a few years later to take part in a debate, posters depicting a caricature of the *Ghostbusters'* ghost went up all over the school with the strap line: 'Take Govey down at the debate!'

'Michael was very much a wit,' one former classmate remembers, 'and a joy to have around. We were never intimates, but he was friendly, intelligent, a nice bloke. He wasn't cool or fashionable, but he was very popular because he would always have a funny rejoinder, and could outwit the teachers. My childhood memories are peppered with laughter because of Michael. One of the things I valued him for was that he prevented me from being bullied. I had glasses and red hair, and I vividly remember being bullied in the changing room, and Michael tried to stop it.'

Gove arrived at Lady Margaret Hall to study English in 1985. The novelist Philip Hensher can still recall watching the freshers arrive, and noticing one dressed in a three-piece green tweed suit. 'It was really a young fogey thing. He seemed a little bit older than he was, but not in a ridiculous way. If there was an element of absurdity to him, he always seemed to be in on it, which is a very attractive characteristic.'

Anthony Goodman was president of the Oxford union when Gove arrived. 'He was one of the most gifted speakers I saw in the union. But he didn't generate any antagonism; he was confident, but not in a pushy, aggressive way. He just seemed like an old head on young shoulders.' Goodman doesn't think Gove was contriving a performance to get in with the elite social set. 'That's pretty much why I did debating,' he jokes, 'but not Gove. He came across as classless.'

The broadcaster and journalist Samira Ahmed edited the union magazine under Gove's presidency, and sums up the consensus: 'I just didn't see why anyone could loathe him, personally. He was a 40-year-old trapped in a 20-year-old's body – but it was totally sincere. There's nothing fake about him at all. He exuded intelligence, and was very grown up for his age. And thinking big political thoughts, on a scale very few of us at that age were thinking. His vision was fully formed at 20.' Another contemporary, Toby Young, agrees. 'He wasn't a work in progress like the rest of us. He seemed to arrive fully formed.'

Gove encountered his first ever setback after graduation, when a job application to the Conservative Research Department was rejected on the grounds that he was 'insufficiently Conservative'. So he returned to Aberdeen and joined the *Press And Journal* as a trainee reporter. Within months, the paper went on strike.

The father of chapel, Iain Campbell, recalls the staff's initial unease about Gove. 'We knew he was a Tory, and our concern was to have a united front. So we spoke to Michael, and he was happy to come on board. He wasn't a typical striker by any means, but he was very articulate, so we asked Michael to come to the European parliament in Strasbourg to lobby MEPs. He was a very good colleague. Being on strike can be very mentally straining, so we used to have parties to keep morale up, and he was someone who would always be there, and always very popular.'

Gove has subsequently said he thought the strike achieved little, and for how long he would have stuck it out we'll never know, for within three months he was offered a job in television, and soon moved south to work for the political programme *On the Record*, and then the *Today* programme. In 1992 he was hired by Channel 4 to present a late-night political comedy show, *A Stab in the Dark*, somewhat to the surprise of his co-presenter, David Baddiel. 'I thought, I've never seen anyone on late-night alternative TV like this. He was rightwing and looked 53. I think he was wearing a three-piece suit. He wasn't cut from the obvious Tory cloth; he is a very bright bloke and a thinking rightwing person, and I'm always interested in intelligent people who think differently from me. I've had many rows with people I've worked with, but not Michael Gove. He was quite humble. He was always very unaggressive. Not trying all the time to intellectually defeat you in that way that politicians can.'

Around the same time Gove appeared as a chaplain in a feature film set in a boarding school. It was a tiny role, but he'd clearly made a big impression on someone along the way, because the lead schoolboy character was given the name M. Gove. Neither the film nor *A Stab in the Dark* were huge hits, though, and in 1996 Gove joined *The Times* as a columnist and leader writer.

Newspaper offices are notoriously fractious places, but staff remember an extravagantly congenial, donnish colleague who would soothe reporters late filing copy with, 'But how *are* you? Yes, of course, should you so wish to file that would be marvellous, that would be very much appreciated. But it's first important that I know how you *are*.' Very much the in-house intellectual, the 'most striking thing about him,' recalls his former editor, Peter Stothard, 'was that he could make people on the other side of the argument not only recognise his argument, but also genuinely like him.'

Gove became friends with the rising young Tory stars Cameron, George Osborne and Steve Hilton, and co-founded the centre-right think tank Policy Exchange. His influence over the party's modernisation project would be difficult to overstate. The exact nature of his contribution, however, is confusing. Everyone tells me his politics owe everything to his humble origins, and are 'all about creating ladders of opportunity; it's all about things you might call progressive, in terms of goals, but using Conservative means'. He is 'ideologically amphibious', interested in ideas from the left, 'on a moral mission, to do with helping the poorest', and responsible for helping to coax his party into the 21st century. Even his political opponents concur. According to a senior Labour party official, 'On sexuality and class and social mobility, on race and gender, he is a genuine liberal.' He is not, Huhne agrees, 'a traditional rightwinger.'

Then I read every word published under his *Times* byline up to his election in 2005, and found that Gove the progressive arch-moderniser simply does not fit with the facts. If you want to understand what Tory modernisation really adds up to, it's a highly instructive read.

Gove's neo-con hawkishness in foreign policy has always been well known. He called for the invasion of Iraq just two days after 9/11, and before the planes hit the towers he'd already published a column that morning calling for action against Saddam Hussein. A committed Zionist and slavish admirer of George W. Bush, a passionate Eurosceptic and staunch defender of British Gibraltar, he regards the Northern Ireland peace process as a shameful capitulation to terrorists, and once wrote a column calling for 'a revival of jingoism'. But where is the evidence in his writing of domestic social liberalism? It doesn't exist.

Passionately pro marriage, he opposes statutory paternity pay, stem cell research, euthanasia and contraception for school children, but supports privatisation of both the BBC and the NHS, and proposes the marketisation of immigration policy, whereby a British passport could, he suggests, be sold for £10,000. He is far ruder about the Lib Dems than New Labour, despairs of the 'absurd belief' that the armed forces ought to reflect the country they serve by recruiting more women and gay men, and takes a robustly bang-em-up approach to law and order. As for supporting public services, Gove can see only one acceptable line: 'The Conservatives could defend public servants from the unjust, unproven and demoralising charge of "institutional racism",' the Macpherson report being, in his view, an outrage.

Why, then, do so many colleagues and political opponents see Gove in this rosier, more moderate light? It has to be because of his debater's gift for according courteous respect to opposing views, creating the impression that he's taken them on board, when he hasn't actually revised his position at all. Everyone tells me how carefully Gove listens, but when asked to recall a single occasion when he has been persuaded to change his mind, to their surprise no one can come up with one. It is a case of manners maketh the impression of a moderniser, for Gove's Tories don't need to be 'inclusive', or 'tolerant'. The important thing is to look as if they are.

He warns the party against 'Social Tone-Deafness', which 'manifests itself in an inability to detect the country's changing mood music', and calls for candidates who 'look like human beings who understand the daily struggles of modern existence'. But a 2003 column tellingly reveals where Gove ranks the importance of actual policy reform: 'The Tories have not yet adopted a tone, style, culture *or even* [my italics] a set of policy priorities appropriate for the 21st century.' A Tory minister and friend of Gove's probably comes closest to the truth when he characterises him as a 'true Conservative, the rightwing conscience of the cabinet. He is a full spectrum, real world Tory; it's all about living in the real world. He would regard the Tory rightwing as completely unrealistic' – which is not the same as wrong. Labour MPs like to say Cameron's Conservatives have modernised on only one solitary issue – homophobia – and I used to think that had to be too cynical. But in all of Gove's writing it's the only example of an authentically abandoned prejudice.

What of Gove's famous passion for social mobility through education? 'His view on social mobility is for people to do what he did – study classical subjects and go to Oxford,' argues a Labour critic. 'It's all slightly "Some working-class people are terribly good at Latin – give them a chance and you never know!"' The former Labour schools minister Jim Knight agrees. 'If he thinks social mobility is getting more poor kids into Oxbridge, then I think that's a massively flawed definition. If you are serious about social mobility, it has to be communities and families, not just individuals.'

Interestingly, in 2000 Gove wrote, 'Too many people go to university', but his columns reveal surprisingly little about the future secretary of state's thoughts on education. For their origins, we need to go back further still, to his old school days. 'He benefited in a life-changing way from a classical liberal education,' as a close ally puts it, 'and would like that privilege to be extended to people from less privileged backgrounds.'

For all its architectural grandeur, Robert Gordon's College during Gove's era was actually Scotland's second cheapest private day school – 'more of a glorified grammar, really,' as a former pupil puts it. About half the boys joined from state primaries, and a quarter received a bursary or scholarship. George Allan and Mike Duncan both assumed Gove had been a scholarship boy, but in fact it was only when his father's business failed in his final year that the family applied for assistance. But every boy had to pass the entrance exam, and the school could operate on the assumption that all pupils would be not merely able, but disposed to work hard.

'When you enter Gordon's and start wearing the blazer and tie, you sort of absorb the traditions of the college,' a former teacher tells me. 'Those kids from poorer economic backgrounds tried to climb upwards, not pull the others down.' When I ask Allan what sort of disciplinary problems he used to deal with, he looks surprised. 'Well, if I had one a term, that was enough for me.' The current acting head says the worst he's encountered was a boy kicking about a plastic bottle who ignored his request to put it in the bin.

Gove has always spoken highly of his old school, and when I visit I can see why. But while I'm admiring its orderly classrooms and general air of cheerful application, a teacher puts into words what I find myself thinking. 'The trouble with anyone's own experience of school,' the teacher points out, 'is that it's so formative it informs all your ideas about education. That's very natural, but not necessarily a good thing.'

From the age of 11, Gove never shared a desk with anyone who struggled to read and write, or who experienced school as an intimidating trauma instead of a golden ticket. 'His prime concern is to make sure that there are safe schools in cities for people like him,' says a columnist who has followed his career closely. 'All this nonsense that free schools are free – they are not, they are Michael Gove schools. He is trying to create a system in which middle-class parents like him can make uses of the state system without having to mix with the rough boys.'

Following his election in 2005, Gove wrote, 'The reason why I'm in Parliament is not really to see my colleagues win power, it is to see us at last in a position where we can give it up.'

But since taking office, he has awarded himself more than 50 new powers, including rules allowing him to acquire land from local authorities and private companies to help him increase the number of academies and free schools. In autumn 2012, 55 new free schools opened, taking the total to 80, the number of academies having risen tenfold to more than 2,300, each one accountable not to local authorities, but to the secretary of state himself. 'He is a High Tory control freak who wants to run every school in the country,' counters the critic of Gove's 'free' school rhetoric. 'He hasn't got a localist bone in his body.'

There are other curious paradoxes. A friend for more than 20 years has never once heard him mention money, and says he regards it with unworldly indifference. But in 2002 Gove wrote about living perennially beyond his means – 'Ever since going up to university, I have accumulated new debt, and new means of becoming indebted'. And when the expenses scandal broke, it emerged that he'd spent £7,000 of taxpayers' money on designer furniture, much of it from Cameron's mother-in-law's interior design company.

Another puzzle was his use of private email addresses to communicate with his team. Everyone says Gove has a practically courtly deference to protocol, but he was plainly breaking the rules. Gove pleaded an innocent failure to master his own departmental technology, and his physical ineptitude is legendary; being driven by Gove is, apparently, a 'terrifying' experience. Whether techno-klutziness explains an arrangement that conveniently kept secrets from hostile civil servants, however, is unclear.

For a man known to be meticulously conscientious, Gove's ministerial career got off to an oddly bumpy start. In the early months, he drew criticism for awarding a grant to a Jewish schools security trust on whose advisory body he had sat (the trust received and administered the grant but made no financial benefit from it), and then there was the botched cancellation of the Building Schools For The Future programme, and confusion over the number of schools wishing to become academies. Gove blamed sabotage by his own department – in a colleague's words, a 'ministerial blooding'. But last year he hired a special adviser who'd been previously blackballed by Andy Coulson, called Dominic Cummings. 'And you could almost feel,' says a senior aide, 'that the moment Dom came to join him, things started getting back on track.'

Earlier this year, Gove leaked to the *Daily Mail* his plan to restore O-Levels, sidestepping departmental and Lib Dem opposition to court the rightwing press, whose praise was predictably rapturous. Issuing every school in the country with a leatherbound King James bible inscribed with the words, 'Presented by the Secretary of State for Education' surely did more for Gove's profile than for the nation's spiritual improvement. At £370,000, it was a pricey gesture, but private donors comprised almost exclusively of rightwing Christian financiers were happy to foot the whole bill. Gove's other big idea this year was pricier still – a new 60-million-pound royal yacht for the Queen as a diamond jubilee present. It was clearly never going to happen, but sent another signal to the right, as did his audacious hymn at the Leveson enquiry to the virtues of 'one of the most impressive and significant figures of the last 50 years', Rupert Murdoch. 'Cummings is a really amazingly effective political street fighter,' the aide says, 'the wily operator he needed. Since then, Michael has felt a new sense of confidence.'

Gove's confidence extends well beyond his existing role. Most cabinet ministers haven't the energy or political courage to discuss their colleagues' policies in any detail; Gove isn't one of them. 'Michael does have an opinion on everything,' says Tim Montgomerie, editor of *Conservative Home*, 'and he talks in cabinet a lot.' One cabinet minister describes him as 'being slightly inclined to go off on a bit of a rant off his own brief', and an aide describes his role as the 'energetic challenger – especially of the system, and of conventional wisdom'. And yet, says another minister firmly, 'I can't think of anyone who sees him as a political rival.'

How could Gove possibly not be seen as a political rival? He may be Osborne's closest ally, but in the opinion of one Lib Dem minister is 'substantially cleverer'. He is Cameron's 'closest friend in politics', helping him prepare for PMQs, feeding jokes into his speeches, and he 'can be quite dazzlingly funny, brilliant at doing impressions', a friend reports. 'I've heard him do what must be a set-piece, in which he does a great impression of Huhne condescending to Clegg in cabinet, that had the whole table in stitches. Genuinely funny satire.'

'The thing you have to appreciate about this group,' an insider explains, 'is that more than any other group in postwar politics, they are a clan. They are in and out of each other's houses, kids and nannies everywhere, they are each others' kids' godparents, their kids go to the same schools. The question of succession doesn't cross their minds.'

The question is whether it crosses Gove's. Just how far does Gove's ambition go? 'At Oxford it was obvious that some people were warming up for the Commons,' Samira Ahmed recalls. 'With Boris Johnson, his plan was obvious. But I never heard that said about Michael.' Former colleagues at *The Times* assumed for a while that he would become their editor, 'But he wasn't seen as someone angling for his own personal promotion at all.' Gove has always insisted he has no interest in leading his party, saying, 'I don't have it in me. I don't have what it takes.' And yet, as Matthew d'Ancona observes, 'You can never assume that a politician who has devoted his life to the game will walk away from the chance to be leader or PM. It's ridiculous for us to think that any politician might.'

A lot of very wealthy Tories presumably agree, for Gove's constituency office last year received five times the party's national average sum of donations. Individual and corporate donors gave Gove, who occupies one of the safest seats in the country, more than £60,000 – almost twice the sum received by Osborne's office and three times more than Cameron's. What exactly are they funding?

Nobody believes Gove would ever challenge Cameron for the leadership. And Gove had always assumed that, when the succession did come, the heir would be Osborne. But now that the chancellor is becoming unelectably damaged goods, and talk of a Johnson leadership bid gathers momentum, few think Gove would simply stand by and watch London's mayor move into Downing Street. If the party needs a Stop Boris candidate, it will be Gove.

Does he have what it takes? Former colleagues are unsure. 'He is an intellectual, not a man of the people, and whether he could operate in an environment in which not very many people knew who Spiro Agnew was I don't know.' I ask his old boss, and

Stothard chuckles. 'I think by common consent the job of home news editor wasn't his natural home. News editors, unless they're hated half the time, are not really on top of their job. Was Michael able to do the throwing the typewriter thing? No. He didn't have the temperament for that role. I don't really believe in pop psychology, so I'm reluctant to go into this very far, but he is quite thin-skinned. Perhaps too sensitive to be home news editor – or prime minister.'

Someone else who knows Gove well agrees that at first he tended to flap when things didn't go smoothly. 'This "I haven't got what it takes" line, I think what he was referring to was this thing of coping with the ups and downs and the crap you get. The relentless roller-coaster and inevitable failures. He previously might have been a bit insecure about his ability to cope with adversity, but I think that has gone now. I think that has changed. If you'd asked me 18 months ago, do you think he could and should aim to be PM one day, I would have said no. But now I think Michael could.' There's some speculation that the decision will ultimately fall to his wife, the *Times* columnist Sarah Vine, but no agreement on which way she'll go.

'I think she adores being a Tory wife,' says one friend. 'The more pictures she can be in with Sam Cam, the better her life becomes.' But another disagrees. 'I've heard people say that, but I don't think she's a scheming Machiavellian political wife, pushing her husband's career.' She has a funny way of going about it if she is, featuring marital anecdotes in her column that render him a faintly absurd eccentric.

The couple met at *The Times*, married in 2001, and live with their daughter and son, nine and seven, in a modest terraced house at the Wormwood Scrubs end of North Kensington, where dinner is 'a standard middle-class set up; completely informal, non matching furniture, child-centred, you can't move for books, the kids are usually up. Sarah does most of the cooking – meat and two veg or pasta, no bought-in food or waitresses or any of that nonsense – and Michael's pouring the wine. It's jolly and cosy and warm and about having fun.'

And if Vine's wider family wind up as Downing Street in-laws, then by all accounts they should provide fabulous entertainment. 'A totally mad, bonkers, crazy family,' a friend laughs. 'They're around in Michael's life in a soap-opera sort of way, fodder for amazing stories and anecdotes and hassle and problems.'

Gove's relationship with his parents has always been 'very tender and loving', another friend says. 'That said, I don't want to sound crude or pompous, but he has a metropolitan London life. There is a gap there.'

But Gove has never looked for his birth mother, and says he never will, out of loyalty to the parents who raised him. 'He is just not a very conflicted person,' another friend offers simply. 'I don't think there's a great deal of inner turmoil there. He regards life as having smiled on him.'

Gove has always been good-humoured about his place in the party's popularity stakes. In fact, he's so accustomed to coming second as the party faithful's choice of after-dinner speaker, he likes to joke that on his gravestone will be carved the words: 'They Couldn't Get Boris.' But though Johnson's sense of humour has got him a long way so far, few would bet on him having the last laugh. 'If you had told me Boris Johnson was going to be mayor of London,' reflects Anthony Goodman, their fellow ex-Oxford union president, 'I definitely would have laughed at you. If you had told me Michael Gove was going to be in government, I would have thought that was pretty obvious.'

9 OCTOBER

Wenlock Edge: in the beautiful sunlight of an October day, butterflies defy the gathering and inevitable gloom

PAUL EVANS

Like a punched ticket, the comma butterfly settled for a second. With apostrophes clipped out of its wings, it was the embodiment of autumn: sunlight through beech and chestnut leaves, earth dark with last night's rain, meadow seeds rattling in the breeze, a hint of late honeysuckle. The comma snapped into the air and was instantly joined by another and they both knot-danced away. It was as if the sun-facing hedges had shaken themselves out, flinging the lives which had been hiding in them into the light.

Speckled wood butterflies, dusty and greying, launched into one last reckless flight. Ruddy darter dragonflies were darting so ruddy fast they seemed to bend the light down a ruby needle. Thousands of hoverflies, true flies and bees with dark, stripy, shiny bodies and transparent wings set up a drone which vibrated through the air and cells of the body. A pair of red admiral butterflies, black, white and red, mirrored each other giddily and with the same colours as the greater spotted woodpecker which not so much perched as appended like an ornate jug handle on a telegraph pole. A brimstone butterfly, as infeasible as a swatch of sunlight, drifted up as charms of goldfinch and chaffinch clattered in and out of tall hedges with trees, holding their subdued little song wrapped up in a parcel.

This all had the feel of a one-last-time party, in which life burst from the shadows into the beautiful sunlight of an October day despite the gathering and inevitable gloom. There was also, in that autumnal melancholic way, a feeling that each of these lives was a memory: the ghost of another life or event or emotion dancing into one last flash of sunlight before fading away, to be swallowed back into the hedge and its darknesses. But not yet. This was a joyous resistance, a wild festival of the living light.

15 OCTOBER

Northern Ireland loyalist shootings: one night of carnage, 18 years of silence

IAIN COBAIN

Shortly after 10 p.m. on 18 June 1994, Ireland were 1–0 up against Italy in the opening match of the 1994 World Cup at the Giants Stadium in New Jersey. The second half had just kicked off, and inside the Heights Bar at Loughinisland, 21 miles south of Belfast, all eyes were on the television. The bar is tiny: there were 15 men inside, and it was packed.

Aidan O'Toole, the owner's 23-year-old son, was serving. 'I heard the door open and then I just heard crack, crack, crack and felt a stabbing pain inside me,' he recalls. 'I just ran. It was instinctive. I didn't know what was happening but I knew I had to get away.'

Others inside the bar turned when the door opened and saw two men in boiler suits, their faces hidden by balaclavas. One of the intruders dropped to one knee and fired three bursts from an automatic rifle. Barney Green was sitting with his back to the door, close enough for the gunmen to reach out and tap his shoulder had they wished. He took the first blast, with around nine rounds passing through him before striking other men. Green, a retired farmer, was 87.

Green's nephew, Dan McCreanor, 59, another farmer, died alongside him. A second burst killed Malcolm Jenkinson, 53, who was at the bar, and Adrian Rogan, 34, who was trying to escape to the lavatory. A third burst aimed at a table to the right of the door missed Willie O'Hare but killed his son-in-law, Eamon Byrne, 39. O'Hare's son Patsy, 35, was also shot and died en route to hospital. Five men were injured: one, who lost part of a foot, would spend nine months in hospital.

O'Toole returned to the bar from a back room after hearing the killers' car screech away. A bullet was lodged in his left kidney and a haze of gunsmoke filled the room. But he could see clearly enough. 'There were bodies piled on top of each other. It was like a dream; a nightmare.'

Loughinisland had been scarcely touched by the Troubles. A village of 600 or so where Catholics and Protestants had lived side by side for generations, none of its sons or daughters had been killed or hurt and none had been accused of terrorist offences. It is not a republican area; many of its Catholic inhabitants were so uninterested in politics that they did not vote even for the nationalist Social Democratic and Labour party and Protestants often drank at the Heights. Ninety minutes after the attack, a loyalist paramilitary group, the Ulster Volunteer Force, telephoned a radio station to claim responsibility.

Despite years of death and destruction in Northern Ireland, people around the world were shocked by the slaughter at the

Heights. The Queen, Pope John Paul II and Bill Clinton sent messages of sympathy. Local Protestant families visited their injured and traumatised neighbours in hospital, expressing shock and disgust.

The morning after the killings, the gunmen's getaway car, a red Triumph Acclaim, was found abandoned in a field seven miles from Loughinisland. The farmer who spotted it called the police at 10.04 a.m. The recovery of such a vehicle was quite rare during the Troubles and police were soon at the scene to take possession. There was no forensic examination of the area around the car, however.

A few weeks later, workmen found a holdall under a bridge a couple of miles away. Inside were three boiler suits, three balaclavas, three pairs of surgical gloves, three handguns, ammunition and a magazine. Not far from the bridge, police found a Czech-made VZ-58 assault rifle, which scientists confirmed was the weapon used to kill the men at the Heights. It had been used the previous October in a UVF attack on a van carrying Catholic painters to work at Shorts aircraft and missile factory in Belfast, in which one man died and five others were wounded.

In the months that followed the Loughinisland shootings, nine people were arrested, questioned and released without charge. A tenth was arrested and released the following year, and two more suspects questioned a year after that, all released without charge. The police repeatedly assured the families that no stone would be left unturned.

Emma Rogan was eight years old when her father, Adrian, was killed at the Heights. 'I was told that these bad men came into the bar, and that my daddy was dead. I didn't really know what they meant. We didn't question the police as I grew up: that's what this area is like. If they said they would leave no stone unturned, you took that at face value.'

By the time the tenth anniversary of the killings came around, Rogan was anxious to learn more about her father's death, and hear of any progress the police had made. A series of meetings was organised between senior investigators of the Royal Ulster Constabulary and the victims' relatives, and later more information emerged when the police ombudsman for Northern Ireland published a report in 2011 on the investigation. Relatives of the dead men came to the conclusion, as Rogan puts it, that 'they had treated us like mushrooms, keeping us in the dark for years'.

The getaway car had passed through four owners in the eight weeks before it was used in the shooting, changing hands so quickly that the first person in the chain remained the registered owner. The morning after the killings, a Belfast police officer was asked to call at this person's home. The officer did so, but found the man was out. The officer then recorded the time of his visit as 9.30 a.m. –34 minutes before a farmer had rung police to tell them he had discovered the car.

Some time between 11 a.m. and noon, a second police officer – a detective with no connection to the murder inquiry – telephoned the second person in the ownership chain, and asked him to come to the local police station to give a statement. How this detective came to know that the car had passed through this man's hands is unclear. But a statement was given, with a note attached to it saying that the individual who gave it could be contacted only through the detective who took it. The Loughinisland families argue this amounts to evidence that the person who gave this statement – one of the people involved in supplying the car used by the killers – was a police informer.

The *Guardian* has interviewed this man. He is Terry Fairfield, and today he runs a pub in the south of England. Fairfield confirms that he was a member of the UVF at the time, but denies he was a police informer. He says he did subsequently receive several thousand pounds from the detective, for helping him take a firearm and some explosives out of circulation. He accepts that being invited to attend a police station, rather than being arrested, was highly unorthodox. The detective says he had known Fairfield for years and contacted him after hearing of the Loughinisland shooting, but that only members of the murder inquiry could decide whether to arrest him.

A second man, who is widely suspected locally of having been in the getaway car, and who is also alleged to have been an informer, has also told the *Guardian* that he has never been arrested.

The families also question the failure to take samples from some of the people arrested for questioning. The *Guardian* understands that at least five of the men arrested in the months after the shootings were not fingerprinted before being released without charge. No DNA swabs were taken from either of the two people arrested in 1996.

One man, Gorman McMullan, who has been named as a suspect in a Northern Ireland newspaper, was arrested the month after the shootings and released without charge. He was one of the people who were released without being fingerprinted and no DNA swab was taken. McMullan firmly denies that he has ever been to Loughinisland or that he was ever in the getaway car, and no further action was taken against him in connection with the shootings. He acknowledges however that he was 'involved in the conflict'.

The police admitted to the families at one of their meetings that they had handed the getaway car to a scrap metal firm to be crushed and baled. They said this had been done because the vehicle was taking up too much space in a police station yard. That decision means it can never again be tested for comparison with samples taken from any new suspects.

Emma Rogan and Aidan O'Toole cannot believe that the destruction of the car or other failings in the investigation were accidental. They believe that this is evidence of police collusion. 'They knew exactly what they were doing,' Rogan says.

The families lodged a complaint with the police ombudsman for Northern Ireland. When the ombudsman, Al Hutchinson, published his report, it contained mild criticism of an investigation that displayed 'a lack of cohesive and focused effort'. To the anger of the families, it refused to state whether or not police informants were suspected of involvement and appeared to gloss over the forensic failures. It concluded that the destruction of the car was 'inappropriate', rather than evidence of corruption or collusion. The report was widely condemned in Northern Ireland. Hutchinson agreed to leave his post, and his successor is now reviewing the report. There will be no examination of the arms shipment that supplied the murder weapons, however, as the ombudsman's remit extends only to the police, not the army.

Much of the suspicion about British involvement in the 1987 arms shipment revolves around Brian Nelson, a former soldier who joined the Ulster Defence Association in the early seventies. In 1985, Nelson offered himself as an informant to the Force Research Unit, a covert section of the army's intelligence corps that recruited and ran agents in Northern Ireland. He quit the UDA the following year and moved to Germany with his wife and children. The FRU persuaded him to return to Belfast to rejoin the UDA as an army agent.

For the next three years, Nelson was paid £200 a week by the government while operating as the UDA's intelligence officer, helping to select targets for assassination. He informed his army handlers in advance of attacks: only two were halted, while at least three people were killed and attempts were made on the lives of at least eight more. A detailed account of this extraordinary operation appears in a report on the loyalist killing of the

Belfast solicitor Pat Finucane that Peter Cory, a retired Canadian supreme court judge, prepared at the request of the government in 2004. An FRU report from July 1985 discloses that the army paid Nelson's travel expenses when he travelled to Durban in South Africa that year to make initial contact with an arms dealer. 'The [British] army appears to have at least encouraged Nelson in his attempt to purchase arms in South Africa for the UDA,' Cory concludes. He adds: 'Whether the transaction was consummated remains an open question.'

In July 1987, the funds to purchase a large consignment of weapons were secured with the robbery of more than £325,000 from a branch of Northern Bank in Portadown, 30 miles south-west of Belfast. The proceeds of the robbery were to be used to purchase weapons that were to be split three ways between the UDA, the UVF and Ulster Resistance, a paramilitary organisation set up by unionists in response to the 1985 Anglo-Irish agreement.

What happened next is described by a former senior employee with South Africa's Armscor, a man who was intimately involved in the plot to smuggle the weapons into Northern Ireland. According to this source, officials in South Africa introduced a senior figure within Ulster Resistance to one of the corporation's representatives in Europe, an American arms dealer called Douglas Bernhardt. Bernhardt was not told where the money had come from, according to the Armscor source. 'When you get that sort of dirty banknote, you don't ask,' the source says. Bernhardt obtained a bank draft which was then sent to an arms dealer in Beirut, who had obtained the weapons from a Lebanese militia.

As the operation progressed, according to the Armscor source, Bernhardt would regularly call his Ulster Resistance contact at his place of work. This man would then call back from a payphone, and they would talk in a simple code, referring to the weapons as 'the parcel of fruit'. At each stage, Bernhardt is said to have been told that the arrangements needed to be agreed by John McMichael and his intelligence officer – Brian Nelson.

Bernhardt is said then to have travelled by ship to Beirut, where arrangements were made to pack the weapons into a shipping container labelled as a consignment of ceramic floor tiles. Bills of lading and a certificate of origin were organised, and the weapons were shipped to Belfast docks via Liverpool. 'There were at least a couple of hundred Czech-made AK47s, the VZ-58,' the Armscor source recalls. 'And 90-plus Browning-type handguns: Hungarian-made P9Ms. About 30,000 rounds of 7.62 x 39 mm ammunition, not the 51 mm Nato rounds. Plus a dozen or so rocket-propelled grenades, and a few hundred fragmentation grenades.' Sources within both the police and the UVF have confirmed that one of the VZ-58s was used at Loughinisland.

According to the Armscor source, the Ulster Resistance member who dealt with Bernhardt was Noel Little, a civil servant and former British soldier. Now in his mid-60s and living quietly in an affluent Belfast suburb, Little denies this. 'My position is that I wasn't involved,' Little says. But he adds: 'I would deny it even if I was.' He confirms, however, that he was a founder member of Ulster Resistance, and a central figure within the organisation at the time that the weapons arrived in Belfast. He also appears to possess detailed knowledge of the way in which the arms were smuggled and distributed.

The weapons arrived in Belfast in December 1987, a few days before McMichael was killed by an IRA car bomb. Early in the new year, they were split three ways at a farmhouse in County Armagh. The UDA lost its entire slice of the pie within minutes: its share of about 100 weapons was loaded into the boot of two hire cars that were stopped a few minutes later at a police road-block near Portadown. The three occupants were later jailed, with their leader, Davy Payne, receiving a 19-year sentence.

The following month, police recovered around half the UVF's weapons after a tip-off led them to an outhouse on the outskirts of north Belfast. Fairfield says he recalls being shown what remained of the UVF's new arsenal, in storage at a house in the city that was being renovated. 'I made the mistake of touching one,' he says, adding that this could result in him being linked to the October 1993 killing outside the Shorts factory. Little was also arrested, after his telephone number was found written on the back of Payne's hand. 'John McMichael had given it to him, in case he got into any trouble in Armagh,' Little says. 'I lost three-quarters of a stone during the seven days I was questioned. The police put me under extreme psychological pressure.' Eventually, he was released without charge. Little says that the Ulster Resistance's weapons were never used. 'They were for the eventuality of the British just walking away after the Anglo-Irish agreement was signed.' As far as he is aware, the consignment has never been decommissioned.

The following year saw Little arrested again, this time in France, in dramatic fashion. He had travelled to Paris with two fellow loyalists, James King and Samuel Quinn, to meet Bernhardt and a South African intelligence officer operating under the name Daniel Storm. Officers of the French security agency, Direction de la Surveillance du Territoire (DST), seized the three Ulstermen and the South African in a raid on a room at the Hilton International, at the same moment that Bernhardt was being grabbed in the foyer of the Hotel George V.

The five had been caught red-handed attempting to trade stolen parts from the sighting system of a ground-to-air missile that was under development at the Shorts factory. The apartheid regime wanted to use the parts in the development of its own missile for use in Angola, where its ground forces were vulnerable to attack by Cuban-piloted MiGs. 'This deal was about speed,' says the Armscor source. 'If you've got Cuban-piloted jets whacking your troops in border wars, you don't have the luxury of saying: "We'll have a research programme over time." You've got to speed up the R&D.'

Storm was set free after claiming diplomatic immunity, while the others were interrogated in the basement of the DST's headquarters in the 15th arrondissement. 'I was slapped about a little,' says Little. 'But not too much.' The DST told Bernhardt it had listened in on a meeting the previous night, through a bug in the chandelier of the room at the George V where the men had gathered. 'They knew all about the fruit code used in 1987,' the Armscor source says. 'They thought the talk about pineapples was a huge joke. They must have been monitoring the phone calls. And they knew all about Lebanon.'My guess is that the British were intercepting those phone calls. But the British didn't get all the weapons. How much did they know in advance? Why didn't they move more quickly? Maybe they were perfectly happy to have that material sort of 'arrive', and put into the hands of the loyalists. Christ knows, the IRA had had enough of their own shipments, everywhere from Boston to Tripoli.'

Noel Little also suspects the British turned a blind eye to the 1987 arms shipment. 'It is a theory I can't discount,' he says. 'Brian Nelson was inserted into the UDA as an agent, he wasn't a recruited member. How could he know about it and not tell his handler?' Little believes that his attempt to hand over stolen missile technology to Armscor in Paris – straying into 'secrets and commerce', as he puts it – would have been a step too far for the British authorities, obliging them to tip off the French.

After eight months on remand, the four men were brought to court charged with arms trafficking, handling stolen goods and terrorism-related conspiracy. Bernhardt told the court that he had helped arrange the Lebanese arms deal for loyalist paramilitaries in 1987. The four were sentenced to time served and fined between 20,000 and 100,000 francs (£2,000–£10,000 then).

Brian Nelson was finally arrested in January 1990 after John Stevens, then deputy chief constable of Cambridgeshire, had been brought in to investigate collusion between the security forces and loyalist paramilitaries in Northern Ireland. While awaiting trial, Nelson wrote a journal in which he recounted his time as an army agent inside the UDA. 'I was bitten by a bug ... hooked is probably a more appropriate word. One becomes enmeshed in a web of intrigue, conspiracies, confidences, dangers ...'

After flying to Durban in 1985, he wrote, his South African contacts had asked whether he would be able to obtain a missile from Shorts. Two years later, while talking about the South African connection with 'Ronnie', his FRU handler, he had been told that 'because of the deep suspicion a seizure would have aroused, to protect me it had been decided to let the first shipment into the country untouched'. Nelson added that 'Ronnie' assured him that the arms consignment would be under surveillance.

In 1993, an intelligence source told the BBC that this had happened: the consignment had indeed been under surveillance by a number of agencies, but the wrong port was watched, with the result that the weapons slipped through. At Nelson's eventual court appearance, a plea deal resulted in Nelson being jailed for 10 years after he admitted 20 offences, including conspiracy to murder. Murder charges were dropped. More than 40 other people were also convicted of terrorism offences as a result of the Stevens investigation. They did not include any of the intelligence officers for whom Nelson worked.

Stevens' investigation team was well aware of concerns surrounding the importation of the weapons. Members of the team talked to former Armscor officials in South Africa, but concluded that an investigation into the matter was so unlikely to produce any results as to be fruitless. However, a senior member of the inquiry team says he believes it feasible that the UK authorities could have been involved in bringing the weapons into Belfast, or at least turned a blind eye. 'It's not at all far-fetched,' he says.

By the time of the Loughinisland massacre, loyalist gunmen with access to the Armscor arsenal were killing at least as many people as the IRA. Czech-made VZ-58 assault rifles were used in many of the killings. A few weeks after the shootings at the Heights Bar, the IRA announced a ceasefire. Many in Northern Ireland are convinced that the importation of the Armscor weapons, and the large numbers of killings that followed, contributed greatly to the IRA's decision. Among them is Noel Little, who says: 'There's no doubt that that shipment did change things.'

With the Loughinisland families no nearer to discovering the truth about the deaths of their loved ones following publication of the ombudsman's report, they embarked on their civil actions against the Ministry of Defence and the police in January this year. Their lawyer, Niall Murphy, says: 'The experience of these six families demonstrates that the current mechanisms for truth recovery do not work.'

Rogan and O'Toole remain tormented by the events of June 1994. 'The people who died in this room didn't know anything about the Troubles, and yet they were slaughtered,' says Rogan. O'Toole, who still has a bullet lodged in his kidney, becomes emotional when he walks into the Heights Bar. 'It's guilt,' he whispers. 'They died in here, while I was keeping the bar.'

Em Grundy's cupboard is bare except for some own-brand biscuits. I am aghast

NANCY BANKS-SMITH KEEPS UP
WITH RADIO 4'S *THE ARCHERS*

Money is skintight in Ambridge. Even at stately Lower Loxley, bookings are down ('We'll have to say "No" to jam sponges!'). Someone who would not say no to a jam sponge is Ed Grundy, who is subsisting on chickpea soup and butter bean casserole, very much like the cowboys in *Blazing Saddles*.

Em Grundy, though evidently a bit of a corker having made mincemeat of both Grundy brothers, is no cook. Her cupboard is bare except for some own-brand biscuits that even the guinea pig rejects. Ed, with a hint of wist, said they eat guinea pigs in Peru. Really, this could be the siege of Rouen: 'They ate doggys, they ate cattys, they ate mysse, horse and rattys.' And their spelling suffered terribly, too.

I would advise Em to watch Nigel Slater, who works wonders with butter beans on TV; but Nigel, I notice, tends to find a half-forgotten duck's breast in the cupboard. Personally, I have never found a half-forgotten duck's breast in the cupboard, although I have looked and looked. Nigel and Nigella must be hell for the hungry Grundys. Particularly Nigella.

I am aghast. Ambridge is flowing with milk and honey and the occasional roadkill. Surely Ed could go pick/poach/shoot/scrump or strangle something? How's about badger en croute? And aren't the Masai said to survive on mingled blood and milk from their cows? I would greatly enjoy the episode where Ed explains this option to Em.

Like a dream in slow motion, everything takes a month to happen in Ambridge. You must have been holding your breath waiting for Joyce and her hip to fall down a hole. You can breathe out now. She has plummeted as per. Matt, the demon developer, had arranged for all her floorboards to be loosened. You can't help loving that man.

17 OCTOBER

How do you cope with not being Felix Baumgartner?

NATASHA BELL

There was something comically audacious about that step. About Felix Baumgartner's nonchalant salute to the watching millions as he plunged from his 24-mile-high perch on a balloon into the abyss, if space (or as near as dammit) can be so called. Less of a plunge, actually. More of a carefree swagger into the unknown.

It thrilled me, spellbound as I was. I couldn't help but be fazed by the colossal indifference to safety. I dare say his mum experienced a different emotion. She probably cared only about the landing, which itself resembled a stroll in the park. But meanwhile Baumgartner had approached orbit in a wafer-thin balloon, travelled faster than a clap of thunder and mercifully lived to tell the tale. As Piers Morgan put it: '"I jump from space." Got to be the best chat-up line ever.'

Whichever way you slice it, this was a feat of endeavour. As alluring as they come. Perhaps more so given the outrageous, vicarious experiencing of it: we might as well have taken that step with him. There is grandeur to the mastery of nature, and Baumgartner, as a falling speck on a curving horizon, delivered that quality in spades.

There is something bewitching about adventurers. My guess is that their gutsy temerity tugs at the latent daredevil in us all. It's just that most of us don't express it, for whatever reason. So we are left to marvel at those who do. And for the most part that's enough. We can identify with the challenge, share in the vastness of the achievement, revel in the relief of a comrade returned safely to us. Adventurers, in their own small way, tighten the common bond that unites us even as they stretch our credulity. If that sounds waywardly romantic, so it should do. This man tumbled from the stars and can tell the world how he did it. That's some story.

Some question the need of it all. Why do it? But this misses the point. Because there isn't one. Daredevil endeavour is akin to existence. Sometimes we do stuff simply because we are who we are, and the need to live it is ineluctable. You might as well try to capture the vacuum that enveloped Felix the leaper, if motive is your bag. Of course, there are the naysayers. Those who focus on the cost of the programme, the technology that enabled it, the frivolous pursuit of the record breaker. And yes, the commercial sponsorship that made it possible. For Baumgartner was but a pawn in the relentless struggle for competitive market advantage. Red Bull stole a march.

There is all of that. But I'm not certain it gets to the heart of the matter. More likely, the likes of Baumgartner test another side to our nature: the cynic. We didn't do it, so let's deflect from the accomplishment of someone who did. Watching the event unfold from my tired-looking garret – he perched on the roof of the world, me in the roof of a tenement block – the contrast in our perspectives could hardly have been more spirit-sapping. Or mocking. The route to work can be interminable, the graft and grind of the day as hapless and hopeless as a march on Moscow. Puncture the balloon and the humdrum becomes that more tolerable, that much more endurable.

That sentiment didn't escape me on the Tube this morning. I can't deny it gave me some *Schadenfreude*-like solace. But I knew it was inauthentic, and brittle. As brittle as the gravity Baumgartner escaped in pursuit of his dream. And therein lies the romance and wonder of the adventurer: fidelity to the clarion call of the dream. Not specifically one we share, not one we necessarily approve of. But a dream that we all at heart aspire to. Would I have swapped my dreary Tube carriage for his tiny capsule? You bet.

This article was commissioned through Comment Is Free's *'You Tell Us'* *scheme, after a suggestion from the writer who comments regularly on* Guardian *articles online under the name Framboise.*

18 OCTOBER

Couple who helped Kenyan village with cannabis profits jailed

HELEN CARTER

A couple who ran a cannabis factory have been jailed despite using most of the proceeds of their illicit activities to help a Kenyan village where they were regular visitors. Michael Foster, 62, and

Susan Cooper, 63, made hundreds of thousands of pounds from a sophisticated cannabis-growing operation at their Lincolnshire farmhouse, which was only discovered when a police officer chasing a burglar recognised the distinctive smell. The affair was described by Lincoln crown court as 'the most unusual cannabis-growing case of this type'.

The couple paid for lifesaving surgery for a villager near Mombasa, purchased computers for an eye hospital, and paid for schooling for children, the court heard. But their philanthropic activity was funded by growing cannabis at their farmhouse in Little Sutton, which was raided by police in June 2010.

Prosecutor Jon Dee told the court: 'The couple were both in their sixties and were of previous good character. For six years, they produced cannabis in significant quantities. It perhaps can be best summed up by Mr Foster, who told police in his own words during his interview that it started off as a hobby and turned into a business.' They were only caught when a police officer was chasing a burglar near their home. 'At the time this couple were completely off the police radar,' Dee said. 'They were caught completely by chance.' The police recovered £20,000 in a carrier bag and 159 cannabis plants, with an estimated value of £20,000, describing it as a 'professional and commercial set up'. The annual electricity bill for the farmhouse had increased by £2,000, which the couple claimed was because they were running a pottery business with a kiln. Bank statements showed that £300,000 had been paid into their joint account over six years from 2004. A further £100,000 had gone into an account held by Cooper.

They admitted four charges of producing cannabis and a single offence of possessing criminal money.

Gareth Wheetman, mitigating for Foster, said the fact they were repeatedly flying off to Kenya in itself required money. 'But the evidence demonstrates much of the money was put to charitable and good use. While in Kenya they bought a computer for a local eye hospital, paid for children to be put through school and paid for a lifesaving operation on a man's gangrenous leg.'

Chris Milligan, mitigating for Cooper, described her as a 'good person who has done a bad thing'. He said there was another side to her. 'She has been a good mother, wife and partner to Mr Foster,' he said. 'She paid for the treatment of the young adult with a gangrenous infection in his leg who was given two days to live.'

Judge Sean Morris, jailing them both for three years, said they were a respectable couple of positive good character. He said: 'You were growing it on a significant scale, jetting off to Kenya on it. I am sure you were doing good things in Kenya with your money, but whether that was to appease your consciences, I can only speculate.'

22 OCTOBER

David Miliband and the Labour art of speaking in code

JOHN HARRIS

Although he has to put up with the gnawing pain of thwarted ambition, it can't be too bad being David Miliband. Never mind that he still seemingly feels too awful to fight the good fight in the shadow cabinet, in the financial year 2011–12, in addition to his salary as an MP, he turned £410,171 in fees for 'consultancy work and speeches', supplied to such worthy causes as an agribusiness firm called Indus Basin Holding and the United Arab Emirates' ministry of foreign affairs.

How he finds time to represent the struggling folk of South Shields as well as overseeing his Movement for Change (which, according to its blurb, works in 'specific areas to support campaigns for change in local communities, to identify and nurture talent and to develop new responses to the challenges that people face') is anyone's guess, though his 45 per cent Commons voting record may say something. Or perhaps he's just given up sleep.

Just to further suggest that's he's bionic, the elder Miliband has also become a prolific polemicist, in the *Guardian* and elsewhere – though then again, maybe 'polemicist' is the wrong word. According to my dictionary, to meet that description, you're meant to be able to turn your hand to 'a controversial argument, especially one refuting or attacking a specific opinion or doctrine'. As far as I can tell, he might be in the habit of doing that, but only in a very strange way.

His latest *Guardian* piece appeared last week and was a master-class in an age-old political art that alumni of the New Labour regime have taken to surreal new heights. The political vernacular terms it 'speaking in code': putting up kites and undermining your adversaries while ensuring that everything is put so nebulously that you can deny any such thing. To the untrained eye, it looks more like the borderline absurd art of saying close to nothing, at great length.

Miliband's latest article was ostensibly about the old Blairite theme of so-called public service reform, which of itself may represent a pop at his younger brother: Ed Miliband does not talk about that stuff very much, and his brother's wing of the Labour party has always used this subject as a club with which to beat its supposedly unreconstructed adversaries. Anyway, the elder Miliband said things such as:

Successful economies in the modern world are not sheepish about the power and responsibility of the state. But there is a catch. We need to be reformers of the state to reboot our economy and build a fairer society ... the fiscal crunch requires a different kind of state. The failure of the government's economic policy makes how much less we spend, and how and where we spend it, a core issue. We cannot meet our goals on jobs, health, education, long-term care and tackling poverty without changing the way government goes about its business.

At first sight, this stuff might be at least mildly interesting. Does he, perhaps, think the approach that has run from the last government into the current one, whereby bits of the public services are chopped up and handed to Serco and Richard Branson, is still a good idea? Has he begun to have doubts? Or is this some fiscally driven grope into entirely new territory? Who knows? Least of all Miliband himself: after 728 words, nothing is clearer than it was at the beginning. One *Guardian* letter writer moaned: 'Having read his piece three times, I haven't a clue what he means by reform. He has one paragraph with two sketchy proposals, but nothing of substance.' Quite so.

To be fair to Miliband, the archives are bursting with this stuff, much of it written by other people. When I spent a joyous few hours researching this piece, it was available in the same volume as french fries at McDonald's, and was similarly taste-free and borderline pointless. In 2005, for example, that bold New Labour outrider Stephen Byers told us:

Achieving renewal in office can play a crucial part in uniting the party. The process itself needs to be inclusive but perhaps even more importantly, it provides Labour with the opportunity to state exactly what it is for, rather than just what it is against ... The task now is to bring forward a policy programme firmly based on the values of the centre-left. The promotion of social justice, opportunity for all and security would maintain that coalition of support that led to landslide victories in '97 and 2001.

Burningly controversial, that was. Among its other disciples, the same rhetorical tradition found another outlet in James Purnell, now of the Institute for Public Policy Research but once hyped as a future Labour leader. Even when liberated from ministerial office, he still tended to speak in the same slightly strangulated way:

The left believes in equality – we disagree about equality of what – but we agree that it should be a goal ... I think we need to widen out from a narrow focus on income, to aiming for equality of capability – giving everyone the power to pursue their goals ... Over time, New Labour became too much of a sect – we went from big-tent politics to small-gazebo politics.

Pardon? But back, anyway, to David Miliband and what's arguably the founding document of his recent outpourings, the leader column he wrote when he guest-edited the *New Statesman* in July:

As the economy stagnates, politics needs to respond with vigour and imagination ... The danger is to confuse being a better opposition with becoming a potential government ... Labour's history is that it wins and governs when it aligns an economic narrative of modernisation with a social agenda of compassion and a political culture of dynamism and progress ... Today, Labour has a disruptive economic narrative – that Britain needs fundamental change in its market structure and culture to compete in the modern world. This is bold. Given the crash, it is also necessary ... The point is that defence of the status quo cannot deliver our goals ... In developing new policies, Labour cannot afford the old politics of a conversation with itself.

Brilliant! While we're here, it's also worth mentioning a recent jointly authored piece in the *Observer* by Miliband and the shadow foreign secretary, Douglas Alexander, who went all the way to the Democratic National Convention and came back brimming with useful thoughts. From the top, then:

We need to be state reformers as well as market reformers ... we win by looking like the whole of the country not just part of it ... we have to find new ways to connect our politics with the small businesswoman in Ipswich, the GP in Fleetwood, the personal trainer in Gloucester.

Sorry, but only people who have spent far too long in the mind-bending environs of Westminster could write a sentence like that. Who knew that things are now so bad there's only one small businesswoman in Ipswich, and a solitary fitness instructor in Gloucester? And why pick on Fleetwood?

You can do this stuff, too, if you're bored: it's like a party game for people who are far too interested in the minutiae of politics. Essentially, you sling together one or two clichés, at least one word or phrase (such as 'reboot') that suggests you own a computer, and a couple of propositions that it would be impossible to argue against (à la 'Feed the world' or 'Make trade fair'). You then chuck in some apparently oxymoronic ideas, to make yourself look a bit clever. Just watch:

We need to represent the whole of Britain, not just some of it. In doing so, we will move into the radical centre, and prove that if you're hard, you can also be soft. In a time of change, we must be the change-makers. Opportunity must be our watchword. Watchwords must be our opportunity. It is time to switch Britain off and on again. We deserve nothing less. And nothing more. Neither does the mechanic in Morecambe, or the wrestler in Rhyl. We will win. Or we might lose. Etc, etc.

What, aside from firing muted shots in some factional battle no one really cares about, is the point? Right when this most miserable of rhetorical traditions is refusing to die, people at the opposite end of the political spectrum are mastering the business of being altogether more blunt and plain-spoken. For proof, read the already-infamous Tory treatise *Britannia Unchained* – which may advocate working until you drop dead and deregulated everything, but is at least coherent and straightforward. Meanwhile, David Miliband and his ilk talk – but say what, exactly? Time to leave the gazebo, disrupt the economic narrative and reboot?

29 OCTOBER

When was the first live blog? 1923, it seems

PAUL OWEN

Regular readers will know how important live blogs have become for the *Guardian*'s web news coverage. For the uninitiated, they are a text version of rolling news on everything from the Arab spring to 'Plebgate'. There has been much debate over who exactly invented the form. It turns out it was none of us. The *Guardian*'s research department has unearthed a fascinating 'hour by hour' running commentary of the 1923 general election that is uncannily like the way it would be covered online today, complete with chronological updates marked by time-stamps. Perhaps even more surprising is the fact that the tone is similar too: brisk, conversational, informal, even jokey, with the writer getting more excitable as the night wears on: 'Is Labour going to sweep Bristol?' 'But what a narrow shave!' 'Mr. Thomas, who threatened to "give 'em an 'ammerin'" in Derby, has made good his word.'

The same format was used in 1924, 1929, 1931, 1935 and 1950. It could all fit quite comfortably into our political blogger Andrew Sparrow's live coverage of election night 2010:

2.31 A.M.: Lembit Opik has lost Montgomeryshire ... A colleague says they are 'very chapel' in Montgomeryshire. Presumably his antics with the Cheeky Girls didn't go down well.

5.15 A.M.: Labour have won Rochdale. Gordon Brown's comment about Gillian Duffy doesn't seem to have done too much damage there.

One of the ideas behind live blogging is to open up the process of journalism to the readers, allowing them to see how news is gathered as it happens. Even there, the *Manchester Guardian* predates us; this confession from the 1929 coverage will be familiar to any live blogger: 'Hardly have we written these lines than by far and away the most sensational of the results of the night comes to hand ...'

The vintage versions are littered with demotic expressions that probably wouldn't get a look-in these days – 'So much for foreign pencils!' remarks the 1935 correspondent, while 1931's notes that 'what Labour men get back will be a flock hard hit for shepherds'. They are also much more openly partisan than today's live blogs. At 10.30 p.m. in the 1929 piece, the reporter writes: 'Here is excellent news. The first blow struck against this Government is by the Liberals at Yarmouth,' while the 1924 version starts: 'The first news is bad news. The Exchange Division of Manchester ... has gone back to Conservatism.'

It seems politicians were not quite as quick as newspapers to embrace the demands of rolling news. The 1931 piece sits alongside a paragraph on Liberal leader David Lloyd George's reaction to the election: 'Mr. Lloyd George decided to withhold any comment on the results until a full list was in his possession.' Nick Clegg would never get away with that.

Of all these proto-live blogs, the 1931 account seems most familiar to modern readers, ending with an attempt by the exhausted writer to put the whole night into perspective: 'Landslide? Debacle? What word quite fits the case of this unprecedented election? Say avalanche and leave it at that!' Although that is the exact opposite of Sparrow's weary conclusion in 2010: 'So much for decision day. This seems to be an election without a result. As Lord Ashdown said earlier: "The country has spoken – but we don't know what they've said."'

6 NOVEMBER

Ugg boots are over – the fashion world rejoices

LAUREN COCHRANE AND TOM MELTZER

It may be an object of derision throughout the fashion industry, but the Ugg boot – a bit like the bootcut jean, or the square-toed office-boy shoe – has refused to die. Over the past ten years, sales continued to rise, and their squat, solid, shearling-lined shapes became the footwear of young Britons nationwide. Until now. The newest sales figures from Deckers, the Ugg parent group, are down 31 per cent. While this has been put down to mild weather, and prices of the boots rising, it's a minor victory for fashion. While not defeated – prices will be reduced in a bid to boost sales – its footwear nemesis is showing signs of weakness.

In truth, these signs have been there for a while. Uggs are undeniably comfortable – they're more often worn as slippers in their native Australia – but the ubiquity of them, and their many imitations, has led to overkill. Bad press has been growing. In a survey in 2010, they were voted one of the ten items men don't like on women and a judge recently ruled they can be dangerous to wear while driving.

They originally gained fashionability in 2001 when they were worn by celebrities including Cameron Diaz, but recent advocates include Joey Essex: hardly an advert for a chic, off-duty look. Rana Reeves, founder of brand agency John Doe, believes this has damaged the reputation of the brand. 'I'd say they're in a similar position to when Daniella Westbrook wore Burberry,' he says. 'They need to go back to basics.' That's certainly not something the brand has been doing recently. Instead, expansion has been the policy. With sales increasing by as much as 67 per cent in one quarter of 2009, confidence has been understandably high – and has led to some questionable ranges appearing alongside the classic boot. The firm has expanded into high-heeled styles with price points over £300, handbags, and even a bridal collection. It might be a case of one spongy step too far. 'Ugg's core product is seasonal,' says Honor Westnedge, senior retail analyst at Verdict Research. 'While it has tried to diversify into new ranges, these have struggled to achieve the same level of popularity as its winter boot collections.' Westnedge points to the relatively high price of Uggs as a problem, 'in a period of limited discretionary spending', and suggests that consumers are unlikely to buy more than one pair. There's also the issue that they may simply be out of vogue. New competitors in the boot market include Hunter, Le Chameau (the brand favoured by the Duchess of Cambridge) and, recently, Converse. In contrast to Ugg, Hunter has seen its profits rise – 38 per cent last year – and style leaders from Kate Moss to Sarah Jessica Parker wear its boots. Reeves believes its success is down to a savvy marketing policy. 'They stay true to what they are,' he says. 'They're functional, they keep your feet dry. Hunter have done some collaborations but they have never tried to be fashion. That's what Ugg did, and that's where they went wrong.' Fashion has long rejected Uggs – it looks like the rest of the populace is finally following its lead.

FIVE USES FOR AN OLD UGG BOOT

1. CRAP GLOVES Uggs are only unfashionable on your feet. Stroll around with them on your hands and people won't know what to think.
2. INSULATION Got an uninsulated pipe about the size of your shin? Whack an Ugg on it. Problem solved.

3. WEASEL BEDS Most weasels find their beds cold and uncomfortable. Let's do something for them, guys.

4. FASHIONISTA REPELLENT A single scrap of Ugg boot worn on a lanyard around the neck will keep away all but the most foolhardy fashion snobs. Win.

5. SAFER THROWING BOOTS Tired of accidentally braining a six-year-old when you hurl your wellingtons across the park? Softer equals safer.

8 NOVEMBER

Justin Welby: a real-world archbishop of Canterbury

STEPHEN BATES

In the 1960s there used to be a favourite children's television character called Mr Pastry. Benign, bespectacled, dressed in black, with a bowler hat and a walrus moustache, he invariably ended up looking surprised and covered in wallpaper paste. Well, the moustache has gone, but otherwise that's vaguely like the modern Church of England which today, having been trumped by betting companies and most of the press, will unveil the next archbishop of Canterbury.

If it is not Justin Welby, the current bishop of Durham, who has been talked about as favourite for weeks, officials will have some explaining to do. A selection process that is supposed to be a) transparent and democratic, and b) confidential – for a candidate has to be passed by the prime minister and authorised by the Queen – has once again been sidestepped and pre-empted. It leaves Church

House, as usual, looking wrongfooted, hapless and drenched in paste. It happened last time too, when Rowan Williams was appointed. The established church ought perhaps to feel pleased there is still so much interest in who gets its top job on Earth.

Welby has excellent credentials, possibly above all that he is not John Sentamu, the archbishop of York, who has been a self-promotional figure not much liked by fellow bishops. Everyone knows where Sentamu stands on most issues (although it does depend on who he is speaking to, or writing for, at any given time), whereas Welby is so new as a bishop – it is less than a year since he was translated to Durham – that his stance on the litmus tests of gay people in the church and women bishops, rather than, say, the nature of the Trinity or substitutionary atonement, remains opaque. This may be a good thing while he remains all things to all men (and, presumably, women) in the pews.

Even more compelling is his interesting background as a 1980s oil trader before he saw the light, gave up a £100,000 salary and trained for the ministry instead. That means he understands the modern holy grail: money and the City, objects of mystery and awe to many in the church. They hope it means he is connected to what they think of as the real world. His experience running Liverpool cathedral and re-energising the diocese of Durham, reorganising its finances in the months he has been there, evidently help.

The C of E's real problem, though, is not so much money as its place in the life and future of the country. It is a mark of the relative thinness of the field of candidates, thanks to the timidity of the episcopal selection processes started under that ultimate grey archbishop George Carey 20 years ago, that the Crown Nominations Commission has opted for a largely unknown and untested figure. No one suggests Welby is another Carey – a man who had also been only briefly a bishop before being inflicted on the church by Margaret Thatcher – but he is being thrust into a job where he will have a high profile. Every move and utterance will be scrutinised for heresy, error or obtuseness by the Pharisees of the church and the soothsayers of the media, not all of them actuated by faith, hope or charity.

Welby certainly looks like an archetypal clergyman and has a thin, harsh voice to match. Some mutter about whether an Old Etonian can keep the church in tune with modern society. People who were at Eton and Trinity, Cambridge, with him say they can't remember him at all, but that may be because he was in the exclusionary God-squad evangelicals of the Christian Union in those days. The death of his baby daughter in a car crash 30 years ago is thought to have impelled him towards ordination. If the C of E is to reconnect with a largely indifferent society, empathy may prove his greatest asset. Maybe charisma will follow.

9 NOVEMBER

US Presidential election as it happened – extracts from the live blog

RICHARD ADAMS

11.14 P.M: EASTERN TIME: Fox News calls Ohio for Obama. They think it's all over. It is now: Barack Obama has been re-elected barring some bizarre miracle.

11.16 P.M: Barack Obama wins re-election as US president. As the news gets out about Ohio, the crowd in Chicago goes wild.

11.20 P.M: It must be official: it's on Twitter.

@BarackObama. Four more years.

801,271 retweets, 299,824 favourites.

11.31 P.M: On Fox News, Republican strategist Karl Rove is refusing to accept reality, calling Fox's own call of Ohio 'premature', says not over yet.

11.40 P.M: Karl Rove goes rogue on Fox News. An intra-channel civil war seems to have broken out on Fox News, as Karl Rove has objected to his employer's decision to call Ohio for Obama. Jonathan Martin tweets from the *New York Times*:

Amazing: Rove rebuking Fox on air.

What follows is truly bizarre: after Rove's fleck-marked objections, a presenter goes to the Fox News decision desk to interrogate those statisticians responsible for the call. They defend their decision and basically say that there was no way Romney could win Ohio.

11.43 P.M: And they are back on Fox News and Karl Rove is still banging on, running through all sorts of numbers that who knows what they mean, but claiming that Ohio was still too close to call. Oh now he is chan-neling 'the Romney people', which is interesting. So is that where he's getting all this from? Funny how he has all these statistics at his fingertips.

By the way, the Associated Press, CBS, NBC, ABC and CNN have also called Ohio for Obama, so, uh.

11.48 P.M: News from Colorado: an amendment that would make it legal in Colorado for individuals to possess and for businesses to sell marijuana for recreational use has passed with 52.7 per cent voting yes and 47.3 per cent voting no, with 1,507,746 votes or more than

50 per cent of active voters counted, according to the Colorado Secretary of State's office. Let's see that get past the Supreme Court.

11.50 P.M: The Empire State Building is lit blue after Obama wins the presidential election on election night.

11.52 P.M: Associated Press calls Colorado for Obama. This seals it, Karl Rove's maths-spinning objections in Ohio notwithstanding: AP has awarded Colorado to Obama, and ABC and CBS have called Nevada for Obama.

11.57 P.M: Is it about to be done and dusted? Karl Rove is still arguing the toss with Michael Barone about the Ohio call with Barone saying that half of Cuyahoga County is still out and likely to swamp the remaining Republican vote. Rove seems to have backtracked somewhat claiming that 'Oh well if I'd seen those numbers ... I was just raising a cautionary note.'

12.11 A.M: Nate Silver is brought down to his *New York Times* work station on a gilded palanquin, and his words are transcribed by flunkies, in which he schools poor old Karl Rove on the subject of Ohio's outstanding votes: 'The vast bulk of precincts that have yet to report their results in Ohio are in counties that have gone for Mr Obama. Cuyahoga County, home to Cleveland, has had only half of its precincts report and could yield another 100,000 votes or so for Mr Obama. Toledoís Lucas County, which has strongly favored Mr Obama so far, has had only 12 per cent of its precincts report. There are also votes outstanding in the Cleveland suburbs, and in Dayton, also areas that have gone for Mr Obama so far. Conversely, the vast majority of areas where Mr Romney leads have reported 100 per cent of their ballots.'

12.14 A.M: Through the thick window panes of the *Guardian*'s Washington DC bureau, you can hear cheering and shouting as the crowds gather outside the White House in celebration.

12.25 A.M: Here are two amazing firsts: Maine and Maryland voters both approve measures to legalise same-sex marriage. That's notable because in the previous 28 attempts to establish or defend a right to marriage equality through referendums, the same-sex marriage side lost.

12.32 A.M: Donald Trump appears to have launched a one-man Twitter frenzy of rage:

@realDonaldTrump This election is a total sham and a travesty. We are not a democracy!

1.01 A.M: Mitt Romney's concession speech in Boston. 'This is a time of great challenges for America and I pray that the president is successful in guiding our nation,' he says. Then there's a lot of praise for his wife Ann. 'She would have been a wonderful first lady,' Romney says in exactly the same tone of voice that he gives his normal campaign speech. When the camera pulls back we can see what a grandiose set the Romney campaign had prepared here. 'I believe in America, I believe in the people of America,' says Romney, which is nice.

But that's about it, this is a short number from Romney, never an inspiring speaker, and so he proves once again. And we'll never have to hear another speech from him.

1.47 A.M: President re-elect Barack Obama walks on stage in Chicago to the sound of 'Signed, Sealed, Delivered' – and the crowd goes wild. 'Tonight, more than 200 years after a former colony won the right to determine its own destiny,' says Obama, starting off with an anti-British note. 'Tonight, in the election, you the American people reminds us that while the road has been long, the journey has been hard, we have picked ourselves. And we know in our hearts, the best is yet to come.' Now some kind words about Mitt Romney. 'In the weeks ahead I also look forward to sitting down with Governor Romney and talk about how we can move this country forward.' Treasury Secretary Romney? Just kidding.

And then it's words for the family, starting with Michelle: 'Let me say this publicly: I have never loved you more.' As for his daughters Sasha and Malia, Obama says: 'I am very proud of you both, but I will say this now: one dog is probably enough.' (The joke there being that he had promised them a dog if he won the election in 2008, hence Bo, the First Dog.)

This was the most-tweeted Guardian *article of the autumn.*

21 NOVEMBER

Typewriters reach the end of the line in the UK

EMINE SANER

It was at 12 p.m. on Friday that the last British-made typewriter was packed into its box at the Brother factory in Wrexham. Its maker, Edward Bryan, 40, has worked in the factory since 1989.

When he started, around 30 people were on the typewriter line. By the end there was just him – the team leader – and another worker. The last CM-1000, an electronic typewriter that retails for around £400, was presented to Rachel Boon, a curator of technologies and engineering at the Science Museum, which will keep the machine. Colleagues gathered around, and the MD of Brother Industries, Craig McCubbin, reminisced about how he had started out on the production line in his school holidays.

'I was a bit sad,' says Bryan, who has been building typewriters for Brother for 23 years. 'You could have ownership of the machine. From taking a little screw at the start, you end up with a typewriter in a box.' He can build one with his eyes closed – he tried it once. 'It took about 40 minutes,' he says with a laugh. (Usually, it would take him just 18.)

The decision was taken six months ago to stop production, says Phil Jones, Brother's UK head. 'Clearly, typewriters have been undergoing a decline in many years. There's always a point where it's not economically viable any more, and we always knew that time was coming.' The factory had been making 300–500 machines a month, accounting for just 0.25 per cent of the company's turnover. 'When a category is such a small percentage, it really isn't worth doing analytics on it,' says Jones when I ask who was still buying typewriters, but he says he thinks many of their customers were older people who don't feel comfortable using a computer. 'And they're popular in prisons – it seems they're still one of the approved technological products that prisoners can use in some prisons.' He also thinks there may be secret government bunkers, where highly classified missives are written on typewriters, 'but that's just speculation'. The international company will still produce typewriters in its Malaysia factory, primarily for the US market and developing countries, 'but it is the end as far as UK manufacturing is concerned'.

As typewriters go, it would be difficult to feel too romantic about the CM-1000 – the large greige machine hardly conjures up the same image as Hemingway hammering away at his trusty black Royal, the clatter of the typing pool or William Boot packing his portable typewriter for assignment in Ishmaelia – but it still feels like a heavy-hearted full stop.

27 NOVEMBER

Career hopes dashed

ROS ASQUITH

29 November

Leveson report:
a nightmare – but only for
the old guard of Fleet Street

NICK DAVIES

Let us look first at the nightmares that have not become real. The government is not being invited to take over the press. All those full-page advertisements linking Lord Justice Leveson to Robert Mugabe and Bashar Assad, all that high-octane coverage in the *Sun* and the *Mail* about his report 'imposing a government leash on papers' and threatening 'state regulation of Britain's free press' has proved to be no more than froth on the lips of propagandists, simply another round of the same old distortion that did so much to create this inquiry in the first place.

Nor does the Leveson report accept that Fleet Street should be rewarded for its repeated abuse of power with the grant of even more power, not only to run its own regulator but to investigate journalists and to impose fines on those it might find wanting. This was the cutting edge of the plan hatched by the conservative end of Fleet Street, still blandly, blindly confident that the rest of us would accept placemen for the *Express* proprietor Richard Desmond ('Ethical? I don't quite know what the word means') policing the ethics of the press; or Paul Dacre (who originally told the Press Complaints Commission that the *Guardian*'s coverage of the phone-hacking scandal was 'highly exaggerated and imaginative') having some role in fining the *Guardian*; or executives from Rupert Murdoch's News International, which misled the press, public and parliament, being granted any kind of role in investigating the truth of other newspapers' stories. Leveson rejected this plan with a neat soundbite: 'It's still the industry marking its own homework.'

Nor is this any kind of catastrophe for British journalism. From a reporter's point of view, there is no obvious problem with the core of Leveson's report, his system of 'independent self-regulation'.

This would have three functions. First, it would handle complaints, but it would do so through an organisation that was neither appointed by nor answerable to Fleet Street. The dark end of the industry may complain that this is all a terrible threat to the free press, echoing the rapist who claims the police are a threat to free love. Why should we fear an independent referee? Why should we not be ashamed of the old Press Complaints Commission which, as the report puts it, 'has failed ... is not actually a regulator at all ... lacks independence ... has proved itself to be aligned with the interests of the press'? It is hard to think of any other decent answer to the evidence of Kate and Gerry McCann, falsely accused of murdering their own child; or of Christopher Jefferies, viciously smeared as a killer; or of any of the other witnesses in the opening module of Leveson's inquiry.

Second, the new regulator would investigate systemic offending. That looks weaker. This is not about investigating crime. There is not (nor should there be) any suggestion that the regulator would have any power to compel the disclosure of documents or to search a reporter's desk. This is about investigating systemic breaches of the code of conduct – taking pictures in breach of their subject's privacy, for example, or interviewing children without the consent of their parents. Without police powers, the regulator would rely on journalists to co-operate. History suggests they will be reluctant to do so for fear of losing their career. Numerous former *News of the World* journalists helped the *Guardian* to uncover the hacking scandal, but only two of them felt able to speak on the record. Weak, but not a threat.

Finally, and most importantly, the regulator would run a new arbitration system as a cheaper and quicker alternative to the civil courts.

That looks like very good news for reporters who currently work with laws on defamation, privacy and confidentiality that really do inhibit the freedom of the press, threatening damages and legal costs on such a scale as to encourage the suppression of the truth. The likes of Jimmy Savile do well in those conditions. Leveson's arbitration system would lighten the load. And, in addition, it offers an incentive for news organisations to volunteer to join a new regulator: their membership, Leveson suggests, would exempt them from the worst of the costs and damages they might face in the event that they do end up being sued in the civil courts. Leveson needs a new law to ensure that the courts recognise the new regulator and deliver those benefits to its members.

There is a nightmare here, but it is for the old guard of Fleet Street. To lose control of the regulator is to lose their licence to do exactly as they please.

While the political attention may focus on Leveson's plans for the future, the real power of his report is in the detailed, damning evidence of just what that licence has allowed. 'Parts of the press have acted as if its own code simply did not exist ... there has been a recklessness in prioritising sensational stories, almost irrespective of the harm that the stories may cause ... a willingness to deploy covert surveillance against or in spite of the public interest ... significant and reckless disregard for accuracy ... some newspapers resorting to high volume, extremely personal attacks on those who challenge them.'

The report takes on the *Daily Mail* and its editor, Paul Dacre, for accusing Hugh Grant of 'mendacious smears' in giving his evidence to the inquiry, finding that the paper 'went too far' and that Dacre 'acted precipitately' and that his explanation for his actions 'does not justify the aggressive line which was adopted'. It tackles the *Sun* over its decision to expose the fact that Gordon Brown's infant son had been diagnosed with cystic fibrosis, finds that 'there was no public interest in the story sufficient to justify publication without the consent of Mr and Mrs Brown', recognises the possibility that the information may have been obtained 'by unlawful or unethical means' and challenges claims by the then editor Rebekah Brooks that the Browns were 'absolutely committed to making this public'. It details the behaviour of the *Mail*, *Sun* and *Telegraph* who, while Leveson was sitting, opted to publish material about the death in a coach crash in Switzerland of the 12-year-old schoolboy Sebastian Bowles, which 'undeniably raises issues under the editors' code'.

This does not mean that the report presents no problems for journalism generally.

In the small print, it seems to suggest that police officers should no longer be able to give non-attributable briefings to reporters. If that rule had been in place over the last few years, it is fair to say that the *Guardian* might not have been able to expose the hacking scandal. There is a section which implies that reporters should be able to conceal the identities of confidential sources only if they have some kind of proof of the undertaking, such as a written agreement with the source – hardly possible if your source is a professional criminal describing alleged police corruption, or a child prostitute talking about her pimp.

But the real problem, of course, is in the power of the beast. This debate is not about to be settled with facts and reasoned argument. It will be conducted under the same old rules – of falsehood, distortion and bullying. Will any government stand up to it? That's where the real nightmare may lie.

30 NOVEMBER

I feel duped and angry at David Cameron's reaction to Leveson

J. K. ROWLING

I am alarmed and dismayed that the prime minister appears to be backing away from assurances he made at the outset of the Leveson inquiry.

I thought long and hard about the possible consequences to my family of giving evidence and finally decided to do so because I have made every possible attempt to protect my children's privacy under the present system – and failed. If I, who can afford the very best lawyers, cannot guarantee the privacy of those dearest to me, what hope did the Dowlers, the McCanns, the Watsons ever have of protecting their own children and their own good names? Those who have suffered the worst, most painful and least justifiable kinds of mistreatment at the hands of the press, people who have become newsworthy because of the press's own errors or through unspeakable private tragedy, are those least likely to be able to defend themselves or to seek proper redress.

My understanding is that Lord Justice Leveson's recommendations would give everybody, whatever their degree of celebrity or their bank balance, a quick, cheap and effective way of holding the press to account. They would also protect the press against frivolous complaints and reduce costly lawsuits. At the moment, only those of us who can afford the immensely expensive, time-consuming and stressful services of the legal system are able to take a stand against serious invasions of privacy, and even this offers little or no protection against the unjustified, insidious and often covert practices highlighted by the Leveson inquiry.

Without statutory underpinning Leveson's recommendations will not work: we will be left with yet another voluntary system from which the press can walk away. If the prime minister did not wish to change the regulatory system, even to the moderate, balanced and proportionate extent proposed by Lord Justice Leveson, I am at a loss to understand why so much public money has been spent and why so many people have been asked to relive extremely painful episodes on the stand in front of millions. Having taken David Cameron's assurances in good faith at the outset of the inquiry he set up, I am merely one among many who feel duped and angry in its wake.

I hope that those who share similar concerns will speak up now and sign the Hacked Off petition. Cameron said that he would implement sensible recommendations: it is time for him to honour that commitment and join the other political leaders by supporting the Leveson recommendations in their entirety.

4 DECEMBER

Bad Sex award goes to Nancy Huston's 'babies and bedazzlements'

MAEV KENNEDY

A long, shuddering gasp of relief will no doubt have been heard from the losers, as the Canadian author Nancy Huston scooped the least coveted book award of the year, the *Literary Review*'s Bad Sex prize, for her 14th novel, *Infrared*, about a woman who likes to snap her lovers in the throes of passion. The judges were seduced by her vivid imagery, which included such descriptions as 'flesh, that archaic kingdom that brings forth tears and terrors, nightmares, babies and bedazzlements', and 'my sex swimming in joy like a fish in water'.

Huston, who now lives in Paris, was either too busy or too bashful to attend the ceremony in London, but 400 guests raised a toast to her, none more heartily than the authors she vanquished, who include the distinguished BBC *Newsnight* economics editor Paul Mason, poet Craig Raine and veteran novelist Tom Wolfe, a previous winner in 2004.

The two authors who had been believed to be a shoo-in for the prize, J. K. Rowling (for her first novel for adults, *The Casual Vacancy*), and *Fifty Shades of Grey* creator E. L. James, were both in the end eliminated reluctantly by the judges before the shortlisting stage – Rowling because her writing wasn't nearly bad enough, and James because the prize, established to draw attention to bad sex writing 'and discourage it' specifically rules out pornographic or intentionally erotic literature.

The prize, presented by the actor Samantha Bond, was collected on Huston's behalf by her publisher, Atlantic, but the author did send a pert statement. 'I hope this prize will incite thousands of British women to take close-up photos of their lovers' bodies in all states of array and disarray,' she said.

Huston was unfancied by *Guardian* readers, who in a poll of the shortlisted authors were far more drawn to Wolfe's *Back to Blood*, Sam Mills's *The Quiddity of Will Self*, and Raine's *The Divine Comedy*, which between them attracted more than 70 per cent of the votes.

But in the end, Huston carried the night. Her prize – a 'semi-abstract trophy representing sex in the 1950s' – will need to find shelf room in an already bursting awards cabinet: Huston has in the past won France's premier literary prize, the *Prix Goncourt*, the *Prix Femina*, and was shortlisted for the Orange Prize in 2010 for her novel *Fault Lines*.

The prize ceremony was held in the august surroundings of the Naval & Military Club in St James. The name by which it is better known undoubtedly explains the choice of venue – The In & Out club.

4 DECEMBER

Pity this royal baby, its future a public obstacle course

SIMON JENKINS

I have no opinion on *hyperemesis gravidarum*. Maternity couture is not my forte. I am weak on Salic Law. As for the logistics of twins as heirs to the throne, I leave that to the department of angels on pinheads. Royal babies are ooh-aah journalism. They soften the brain.

Yet after so much relentless bad news, we gulp down anything heart-warming like parched travellers stumbling into an oasis. In mid-recession, Britain went ecstatic when William and Kate wed. It cooed with pleasure over a royal jubilee. 'Olympic heroes' sent it weak at the knees. Now comes a royal pregnancy, and a thumping great smile crosses the nation's face.

At four o'clock on Monday afternoon, every office, shop floor, canteen and playground was uplifted, or so the media told us. David Cameron emerged from Downing Street, like a mole scenting the dawn, for his Tony Blair royal moment. He said he was 'absolutely delighted', over and again. I swear I saw the ghost of Alastair Campbell murmuring at his shoulder, 'The people's pregnancy'.

This is the danger of media simplification. When front pages used all to carry a dozen news stories, the world's ups and downs tended to cancel each other out. The window on the world had many openings, good and bad. Tabloidisation has turned this into a single daily headbang, one dominant story, overwritten and slammed in front of the reader's eyes to the exclusion of all else. Whether it is bankers' bonuses or phone hacking or the Olympics or Jimmy Savile, single-issue coverage distorts perception and encourages a gloomy cynicism towards the world. Bad news is always catastrophe, good news is hysteria.

The prospective birth of a third in line to the throne is significant, since the constitution requires the headship of the British state to be inherited. What is not given is that those down that line of inheritance, and their potential children, be accorded such massive fame. Britain is exceptional, even among surviving crowned heads of state, in treating its monarchy as a royal collective. While republicanism has the rational high ground in the matter of heredity, it has failed to dent the emotional attachment of the English (I hesitate to speak for other Britons) to constitutional monarchy. But that attachment has never been unqualified. When monarchy does not play ball with democracy, it is monarchy that is in trouble. It wobbled during the parliamentary crisis of 1910 and on the abdication of 1936. It wobbled, briefly, after the death of Princess Diana in 1997.

Wobbling opens the usual can of worms, such as why not female inheritance and why not a Catholic or an atheist. Female succession is now confirmed. But each move to a more 'relevant' monarchy leads to more ideas for reform, until it comes dangerously close to making the person of the monarch signify something specific, which it must not. Traditional institutions are always at their most vulnerable when being changed, as Alexis de Tocqueville warned and of which the Anglican church is now an awful example.

Who is monarch must not matter. He or she is required to be no more than the anthropomorphic embodiment of statehood. Inheritance is a security against monarchical power, since its indefensibility ensures the powerlessness of the head of state. By being random in age, merit or inclination, it detaches the head of state from all claim to influence.

Despite the paranoia of the left, the monarch has no constitutional potency. The power-grasping Stuarts brought Britain to rebellion, civil war and chaos. The power-averse Hanoverians buried themselves in their cards and their mistresses. Parliamentary freedom flourished as a result. The Prince of Wales can say what he likes. He does not award planning permission or run the NHS. The body politic is robust enough to stand a few eccentric occupants of the constitutional display case.

When kings and queens mattered, royal babies were serious tokens of national continuity. Since their sovereignty was, at least in theory, beyond dispute, they were the crown in flesh and blood. The infant Henry III, the feeble Henry VI, the sickly Edward VI were all treated as ciphers by the courtiers round them, but they still breathed an authority that could not be gainsaid.

Today an heir to the throne is a mere echo of that continuity. He or she embodies custom and practice, history, nationhood, much as do the crown jewels, Buckingham Palace and the houses of parliament. It does not matter if the heir is a boy or a girl, a giant or an imp, a genius or a fool. It should not matter if it is Protestant or Catholic, white or black, gay or heterosexual. Monarchy is just the way Britons have long chosen to express their inanimate throne, largely because it would look empty otherwise.

The crown has made few mistakes in the lifetimes of most Britons. But one error, made under PR advice back in the 1960s, was to elevate the 'royal family' to significance, its members adorning ceremonial and public occasions, however trivial, and drawing on a civil list in consequence. This confused the empty concept of 'being in line to the throne' with actual headship of state. It set apart a collection of individuals, who could not do proper jobs and often irritated the public by their behaviour, in a cocoon of costly protection. This last was unnecessary, since a virtue of heredity is an ample supply of replacements.

The resulting pressures on the family members are well documented. Few couples can stand the weight of expectation – to be ecstatically happy – loaded on to them by celebrity status. Scandinavians put their royals under nothing like this pressure. They lead a normal life unless and until called on to take office. In the case of Prince William and his wife, the 'wait' to ascend the throne, under the gaze of the entire world, stretches ahead like a ghastly obstacle course. It will last probably most of their lives.

A 'royal family' was the biggest risk run by the British monarchy in modern times. The ferocity of the spotlight helped undermine three royal marriages, from which the monarchy is lucky to have escaped unscathed, largely through the personality of the Queen. Now the same terrible glare is being turned on the next young couple, and what seems to be a difficult pregnancy. We can smile and wish them well. But it is not morning sickness that this family has most to fear, it is the demons that follow.

Women in theatre: why do so few make it to the top?

CHARLOTTE HIGGINS

'It's a big world in here' is the ringing phrase the Young Vic theatre in London has adopted as its motto. It's a nice play on Shakespeare, for, as he said, all the world's a stage (not for nothing did he call his own theatre the Globe). On stage, real people act out human desires and dilemmas in front of a live audience: at its best, theatre is the art form that best represents the world.

Except that it doesn't. Some months ago, the staging of two all-male Shakespeare productions at the Hampstead theatre in London uncorked an explosion of frustration from women actors, writers and directors. There was a sense of basic injustice – actor Janet Suzman talked of a 'really frustrating' career where there 'aren't bloody well enough parts for women'; deeper concerns were also expressed.

This failure to represent women, argued the actor, writer and director Stella Duffy, was deeply entwined with society's wider failure to put women's voices on an equal footing with men's. A sense of responsibility to the world was, she said, being ducked – particularly by our larger national stages. In an impassioned blogpost, she wrote: 'When we do not see ourselves on stage we are reminded, yet again, that the people running our world (count the women in the front benches if you are at all unsure) do not notice when we are not there. That they think men (and yes, white, middle-class, middle-aged, able-bodied men at that) are all we need to see.'

After I wrote an article quoting Suzman and others, Elizabeth Freestone, artistic director of Pentabus Theatre, wrote to me. While an artist-in-residence at the National Theatre, she had done her own research into women in theatre, which she offered to show me. She had also done fascinating work on Shakespeare, unlocking some of the root causes of this imbalance. The *Guardian* teamed up with Freestone, and we extended and updated her research. Her headline figure had been that there was a '2:1 problem' in English theatre, or two men for every woman; this was borne out by our new findings, too. Women are seriously underrepresented on stage, among playwrights and artistic directors, and in creative roles such as designers and composers. On the other hand, women are a substantial majority when it comes to the audience. According to Ipsos Mori figures produced for the Society of London Theatre in 2010, women make up 68 per cent of theatregoers.

We looked at the top ten subsidised theatres in England – those best placed to provide leadership – and at their record in the financial year 2011–12. (One important detail to bear in mind: the National Theatre and the Royal Shakespeare Company received at least six times more subsidy than the next-best-funded theatre, the Royal Court in London.)

The 2:1 problem begins at board level. Our sample had an average of 33 per cent women on their boards; only one, the Royal Court, has a majority female board. Women accounted for 36 per cent of the artistic directors; executive directors were much better represented at 67 per cent. Of the actors employed by the 10 theatres, 38 per cent were female, with the National coming out worst at 34 per cent. Of directors, only 24 per cent employed were women; and when we examined creative teams (directors, designers, sound designers, composers), 23 per cent were women. We found, too, that women in creative roles were less celebrated.

In 36 years of Olivier awards, women have won only twice for director (Deborah Warner, in 1988 and 1992) and four times for playwright (Caryl Churchill, Timberlake Wertenbaker, Pam Gems and Katori Hall).

We were aware that our statistics did not dig into the subtleties of women's careers. Josie Rourke and Kate Pakenham, the artistic and executive directors of the Donmar Warehouse, tell me their office is almost entirely staffed by women in their twenties and early thirties. But will they rise through the ranks? 'For me,' says Rourke, 'a huge part of the conversation is how you stick at it in your thirties, and what motivates you to move from middle to senior management.' For those in freelance roles, the theatre is a hard place to sustain a career and children: no pension, no maternity leave, a nomadic lifestyle, unsociable hours. 'It will take huge wisdom and honesty for theatre to investigate its culture,' says Rourke.

The weight of history is not on the side of female playwrights: the canon is overwhelmingly male. Even so, we were surprised to learn that one of our top ten, Chichester festival theatre, employed no female directors and produced no plays by women over the period we looked at. Artistic director Jonathan Church suggested this was an anomalous sample; he also pointed to the financial pressures on regional theatres and the need, when programming contemporary or 20th-century work for a big auditorium, to put on 'names' that have had West End success, such as Coward, Ayckbourn, Stoppard, Hare, Rattigan: all men.

There is currently a blooming of extraordinary female voices in theatre, among them Lucy Kirkwood, Lucy Prebble and E. V. Crowe, yet we found that women writers accounted for only 35 per cent of the new plays produced – another expression of the '2:1 problem'. There is, however, some cause for hope: 41 per cent of the plays commissioned by our theatres, but yet to reach the stage, are by women. Nicholas Hytner, artistic director of the National, sees this as a hugely positive sign: 'I won't put a date on it, but in not too many years the gender balance of directors and writers will be 50:50. I can say that with confidence because I look at directors and writers in their twenties and thirties and it is 50:50.'

Still, there are nuances behind such figures. Of the seven plays by women produced at the Royal Court in this period, all but one were staged in its smaller auditorium: meaning a smaller fee, fewer royalties, a lower profile. If these women are being nurtured towards bigger careers, so much the better; but will they be allowed to make the leap? The playwrights I spoke to talked of careers that had sparkled in their twenties and stalled in their thirties. The really big commissions had never come, and they found their male peers outstripping them. Some had turned to screenwriting: still tough, but, according to playwright Zinnie Harris, 'In TV, I haven't encountered the feeling that you're not going to get to the top because you are a woman.'

Only two original plays by women have ever been staged in the largest auditorium at the National: Rebecca Lenkiewicz's *Her Naked Skin* in 2008, and Moira Buffini's *Welcome to Thebes* in 2010. According to writer Tanika Gupta, who has a new play at the Swan in Stratford next year, there is an underlying doubt about the material women are capable of taking on. 'The argument is that women can write very good domestic drama, but are not intellectually rigorous enough to do the big plays. We need to be given the chance to write those state-of-the-nation plays.' Harris adds: 'It is somehow harder for people to embrace a play written by a woman, whatever its quality. There is something slightly unseemly about filling stages with our voices, whereas men have a sense of filling Chekhov's or Ibsen's shoes. The woman who raises her voice becomes shrill and hectoring; the man becomes authoritative.' She believes the media is at fault, too. 'When plays by women don't work, they are over-condemned. With men, they are seen as a step on the way to developing an interesting voice.' The statistics bore out what we had suspected: women playwrights write more roles for women than their male counterparts. Women wrote 49 per cent of their parts for women; men wrote 37 per cent.

A clear message began to emerge about the importance of women running instititutions. Female artistic directors had staged many more plays by women than their male counterparts. Roxana Silbert at the Birmingham Rep came out top: 32 per cent of the plays she has directed are by women. She was followed by all the remaining women. Then came David Lan at the Young Vic (15 per cent), followed by all the remaining men. Neither Hytner nor Gregory Doran, artistic director of the RSC, has ever directed a play by a woman.

It is clear that history comes into play here: both men have had careers that focus on the classics, with Doran a specialist in the 16th- and 17th-century repertoire. When I put this to Hytner, he said he believed his own record was 'irrelevant: there are all sorts of things I have never directed because I am not very good at directing that kind of thing'. Freestone disagrees: 'Profile and visibility matter. Those in charge of national organisations have a responsibility to show leadership.' Vicky Featherstone, who in April becomes artistic director of the Royal Court (England's most important theatre for new writing), says: 'It is a no-brainer that there should be equal representation of men and women in the theatre. It is absolute common sense and I expect nothing less.'

Our research was not intended to browbeat individuals. Rather, it was meant to focus debate on fact rather than anecdote, and to encourage theatres to take gender into account. As Freestone puts it, 'This is about asking: are you thinking about gender balance?

Do you ask the question? If you have 10 writers under commission do you think about it if they are all men? If you never think to ask, that's when you are in trouble.' She argues that much more needs to be done. 'The theatre world remains strangely passive in the face of overwhelming evidence of its failure to address the gender imbalance both on and off stage. Programming, commissioning and casting decisions are routinely made without any consideration of gender.'

Why is this 2:1 ratio so stubborn? Like so much else in English theatre, it goes back to Shakespeare. He was, of course, writing for all-male companies; and, though he wrote transcendent parts for women, there aren't very many. Of his 981 characters, 826 are male and 155 female: 16 per cent. Women have less to say, too: of roles with more than 500 lines, only 13 per cent are female. The most wordy of Shakespeare's heroines, Rosalind, has 730 lines. Hamlet, his most loquacious hero, has 1,539.

This means less work for women actors, and fewer opportunities for them to develop their skills via the many workaday parts available to men. The Shakespeare problem has persisted because, until relatively recently, much of British theatre relied on the repertory system: a company of actors performing a handful of different plays in a season. Shakespeare would frequently sit at the heart of such a company; many new plays would therefore tend to be written for a similar gender balance. There is something deeply culturally engrained about this: it runs so deep that we have become used to not seeing women equally represented, arguably aided by a culture of complacency. The Shakespeare inheritance has meant, says Freestone, 'we've been caught thinking that 30 per cent women is good enough. I'm not saying there's been institutional sexism, but there has been a sort of blindness to female actors because of the burden of the classical canon.'

The answer to this is, surely, gender-blind casting, especially in the classics, where colour-blind casting has ceased to be a matter for comment. Phyllida Lloyd, whose current all-female *Julius Caesar* at the Donmar has provided a focus for recent debate, is clear: 'If I were running the RSC, I would make it 50 per cent male and 50 per cent female actors – and then I would work out how to do the plays,' she says. 'It wouldn't be a stranglehold, it would be liberating.'

When I speak to Doran, he tells me he has invited Lloyd to run a company of actors at the RSC on precisely those lines. 'Watch this space,' he says. Hytner believes he cannot impose strictures, that directors' casting decisions have to be based on their own instincts: 'I am very interested in gender-blind casting and often think it is excellent. But I can't tell writers how they should write and directors how they should cast. What I admire is that the Donmar Warehouse responded to Phyllida Lloyd's desire to do *Julius Caesar* that way.' When the National staged *Timon of Athens* this year (Shakespeare's most male-heavy play), five male parts were given to women – though the share of female lines increased only from 0.67 per cent to 14 per cent. For many, this is not enough. 'I really believe that a more imaginative approach to casting the classics will unlock all kinds of creative interpretations, and naturally feed in to all other areas – male playwrights writing female parts, more confidence in female creative teams,' says Freestone. Duffy argues that fringe theatre is better balanced, and that the national companies should be leading by example – 'and they are not, and I find it heartbreaking'. She adds: 'We have a responsibility to make the world a fairer place, and sometimes you have to do a little social engineering to make that happen.' In the end, she says, 'I don't know why people don't just suck that up and get on with it.'

From Euro 2012 to 'Gangnam Style': what Britons Googled most this year

JEMIMA KISS

Like the Oxford Dictionaries' word of the year (2012: omnishambles), Google's annual Zeitgeist list of the year's top UK internet search terms is becoming a handy barometer of what is on the nation's mind. In 2012 the top UK search terms included Whitney Houston, Kate Middleton, 'Gangnam Style' and April Jones, the Welsh five-year-old who went missing in October.

Zeitgeist measures the year's fastest-growing search terms, rather than the largest volume of searches. The top 10 overall list of trending terms features familiar online preoccupations – sport, celebrity, the royal family, viral videos, Apple product launches – along with others relating to big stories of 2012, including NatWest Online, which went down in July leaving customers with no access to their internet accounts and unable to use debit cards, and the disappearance of April Jones, who remains missing despite a massive search effort.

Sport is represented by Euro 2012, the fastest growing Google UK search term of the year, ahead of Olympic tickets (possibly because these went on sale in 2011). Houston, the US singer who died in February, is at number three, followed by the Duchess of Cambridge. Also in the top 10 list are Netflix, the US video-on-demand service launched in the UK in early 2012; iPad 3; Gary Barlow; and South Korean pop star Psy's song 'Gangnam

Style', the video for which has become YouTube's biggest ever hit, approaching 1 billion views four months after going online.

The top-10 trending politician was Conservative minister Jeremy Hunt, who as culture secretary survived a grilling at the Leveson inquiry over his relationship with News Corporation, before inheriting the controversial NHS reform brief. Tories dominate the political list – Boris Johnson, Justine Greening, Michael Gove, George Osborne, Louise Mensch and Nadine Dorries also feature. Andy Murray, Tom Daley and Jessica Ennis were the top three on the British Olympians list, with Usain Bolt, Michael Phelps and Roger Federer heading the list of foreign Olympians. The fastest-growing sports-related searches were dominated by Olympic events, with synchronised swimming, murderball (officially known as wheelchair rugby), wheelchair basketball, volleyball and archery all ahead of the 100 metre sprint. Rio de Janeiro, which is hosting the 2016 Games, was the top travel destination search term. Bond film *Skyfall* and 'Gangnam Style' topped the movie and song top 10s but other Zeitgeist lists produced some surprises. BBC children's show *Mike the Knight* was top of the TV shows and Lucy Spraggan, an *X Factor* contestant who fell ill and quit in November, topped the music artists category.

Dr Grant Blank of the Oxford Internet Institute said the Google Zeitgeist results reflected popular concerns and highlighted the perennial question of whether popular culture is really important. 'To many people it is, though it's outside institutional society, politics and foreign affairs,' he said. 'Popular culture is a way for people to be connected to larger society, to something bigger than they are, and it's easier to connect to a person than to something more abstract.' Blank pointed out that Google's search trends can only reflect the UK's online population, with as much as 25 per cent of the country – likely to be poorer, older and less educated – not yet online. Another unspoken constituency omitted from

Google's trend reports is the adult content market. Metrics firm comScore declined to provide statistics on adult content, although a 2010 figure from researchers at Nielsen estimated that as much as 27 per cent of UK web traffic was porn-related. 'Searches for adult keywords are pretty constant, and although unquestionably popular, we don't think they define the Zeitgeist for any one year,' said a Google spokesperson, though the company would not release trending data on adult content. 'We apply the same kinds of filters to the Zeitgeist that we use for SafeSearch, so no adult keywords are included.'Google retains a near monopoly on UK search engine traffic with, according to comScore, a 90.2 per cent share of the market. It faces a challenge as consumers come to rely more heavily on their mobile devices for internet services, changing the nature of how and what people search, and because information stored in mobile apps cannot be indexed by the search engine.

Google would not break out what proportion of its traffic is mobile, but said the volume of combined searches had nearly doubled year on year. Blank is confident that Google will continue to dominate as the most intimate relationship we have with technology. 'There are people who feel that the coming wave of machines are going to be making decisions for people in a way they don't understand, though I think that's a little overstated,' he said. 'But power stations are now automated to some extent, and we're looking at automated landing systems for airplanes and cars that don't need drivers. There is research into how these things might fail, but they will be easier and safer because the machine makes decisions faster and without distraction. Where the balance lies is yet to be determined.'

29 DECEMBER

Revealed: how the FBI coordinated the crackdown on Occupy

NAOMI WOLF

It was more sophisticated than we had imagined: new documents show that the violent crackdown on Occupy last fall – so mystifying at the time – was not just coordinated at the level of Department of Homeland Security, and local police. The crackdown, which involved, as you may recall, violent arrests, group disruption, canister missiles to the skulls of protesters, people held in handcuffs so tight they were injured, people held in bondage till they were forced to wet or soil themselves, was coordinated with the big banks themselves.

The Partnership for Civil Justice Fund, in a groundbreaking scoop that should once more shame major US media outlets (why are nonprofits now some of the only entities in America left breaking major civil liberties news?), filed this request. The document shows a terrifying network of coordinated DHS, FBI, police, regional fusion center, and private-sector activity so completely merged into one another that the monstrous whole is, in fact, one entity: in some cases, bearing a single name, the Domestic Security Alliance Council. And it reveals this merged entity to have one centrally planned, locally executed mission. The documents, in short, show the cops and DHS working for and with banks to target, arrest, and politically disable peaceful American citizens.

The documents, released after long delay in the week between Christmas and New Year, show a nationwide meta-plot unfolding in city after city in an Orwellian world: six American universities are sites where campus police funneled information about students involved with OWS to the FBI, with the administrations' knowledge (p. 51); banks sat down with FBI officials to pool information about OWS protesters harvested by private security; plans to crush Occupy events, planned for a month down the road, were made by the FBI – and offered to the representatives of the same organisations that the protests would target; and even threats of the assassination of OWS leaders by sniper fire – by whom? Where? – now remain redacted and undisclosed to those American citizens in danger, contrary to standard FBI practice to inform the person concerned when there is a threat against a political leader (p. 61).

As Mara Verheyden-Hilliard, executive director of the Partnership for Civil Justice Fund (PCJF), put it, the documents show that from the start, the FBI – though it acknowledges the Occupy movement as being, in fact, a peaceful organisation – nonetheless designated OWS repeatedly as a 'terrorist threat':

> FBI documents just obtained by the Partnership for Civil Justice Fund (PCJF) reveal that from its inception, the FBI treated the Occupy movement as a potential criminal and terrorist threat. The PCJF has obtained heavily redacted documents showing that FBI offices and agents around the country were in high gear conducting surveillance against the movement even as early as August 2011, a month prior to the establishment of the OWS encampment in Zuccotti Park and other Occupy actions around the country.

Verheyden-Hilliard points out the close partnering of banks, the New York Stock Exchange and at least one local Federal Reserve with the FBI and DHS, and calls it 'police-statism':

This production [of documents], which we believe is just the tip of the iceberg, is a window into the nationwide scope of the FBI's surveillance, monitoring, and reporting on peaceful protestors organising with the Occupy movement ... These documents also show these federal agencies functioning as a de facto intelligence arm of Wall Street and Corporate America.

The documents show stunning range: in Denver, Colorado, that branch of the FBI and a 'Bank Fraud Working Group' met in November 2011 – during the Occupy protests – to surveil the group. The Federal Reserve of Richmond, Virginia had its own private security surveilling Occupy Tampa and Tampa Veterans for Peace and passing privately collected information on activists back to the Richmond FBI, which, in turn, categorised OWS activities under its 'domestic terrorism' unit. The Anchorage, Alaska 'terrorism task force' was watching Occupy Anchorage. The Jackson, Mississippi 'joint terrorism task force' was issuing a 'counterterrorism preparedness alert' about the ill-organised grandmas and college sophomores in Occupy there. Also in Jackson, Mississippi, the FBI and the 'Bank Security Group' – multiple private banks – met to discuss the reaction to 'National Bad Bank Sit-in Day' (the response was violent, as you may recall). The Virginia FBI sent that state's Occupy members' details to the Virginia terrorism fusion center. The Memphis FBI tracked OWS under its 'joint terrorism task force' aegis, too. And so on, for over 100 pages. Jason Leopold, at Truthout.org, who has sought similar documents for more than a year, reported that the FBI falsely asserted in response to his own FOIA requests that no documents related to its infiltration of Occupy Wall Street existed at all. But the release may be strategic: if you are an Occupy activist and see how your information is being sent to terrorism task forces and fusion centers, not to mention the 'long-term plans' of some redacted group to shoot you, this document is quite the deterrent.

There is a new twist: the merger of the private sector, DHS and the FBI means that any of us can become WikiLeaks, a point that Julian Assange was trying to make in explaining the argument behind his recent book. The fusion of the tracking of money and the suppression of dissent means that a huge area of vulnerability in civil society – people's income streams and financial records – is now firmly in the hands of the banks, which are, in turn, now in the business of tracking your dissent. Remember that only ten per cent of the money donated to WikiLeaks can be processed – because of financial sector and DHS-sponsored targeting of PayPal data. With this merger, that crushing of one's personal or business financial freedom can happen to any of us. How messy, criminalising and prosecuting dissent. How simple, by contrast, just to label an entity a 'terrorist organisation' and choke off, disrupt or indict its sources of financing.

Why the huge push for counterterrorism 'fusion centers', the DHS militarising of police departments, and so on? It was never really about 'the terrorists'. It was not even about civil unrest. It was always about this moment, when vast crimes might be uncovered by citizens – it was always, that is to say, meant to be about you.

This article was the subject of more references and links on Facebook than any other in the quarter.

Winter

Can vegans stomach the unpalatable truth about quinoa?

JOANNA BLYTHMAN

We struggled to pronounce it (it's keen-wa, not qui-no-a), yet it was feted by food lovers as a novel addition to the familiar ranks of couscous and rice. Dieticians clucked over quinoa approvingly because it ticked the low-fat box and fitted in with government healthy eating advice to 'base your meals on starchy foods'. Adventurous eaters liked its slightly bitter taste and the little white curls that formed around the grains. Vegans embraced quinoa as a credibly nutritious substitute for meat. Unusual among grains, quinoa has a high protein content (between 14 and 18 per cent), and it contains all those pesky, yet essential, amino acids needed for good health that can prove so elusive to vegetarians who prefer not to pop food supplements.

Sales took off. Quinoa was, in marketing speak, the 'miracle grain of the Andes', a healthy, right-on, ethical addition to the meat avoider's larder (no dead animals, just a crop that doesn't feel pain). Consequently, the price shot up – it has tripled since 2006 – with more rarified black, red and 'royal' types commanding particularly handsome premiums.

But there is an unpalatable truth to face for those of us with a bag of quinoa in the larder. The appetite of countries such as ours for this grain has pushed up prices to such an extent that poorer people in Peru and Bolivia, for whom it was once a nourishing staple food, can no longer afford to eat it. Imported junk food is cheaper. In Lima, quinoa now costs more than chicken. Outside the cities, and fuelled by overseas demand, the pressure is on to turn land that once produced a portfolio of diverse crops into quinoa monoculture. In fact, the quinoa trade is yet another troubling example of a damaging north-south exchange, with well-intentioned health and ethics-led consumers here unwittingly driving poverty there. It's beginning to look like a cautionary tale of how a focus on exporting premium foods can damage the producer country's food security. Feeding our apparently insatiable 365-day-a-year hunger for this luxury vegetable, Peru has also cornered the world market in asparagus. Result? In the arid Ica region where Peruvian asparagus production is concentrated, this thirsty export vegetable has depleted the water resources on which local people depend. NGOs report that asparagus labourers toil in substandard conditions and cannot afford to feed their children while fat-cat exporters and foreign supermarkets cream off the profits. That's the pedigree of all those bunches of pricy spears on supermarket shelves.

Soya, a foodstuff beloved of the vegan lobby as an alternative to dairy products, is another problematic import, one that drives environmental destruction. Embarrassingly, for those who portray it as a progressive alternative to planet-destroying meat, soya production is now one of the two main causes of deforestation in South America, along with cattle ranching, where vast expanses of forest and grassland have been felled to make way for huge plantations. [Although soya is found in a variety of health products, the majority of production – 97 per cent according to the UN report of 2006 – is used for animal feed.]

Three years ago, the pioneering Fife Diet, Europe's biggest local food-eating project, sowed an experimental crop of quinoa. It failed, and the experiment has not been repeated. But the attempt at least recognised the need to strengthen our own food security by lessening our reliance on imported foods, and looking first and foremost to what can be grown, or reared, on our doorstep. In this respect, omnivores have it easy. Britain excels in producing meat and dairy foods for them to enjoy. However, a rummage through the shopping baskets of vegetarians and vegans swiftly clocks up the food miles, a consequence of their higher dependency on products imported from faraway places. From tofu and tamari to carob and chickpeas, the axis of the vegetarian shopping list is heavily skewed to global.

There are promising initiatives: one enterprising Norfolk company, for instance, has just started marketing UK-grown fava beans (the sort used to make falafel) as a protein-rich alternative to meat. But in the case of quinoa, there's a ghastly irony when the Andean peasant's staple grain becomes too expensive at home because it has acquired hero product status among affluent foreigners preoccupied with personal health, animal welfare and reducing their carbon 'foodprint'. Viewed through a lens of food security, our current enthusiasm for quinoa looks increasingly misplaced.

This was the most-read article in the quarter on the Guardian *website and the fifth most popular of the year.*

11 JANUARY

Guardian cryptic crossword

ARAUCARIA

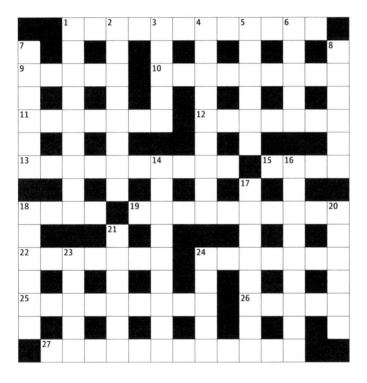

Araucaria has 18 down of the 19, which is being treated with 13 15.

This puzzle was first published in the December 2012 issue of the crossword magazine 1 Across © *and is reprinted here by kind permission.*

ACROSS

1 Subject to town hall causing milieu's panic (12)

9 Encounter dog's home (5)

10 Araucaria beginning to recite old poetry books, bringing Christmas cheer (9)

11 Man with a first having common sense? That's terrible (7)

12 Scouse blues go green in time for energy supplier (7)

13,15 Friendly (say) vicar at ease (say) with arrangement for coping with 18 down (10,4)

18 101° under the ice? (4)

19 Food transporter heard to gradually reduce an endless effusion (10)

22 Place(s) of non-vintage vintage? (7)

24 Food related to cake of soap? (4,3)

25 Complete very large reproduction with look at 19 etc (9)

26 See 1 down

27 Bargain keeping mum to deal with 18 down (12)

DOWN

1,26 18 down worker gives coat to factory girl and father of archbishop's killer? (9,5)

2 Northern ocean hides love which could give ultimate 13 15 (8)

3 French writer passed, only first out of university (5)

4 Overplay muddle over old Frenchman (9)

5 Hang about to see the Queen of Italy? (6)

6 Scamp item to expand 19, for example (5)

7 Accident on motorway summit? (6)

8 Case lacking in posture (6)

14 Corrupt dealing with crime, the French abandoning the leader of the march? (9)

16 Gray's works (in two volumes?) contain opening of Byzantine controversy (4-5)

17 Plant reported to be enemy to skin complaint (8)

18 Sign of growth (6)

20 Fat round Poles at end of day (6)

21 Beast of Oz whose subject was cats (6)

23 Dimension accompanying outside number (5)

24 Cook said to be lawman and impresario (5)

Solution on page 300.

18 January

Rev John Galbraith Graham, aka Araucaria: 'Crosswords are a way of life'

AIDA EDEMARIAM

Just over a week ago, thousands of people turned to the *Guardian* cryptic crossword, saw it was by Araucaria, and settled in for a quiet hour of pleasurable frustration, but soon found themselves assailed by a growing sense of foreboding. 'For me, there was chutzpah in making that 18 down easy for regular solvers,' wrote a puzzle reviewer, a few days later. 'The rubric sends your eye down to that clue, you run through the six-letter signs of the zodiac, and before even writing it in, your stomach has lurched.' A colleague, who did the crossword with her daughter, said: 'It was like watching a photograph slowly appearing out of developing fluid.' And her daughter turned to her in shock, and said: 'I think this must mean he's dying of cancer.'

The reaction online is extraordinarily heartfelt and moving. Some admitted to completing their crosswords through tears; others devoted their comments to trying to explain why Araucaria has meant so much to them over the years. It is a 'brain-joy' doing his puzzles, wrote one. 'No other setter comes near to attaining his fusion of knowledge, originality, humour and consistency,' said another. 'It's not a solo pursuit, it's an intimate exercise,' said brighton2k. 'Your vocabulary, intelligence, wit and imagination being teased and excited by the setter. I've never seen crosswords as a challenge: they're a unique way of engaging with another person's mind. Araucaria's puzzles are fair, honest, complex and have a deft wit. I imagine the person being just the same.'

The Reverend John Galbraith Graham – aka Araucaria, the Latin name for the monkey puzzle tree – has for the past 18 years lived in a tiny cottage in the village of Somersham, Cambridgeshire. Flat, frost-rimed fields stretch for miles around. Inside, it is ordered and cosy, calm and quiet except for two clocks ticking a hurried, insistent counterpoint. Graham, who set his first puzzle for the Guardian 55 years ago, seems younger than his 91 years. Partly this is because his default expression is a smile that lights up his face, but mostly it is because of his engaged, amused intelligence.

Your solvers feel they know you, I say, because they have spent much of the last half-century puzzling out your character. 'It seems to work that way, yes.' And does he feel he knows them? 'It's hard to say. I suppose I have a vague picture in my mind of a sort of idealised solver, who is a combination of everybody I've loved. When I meet or correspond with any of them, it's some-times quite a shock, because they don't always react the way I think they're going to.'

The cryptic crossword turns one hundred this year, and like every established religion or party, has its own schisms: in the stand-off between Ximenian (named after a setter called Ximenes, and requiring an absolute adherence to set rules) and Libertaria crosswords, Graham falls into the latter camp, which depends more on the solver's trust in the setter; trust that the answers will be in the reasonable purview of the average, educated reader with a decent amount of life experience.

Crossword buffs such as the historian and former *Guardian* columnist David McKie point to the layers of interest that make up the peculiar joy of an Araucaria puzzle. 'The first thing is if you look at the clues, they're entertaining to read just on their own, without starting to solve them.' He's also, having invented his own forms of the crossword, such as the alphabetical jigsaw, 'amazingly ingenious'. And then there's his range: a recent crossword contained references to *A Winter's Tale* ('exit, pursued by a bear'), Twickenham, Lysistrata, Methuselah, oscilloscopes, raspberry bushes, Orville Wright and Penang. Graham does admit that, while he reads the papers with half a mind to keeping up to date, 'modern music, modern art, modern poetry is outside my range, really'. Having said which, he did once devote a crossword to the Spice Girls. And he has a checker, a woman in Wiltshire, who keeps an eye on his factual accuracy.

Graham, who produces 14 crosswords a month, for various publications, with an average of 30 clues in each, says he sees crossword clues in everything, all the time, which is not always a blessing. 'It can be very destructive of life, in a way – you can be reading a beautiful poem and then something occurs to you in the middle, that this could be a big part of a crossword clue. And of course the enjoyment of the poem is spoilt completely.' He actively enjoys setting crosswords, as a creative process. 'It's a voyage of discovery. I love the way the word invention both means discovering something and producing something new. That's how it works. Clues are not something you've invented in the sense that they're completely new – they're something you discover, about words and about connections. And that's exciting. The art of the crossword is getting all this stuff into a form that makes sense to people and brings the connection to them.' But he resists the quote attributed to the famous setter Barbara Hall, formerly of the *Sunday Times*, who also devised codes for the navy during the Second World War, that crosswords can be a refuge from the world. 'For me, it's a way of life – it's just what I do, you know.' If he wanted a pleasure to disappear into, what would it be? Poetry, it turns out; especially the Shakespeare of *A Midsummer*

Night's Dream – an answer which, in its appreciation of serious lightness, of joy in words and in the worlds each word can hold, is entirely unsurprising.

Graham is the oldest of six children; his father, dean of Oriel College, Oxford, when John was born, became a bishop; his mother, when she was not managing her large household, wrote 'children's religious books, which weren't very good, but she also wrote a companion to children's worship, which was'. The novelist Penelope Fitzgerald, who wrote a memoir, *The Knox Brothers*, about four brilliant uncles born in the 1880s, once said in an interview that: 'They were a vicarage family and vicarages were the intellectual powerhouses of 19th-century England.' Although his family did not hit the same heights, it's a description Graham, who was born in 1921, recognises. The six children had to find their own entertainment, and they often found it in wordplay: charades and puzzles. One of the online comments on his announcement of cancer is from a nephew: 'The young John used to grab *The Times* as soon as it was delivered to his father's home, put it on the upright piano in the drawing room, and stand to excitedly solve the whole thing before breakfast – he was around eight or nine at the time.'

Religious faith was an integral part of his childhood, but in his teens he began to question it, and by the time he went to read classics at Cambridge, he was an atheist. This was at the beginning of the Second World War. 'I thought I'd better go and join up or something. [But] there were so many people queuing that I couldn't be bothered, so I thought, I'll do it another time, but I never did. I hung around for a bit, and then I thought, I don't think I really like this war – for a couple of years, I suppose, I was probably a pacifist.' For reasons he cannot clearly remember now, he changed his mind about two years into the war, and with a vengeance: 'I thought to myself then, if I'm going to fight, I must do the nastiest job I can think of [in terms of killing people], and the best way to do that is to be a bomber pilot. I finished up as the person who drops the bombs, not the pilot – an observer, they were called in those days.' He flew missions over Italy, 'night-intruding', until their plane was hit, and he had to bale out. Two of the four crew – he and the pilot – survived, and he was mentioned in dispatches, although he is dismissive of this. 'It was because I baled out and got safely back,' he told Kirsty Young on *Desert Island Discs*. 'It was automatic. Anyone who did that was mentioned in dispatches.' He found refuge with an Italian family, who hid him in a stable, 'nice and warm, full of rats' and then in a hide in a field. He took Italian lessons from a schoolteacher billeted with the family; he taught her English and Latin.

When he returned, he switched from classics to theology, because he already knew Greek, was bored with the classics, and couldn't understand the maths lectures. But later that year, he felt a positive calling. 'I was saying me prayers,' he told Young, trying to distance himself from the sincerity by slipping into uncharacteristic demotic, 'and I just somehow knew. It's the only time something [like that] happened to me, I may say, but it did seem as though I was being spoken to.'

When he left university, it was to work in a parish in south London, under his old air force chaplain. This did not last long, because he fell in love. Although it seems surprising now, this was a Church of England parish that demanded celibacy from its priests, so Graham was sent to Durham. 'It was a job that was right for me. I loved it there. But Nesta remained in London. We had three years to wait. We got married at the end of those three years and I went as a curate to a parish.' They were married for 26 years, though many of the latter years were increasingly unhappy, and eventually he left to be with the woman who would eventually become his second wife, Margaret. The church intervened again:

divorced priests could not then serve in the ministry, and so he had to leave his job and his home, as well as his marriage. It seems an extraordinarily harsh outcome. 'It wouldn't happen now. But they were still struggling, really – it's always been the church's teaching that marriage is indissoluble. I mean, sex has always been a problem for the church, from way back. It still is.' He must have resented it, terribly. 'No, because I knew the rules when I started, and I knew I was breaking the rules. I had to choose between keeping to the rulebook, or a spot of happiness for all concerned. It wasn't a difficult choice. It was a painful choice, but there was never much doubt about what I was going to do.'

Margaret, whose husband had died, had her own home, so he moved in there. He had been setting crosswords since 1958, but in secret, because his wife, in particular, felt it would not look good if a priest was seen to be moonlighting; suddenly it became his only source of income. 'I was living with Margaret for seven years. We got married, but even that wasn't enough. When Nesta died [in the mid-1980s] I was no longer living in sin, technically, you see. So they recognised the second marriage', and finally allowed him to return to the ministry. 'We had a very happy 14 years. It's more than 14 years since she died, which is strange. You remember the earlier part of your life better than the middle part, in my experience. And it was the middle part, in a sense.'

He had had his suspicions about what was wrong with him, and his official diagnosis of oesophageal cancer, a few weeks ago, did not come as much of a surprise. He seems to have met it with a striking measure of calm. Although he was exhausted for a couple of months, 'really quite depressed, though I've not realised it. Being anaemic, I haven't been able to do anything.' But a few days ago he was given iron tablets, and they're finally kicking in. 'Now, I hope I'm going to feel very fit and happy, and able to do anything. Until whatever happens next.'

25 JANUARY

A tribute to Frank Keating, the gentle monarch of sports writers

MATTHEW ENGEL

We have lost the lion king of *Guardian* sports journalism and the pride will never be quite the same again. Frank Keating, who died early on Friday aged 75, epitomised the sporting traditions of this paper but he never exemplified them. He was too much a one-off for that.

His colleagues took delight in imitating his verbal mannerisms: 'Oh, m'dear,' he would cry with delight on answering the phone; or, on the rare occasions when he moved into attack-mode, 'I love him dearly but ...' No one tried to imitate his writing. It was inimitable.

Nonetheless he effectively invented modern posh-paper sports writing. In 1971, when the sports editor John Samuel discovered he was harbouring a genius among his sub-editors and unleashed Frank on the unsuspecting public, posh papers had a time-honoured way of reporting sport. The *Guardian* way was more elegant than anyone else's but it was still mainly formal and the players were largely anonymous: they had surnames and perhaps initials but they rarely had personalities.

Frank simply tore up the rulebook. First he reinvented the language, turning adjectives into nouns and nouns into adjectives, and making everything fizz with the sheer *joie de vivre* of word play. For some time the subs in Manchester, who still produced their own version of the paper, refused to have anything to do with this stuff. Secondly he treated competitors as real people. Many of his greatest pieces were interviews, in which his disarmingly gentle manner lulled his subjects into revealing themselves, often just by what they ordered for lunch.

There were many sides to Frank: he could be simultaneously West Country, Welsh and Irish without anyone minding; in his youth he was a London *boulevardier* and an actor *manqué*. There was always a vague hint of the defrocked priest. But his finest and most enduring role was that of little boy lost. He never made a convincing grand old man.

He would always talk about 'dashing off a piece' or 'cribbing something'. Many journalists mistake cribbing for research; he was the other way round. His casualness disguised the cunning of his writing and the breadth of his memory (and his library). Self-deprecation was so much part of the act that he probably convinced even himself.

I learned the hard way never to underestimate the old devil on what might have been the very first day I met him: in the press box at Northamptonshire when I was the evening paper cricket reporter circa 1974. I was discussing with a local colleague when we might announce the information we had about some trivial injury or team selection news, and assumed there was no risk talking when there was only fey, polysyllabic Mr Keating in earshot. The decision was made for us: Mr Keating announced the news in next morning's paper.

His heyday as a sports reporter was all too brief. From the late 1980s, when he settled into his wonderfully successful marriage to Jane and adoring fatherhood, he lost the urge to travel. He never cared for modern football, and his heroes remained those of his youth.

After a last hurrah (well, not much of a hurrah – he hated the whole fiasco) at the 1996 Atlanta Olympics, the first hints of ill-health began to intrude. But he kept writing and became a master-nostalgist, another role he played with complete conviction. He loved to talk about Usain Bolt winning the 100 yards.

In a way sport had left him. For Frank it was always a joyous business, about lovable people doing beautiful things with the ball on the field and having fun afterwards. When it started to be grim-faced and serious and unsmiling – even rugby ... especially rugby – the jollity drained out of it. It was no longer possible to build a rapport with the new characters, if they had any character at all.

Though he loved to celebrate sportsmen and their achievements – the centuries, the goals, the magnificent tries – the rarity of his anger made it perhaps his most effective weapon. When he went into attack mode, you didn't half know about it.

He was merciless in his coverage of the ludicrous, rain-lashed 1986 Commonwealth Games in Edinburgh 'saved' from financial ruin by the intervention of the absurd Robert Maxwell. 'Wellies and wallies,' he called it, and then there were the caterwauling bagpipes: 'These Games have sounded like carving-knife time in an Isle of Man cattery.'

Phrases stick in the memory. Some of his best early pieces were essays about watching Fulham from the terraces 'in the days when dope was Bedford Jezzard's latest signing'. Sometimes a line would just whack you between the eyes, as when one of the monks at school promised to take him to watch Bradman at Worcester 'but the black-cowled swine reneged'.

But his finest pieces of all were his most emotional. On the traumatic England tour of the West Indies in 1980–1 – which brought forth his finest book, *Another Bloody Day in Paradise* – he was confronted with the sudden death of the beaky, beloved Mrs Malaprop of an England coach, Ken Barrington, just when his team had got on top of the mighty West Indians. 'He had been so hale and full of beans,' he began. 'So dynamite chuffed

... his nose crowded out the already jammed pavilion long room bar. His smile illuminated it ...' Later Keating listed some of his favourite Barringtonianisms – 'caught in two-man's land' and 'sleep like a lark', and he concluded, 'between their sobs yesterday his boys could only have faith that he will "sleep like a lark" in eternal peace'.

Only the revered and knighted Neville Cardus, who reigned as cricket correspondent between the wars, had as much influence on the paper's sports coverage and its reputation as Frank did. In-house he was master of the revels. On the page he was something more than an enjoyable read; the wider *Guardian* community regarded him as a personal friend who saw sport with the same unjaundiced eye that they did and wanted to believe the best of their heroes. The warmth of the tributes on the website from readers who can never have met him is testament to that.

And he was adored by young sports writers, who took their cue from Frank and for years after he retreated would make pilgrimages to his Herefordshire fastness to see him. And, as post-Atlanta major sports events came and went without his presence, some of us would always refer to the Media Entrance as the M'dear Entrance in his honour.

For me he was colleague, friend, mentor, neighbour and inspiration. Since he got an infection just before Christmas one has feared the worst. But on Thursday afternoon, he was laughing with Jane in the hospice and talking about returning to his column.

On one web page yesterday the news of his death appeared just above a link to a story about *Guardian* cutbacks. He would have laughed at that. I just wish I could tell him. Good night, m'dear. Sleep like a lark.

30 JANUARY

Mice invasion: don't panic!

PAULA COCOZZA

Radio presenter Shelagh Fogarty was live on air, discussing drugs harm with Detective Inspector Ian Golsborough, when he interrupted her with words to strike fear into even the brave: 'Sorry, I just saw a mouse.' At this Fogarty's voice rose an octave to something approaching a squeal. 'Oh my God! Oh! Oh, how horrible!' Within moments the DJ was hurriedly rounding off the conversation, knees safely on the chair – only for the creature to reappear, with Fogarty screaming, 'It's on the bloody table!'

What is it about mice that scares or upsets us so? In theory, we share our indoor space with all kinds of creatures. If a mouse wants to warm him or herself beneath your floorboards and surface now and then for the odd snack, what harm is there in that? In practice, however, it can be tricky to remain composed. There are countless mouse-in-house stories. One colleague tells of the time he fancied a bagel, put it in the toaster, only to return and hear a strange squeaking noise. You can possibly guess the rest, at least up to the part where, unsure what to do, he left the mouse and bagel in place and Googled 'mouse in toaster'. Apparently, it's a common problem: he opted to bin the toaster without retrieving the bagel.

There are stories of mice who, finding no other escape route, have politely been shown the front door and, accommodatingly, departed. But these are rare. I have spent many winters in pursuit of mice: one was so bold and complacent about the kitchen that I even managed to catch him by slamming down the bin on top of him. But his little tail poked out and the surprisingly deep mewling (was he in pain, or just scared under there?) went on for long enough to make me relent and let him go. 'That'll teach you!' I yelled at the tail disappearing under the cupboards. But within moments, he was back. It had to be the same one. It was like the film *Duel*, with the mouse as the invisibly driven truck.

'There's been a big increase in mice activity – domestic and businesses,' says Andrew Chowdhury, who manages the Manchester branch of Prokill Pest Control. He says Fogarty's mouse isn't a rarity; both Manchester United and Manchester City have had mice incidents in recent weeks. What makes mice so unsettling? 'It's the volumes,' Chowdhury says. 'You very rarely get one mouse. You can have hundreds in one property. They'll eat through your skirting, they'll eat through your doors.' At which point, presumably, all the other mice can just walk right in. Comfortingly, Chowdhury says that even he, pro killer, starts when he sees one. 'You tend to catch them out of the corner of your eye, the periphery of your vision, and you'll jump.'

So what is it about mice that is so unnerving? Is it the way they move, or the way they seem to break into not only your home, but your head space, gnawing away at your imagination until even knots on floorboards look as if they are about to jump? All ideas and stories gratefully received.

There were 387 responses to this piece. Here are some of them:

GREENFINGER: Some years ago I had a house in Chichester, with an active cat. The house had fields almost at the end of the garden, with a good section of rough stuff intervening.

One evening Armstrong (the cat) sauntered in through the cat flap just as I caught sight of a *field mouse in his food bowl*. Armstrong obviously wasn't hungry and so failed to notice the now *motionless mouse*, stood up in the bowl. He strolled past and upstairs for a well-deserved rest. I like mice in general, though not an over abundance of them; so I failed to point the situation out to him. Mice 1 Cats 0.

COMMEDAGH1: To catch a mouse my friend's mum fried a slice of streaky bacon and wrapped it around a piece of Green & Black's butterscotch chocolate and set it in the trap. In the morning the bacon was there and the chocolate gone and no sign of the mouse ... clever mouse.

EYESALIVE: My cat once caught a baby mouse, scratching at the door to get in with the poor deceased rodent in its mouth. As I reached for the door, a gigantic adult mouse, at least as big as a terrier, pounced on my cat from the eaves, and took her down like a lion would a wildebeest.

The big ones are reclusive, but are a true danger when roused. Don't mess with mice.

18–22 FEBRUARY

The Oscar Pistorius bail hearing in Pretoria

DAVID SMITH (@SMITHINAFRICA)

This is a selection from the 387 tweets that were written alongside stories from the court for the paper and web

18 FEBRUARY

Furious media scrum outside Pistorius court hearing. I got past the police line with brute force. Another reporter did it by crying.

Prosecutor Gerrie Nel: Murder charge. 'The applicant shot an unarmed and innocent woman.' Pistorius slumps forward, head in hands.

Pistorius's brother Carl kneels on the floor, resting his hand on the right side of the athlete's back. Pistorius staring at the ground.

Magistrate Nair: 'Mr Pistorius, do you understand what's going on?' Pistorius gives a small nod and says 'Yes'.

Defence Roux: 'The accused wants to take the court into his confidence.' He will give full account of what happened in an affidavit.

Roux: 'Are we immune to what's happening in the world out there?' I will put forward case after case where husbands shot wives through door.

Nel: 'He got up from a bed, put on his prosthesis, armed himself and walked 7 metres.' It's not: 'There was someone standing over my bed.'

Nel: It was a 1.4 x 1.4m room. 'It must have been horrific.' She couldn't get away.

Magistrate Nair talks about possibility of premeditated murder charge and prison. Pistorius sobs, puts tissue to eyes, head bowed.

19 FEBRUARY

Pistorius family grouped in small circle, weeping, arms around each other. Cameras clicking and filming from every angle.

Pistorius: 'I have no intention to relocate to any other country as I love my country.' House is valued at approximately 5 million rand.

Pistorius: 'We were deeply in love.' She felt the same way.

Pistorius: 'As I did not have my prosthetic legs on, I felt vulnerable for myself and Reeva.' Feared danger posed by intruders.

Witness Samantha: 'Reeva said if Oscar asked her to marry him, she would probably say yes.' Pistorius bows head in grief again.

20 FEBRUARY

Pistorius looking more calm and collected. His legal team is winning and the investigating officer is crumbling.

Outside Pretoria magistrates court met another Oscar, Oscar Ngcobo, homeless and complaining: 'The president built a big house.'

More chaos in Pretoria as officials have no clue how to handle media interest. Had to sprint up four flights of stairs and scrape into court.

21 FEBRUARY

Has the Pistorius case got the rainbow nation talking? Heard a white man and black woman discussing it animatedly on a station platform.

Spoke to Pistorius's uncle Arnold on way into court. 'I'm hopeful,' he said about the bail decision, but added: 'Maybe I should ask you.'

22 FEBRUARY

Nair: I have difficulty in understanding why the accused did not check where girlfriend was or ask who was in the toilet.

Nair: The issue is whether he would seek to 'duck and dive all over the world' when he might face a charge of culpable homicide.

Pistorius family together in a circle praying.

Nair: 'Bail is fixed at an amount of R1 million' including R100,000 in cash.

David Smith gained thousands of new Twitter followers every day during the Pistorius hearings, a phenomenon shared by other writers live-tweeting as stories developed.

The school where they speak 20 languages: a day at Gladstone Primary

PATRICK BARKHAM

'We're using a thesaurus and finding different words to make "sad",' explains Rehan, eight. The Year 3 pupil reads from the list his English class has assembled. 'Grief-stricken, heartbroken, distressing.' 'Heartbroken,' interjects Christine Parker, the head-teacher. 'I think that's how I felt in November 2011.'

That was when Gladstone Primary School in Peterborough was judged 'inadequate' by Ofsted, the teaching inspectorate's lowest mark. The school was ordered to improve, and was inspected with alarming regularity until it did. After a stressful 16 months, Ofsted has finally issued a glowing report. 'Standards are rising rapidly. Pupils are making good progress often from a low starting point,' judged inspectors. The behaviour of children at the school had always been good – in one report last year inspectors described pupils as 'delightful' – but now the school was performing well academically. The head was praised for expecting high standards and for having 'significantly improved the school'; the school was graded 'good' in every aspect.

A decent Ofsted is not, though, why the 450-pupil school has made the national news. Gladstone Primary is believed to be the only school in the country where none of its children speak English as their first language. This fact fascinates and repels media commentators. 'If you wonder what's gone wrong with Britain look no further than Gladstone Primary School, Peterborough, where not one pupil speaks English as a first language,' thundered Peter Hill in the *Express*, without actually explaining why. Is Gladstone Primary a vision of a dystopian future or a triumph of multiculturalism? And what is it like to be a pupil and a teacher there?

The colourful displays, the smell of crayons, and the hush of mid-morning lessons feels the same as any primary school in Britain, and the children huddled around tables wouldn't alarm the most bigoted of columnists: they speak perfect English and there are a number of white faces because of the recent arrival of Latvian, Lithuanian and Polish children from families drawn to agricultural jobs in the area. Peterborough has welcomed other nationalities ever since Seaxwulf – said to be an orphaned foreigner – established a seventh-century monastery in heathen East Anglia. The town that grew up on the edge of the Fens became a major centre for Italian immigrants in the 1950s, who laboured in the brickworks and, later, Pakistani and Bangladeshi workers. There are more than 100 languages spoken and more than a third of children in Peterborough speak English as their second language, up from one in five in 2008.

Across Britain, schools are becoming more multicultural. Just over one million primary and secondary pupils spoke a first language other than English in 2012 compared with around 800,000 in 2007. On average, one in six (17.5 per cent) primary school pupils in 2012 spoke another language at home, up from 16.8 per cent in 2011. The challenges facing Gladstone Primary, though, seem particularly acute. About 80 per cent of its pupils are from a Pakistani background: most speak Punjabi, but the school's 20 other languages include Dari, Pashto, Gujarati, Kurdish, Arabic, Lithuanian, Latvian, Russian, Polish, Slovakian, Czech, German and French. One child is from the Seychelles;

another from Guinea Bissau. At break, six Year 5 girls all cheerily admit they couldn't speak English when they arrived at school.

Where does a school begin when faced with so many foreign languages? 'Bilingualism isn't a learning difficulty. A positive view of the bilingual child is the key,' says Parker firmly. She was born in Orpington, Kent and her view of teaching was transformed in 1986 when she began teaching at a school in Sheffield where a third of pupils were of Pakistani descent. Inspired, she worked in Pakistan in the late eighties, picked up Urdu, and has taught in diverse schools ever since. Some teachers (or people in general) can be put off finding out about another community, frightened of asking questions that cause offence, but Parker found that getting to know Urdu speakers gave her the confidence to explore other communities. 'I remember in 1986 being very inquisitive in asking the children about their lives,' she says.

To help Gladstone's staff with their learning, a teacher gives a short presentation about one of their pupils' countries at the weekly staff briefing: last week it was Latvia; next week is Lithuania. This is just one small way in which Gladstone bridges the language gap. With pupils aged four and five, the teachers give a running commentary on work and group play. 'Being a talkative adult helps. I've got a lot of talkative adults in the early years,' laughs Parker. The emphasis is matching actions and objects with words, not on asking intimidating questions. In later years, Chris Wells, a young teacher in charge of a Year 6 class, explains he always runs through the words and vocabulary of a topic before they begin. When the class studied chocolate, for instance, there were a lot of new words to learn. In this environment, he says, pupils become completely unafraid to ask questions that may reveal when they don't know something.

'Diet!' shouts Wells to his class of 30. 'It can be used as a verb, to diet, but in this case it is a noun – Diet Coke.'

'Is it a proper noun?' pipes up a boy at the front. This lesson is already going over my head.

Not speaking English as a first language could amplify differences of ability within classrooms but in the Year 3 lesson with the thesaurus, pupils are engaged in vastly different tasks, according to their linguistic attainment. While some are learning sophisticated words such as 'distressing', those who are currently less proficient in English are sorting words according to their place in the alphabet.

Gladstone has 18 teaching assistants – one for each class – and 10 of these are bilingual, which can be crucial in the classroom. Wells hails from nearby Grantham. Does he ever feel disadvantaged if pupils speak their own (secret) language that he cannot understand? 'I can feel a little outnumbered but it's never been a big issue for me,' he says. His teaching assistant speaks seven languages, and quickly notices if pupils are behaving badly.

Teaching assistant Daleep Wahiwala has worked at Gladstone for 30 years. Even when she started, the majority of the pupils were Muslim. Her three sons went here, and they are now an accountant, surveyor and optician – proof the school works well, she says. But Wahiwala has also served as a school governor, and says that some years ago the other governors became increasingly concerned that their children had so few opportunities to speak, and learn, English. 'It was getting to a situation where our children didn't need to speak English when they were going out. They'd go to the local shops, which were Asian, and the doctors were Asian. We talked about what needed to be done, and Christine has actually done it,' she says.

Those who fear that parts of Britain are becoming ghettos wonder whether the children of non-British parents are sufficiently encouraged to learn English. When I ask if Parker has ever encountered a child who doesn't want to learn the language,

Parker looks at me as if I am talking gobbledegook. 'No,' she says, amazed that anyone would consider this to be a possibility. And does Gladstone ever forbid foreign languages being spoken at school? 'Why would you do that?' she asks, mystified. Actually, though, she remembers there was one time when she told their cricket team not to speak in Punjabi when playing an opposing school. But surely it could be a competitive advantage? 'Of course, we do want to win!' laughs Parker.

The school is helped by additional local-authority funding for newly arrived pupils in their first three years at school. Around £97,000 this year has funded innovations such as a new 'family support worker' who liaises with parents (who may struggle with English) and visits families at home if pupils are absent from school. Other unique features include a buddy system, so new arrivals are paired up with schoolmates who speak their 'specialist' language, as well as Gladstone's determination to forge links with other schools. Sixth formers from The King's School in Peterborough visit to teach science; others from Oundle public school also take English classes. 'Although I have socialist leanings, if somebody offers me something that benefits the children, I'll take it,' jokes Parker. Then there is a regular arrangement with a school in Stamford in which Year 5 pupils spend time at each other's schools every fortnight. 'What I'm really pleased about is that they are really learning together,' adds Parker. 'It's really good to have peers speak English as a first language.'

If Gladstone has problems, they seem fairly typical of any school. When I arrive, a mother has turned up to discuss her daughter being bullied. (When I ask about racist bullying, Parker says the school addresses any incidents in the same way: 'We are very open with children and we believe in restorative justice,' she says.) The repeated Ofsted scrutiny was enormously stressful. 'There is no doubt it has a negative impact on staff health and wellbeing, and it wouldn't be fair to gloss over that,' admits Parker. However, a morning at the school is a genuinely uplifting experience. 'I find it much more rewarding,' says Wells of teaching at Gladstone compared with his experiences at other schools. 'There's that wonderful spark you see when children understand. With these children, it's much, much bigger and you see the sense of pride when they've got it. It sounds horribly clichéd but teaching here is the best thing I've ever done.'

Teachers know when to be diplomatic but the beauty of children is they cannot be media trained. What's the best thing about the school? 'We're famous!' cries Sarah, eight. 'We've been on TV. We've been on the newspapers. We've been everywhere.' Areesha, also eight, says Gladstone is 'better than any other school. It's better than the whole wide world.' Zohib and Maadina are 10 and more circumspect but still extremely positive. 'The learning is good because if you don't understand something and don't want to tell the whole class, you can have a one-on-one with the teacher,' says Zohib. 'Everyone is a friend,' adds Maadina. 'If someone is upset, someone else goes and cheers them up.' Peter, 11, came to Britain from Slovakia when he was eight, and only arrived at Gladstone last year. His previous school contained more English pupils. 'It was a bit difficult because some English people speak fast and use different words so I didn't understand it,' he says.

For all this positivity, it is not only rightwingers who sometimes wonder if it would be better if schools like Gladstone contained pupils who speak English as their first language as well. It would save the need for trips to other schools for one thing. 'This is representative of the community that is here,' says Parker – and all of the few English-as-a-first-language pupils at the school during her tenure left at 11; none were prematurely removed by concerned or prejudiced parents. She doesn't see Gladstone as a ghetto. 'We've got more diversity and we're very celebratory about that diversity,' she says of the school's changing cultural mix. 'It's my job to ensure that when the children leave they are well-balanced, achieving what is expected of them and having a perspective of Peterborough that is not just of one area.' She argues that other predominantly white British schools (and there are plenty in the region) should forge links with multicultural schools. 'They have as much of a responsibility to ensure that the children in their schools understand the diversity of Peterborough and have some real experience of that.'

Parker is running a school, not a crusade, but I can see how Gladstone Primary might educate adults as well as children. As Parker puts it, 'Not only is most of the world bilingual, a lot of the world is multilingual. We're the odd ones out. When I was working in Pakistan, many of our friends spoke five, six, seven languages. We tend to have a fear about language but different languages bring different ways of seeing the world.'

4 MARCH

No comments? No thank you

ALLY FOGG

I have a rule which I try to observe while browsing news sites online: to try and keep my sanity intact. I rarely succeed, it must be said. The temptation to peek is just too strong. I know I will be annoyed, upset and occasionally disturbed by some of the ugly and stupid things written by ill-informed, ignorant, bigoted souls with an over-inflated sense of their own worth and importance. I know I am sometimes suckered by provocative trolling, attention-seeking idiocy or corrupt promotion of vested interests, but next time it will be different. But one day, I will manage to obey my own golden rule: never read the top half of the internet.

Yes, you read that correctly. I know the received wisdom among journalists and opinion-pedlars is the opposite: never read the bottom half of the internet. If I may put it politely, sod that. I'm old enough to remember the internet before the world wide web, when it was used as nature intended: to share incontrovertible proof of alien invasions. In the days of newsgroups and lists, the bottom half was the internet, and it remains the raw, beating heart of the beast.

I still treasure the optimism of those years – a future of limitless knowledge, the democratisation of debate, the end of political censorship. A quarter of a century later, the miracle of the digital revolution has created the means to connect the world, allowing us to reach out and talk directly to people across the planet, from a suburban Melbourne housewife to a street kid from São Paulo or a professor from Sacramento. We can listen to their views, learn from their experiences and then call them a dick. Technology is a wonderful thing.

There is no denying that people are rude to one another online, and especially rude to journalists. It seems many of my fellow hacks have had enough. Charlie Brooker has said recently that opening comments online was the worst thing to have happened to newspapers. Robert Fisk wrote that those who abuse journalists online are exactly like Adolf Hitler and Anders Breivik. No really, he did.

Meanwhile the tabloids' war on trolls has reached the point where a Twitter user was branded thus for responding to the news that Fearne Cotton had named her son Rex Rayne with the question: 'Who the fuck suggested that name? Scooby Doo?' If that type of wit is now classed as trolling, then we're gonna need a bigger bridge.

But do not despair, dear commenters, because the fightback has begun. At the recent social media conference The Story, Rob

Manuel, co-founder of B3ta.com, offered a passionate defence of online comments. His talk inspired Hannah Waldram, a *Guardian* community staffer, to mount a brilliant volley of praise for commenting on her blog, and to establish a new Tumblr, entitled *The Bottom Half of the Internet*, devoted to the very best, most informative, constructive and helpful contributions, submitted to the *Guardian* and elsewhere. In the first few days, the site has already illustrated how frequently comments add specialist knowledge, perspective and insight to the original articles.

I've learned a hell of a lot from reading the internet, and I'd guess that I've learned at least as much from the comments and amateur blogs as from professional writers. To take just one example, it was the commenters on *Comment is Free* who were railing against the injustices of work capability assessments introduced by this government and conducted by ATOS, long before mainstream political journalists, even the most left-leaning *Guardian* columnists, picked up on the story. As a journalist, I am forever picking up nuggets of information on topics of interest from below the line. Of course, many turn out to be somehow (or entirely) inaccurate or misunderstood, but a significant minority are immensely useful. I find it genuinely unfathomable that other writers would cut themselves off from this goldmine of knowledge.

As I hope you've realised, I was joking about never reading the top half of the internet. Across the spectrum of news media, there is near endless provision of fantastic writing, intelligent analysis, informed wisdom and brilliant wit. There is also near endless provision of dross that can be easily ignored, and ugly and offensive opinions that probably should be. Sound familiar?

So if you've read this article all the way down here, I thank you. If you've skipped my ramblings and jumped straight down to the comments for a barney, I applaud you and thank you for that, too, even though you'll never know. Because, whatever other topside writers may tell you, whatever abuse we get, whatever furious disagreement, whatever cruel jokes come at our expense, there is only message beneath our articles that we honestly, truly dread. It's the one that says: Comments [0].

5 MARCH

Human rights laws: supremely serious judgment

GUARDIAN LEADER

Britain's judges have traditionally disliked involving themselves in public controversy almost as strongly as Britain's politicians wish the judges would keep their criticisms firmly under their wigs. That is why Tuesday's *Guardian* interview with the president of the UK supreme court, Lord Neuberger, is such an important and even astonishing event. The wigless Lord Neuberger warns that, in order to deport unwelcome terrorist suspects to lands where basic rights may not be observed, Britain risks having to withdraw not merely from the European court of human rights but also even from the United Nations. This is a formidable challenge to the government in general and to Conservative ministers in particular to weigh their options with great care. It needs to be taken with the utmost seriousness.

It is nevertheless hard to think of a challenge with more destabilising implications for relations between government and the judiciary. Lord Neuberger must have given considerable thought to his words before uttering them. That he said what he did is therefore evidence of the depth of the anxieties felt by senior judges about the way ministers are increasingly tempted to defy not just the European human rights court, and thus the UK courts which defer to European rulings, but also the international treaties and conventions to which the UK is a signatory – and which in many cases were drafted by British lawyers. It suggests that relations between ministers and the judges are in an unhappy state. There is a great deal at stake here for the working of the rule of law. One side or the other is going to have to back down. Serious politicians should therefore think very carefully indeed before they choose how to respond.

Lord Neuberger's warning has old roots but recent causes. It is the result of a combustible collision between two increasingly unmanageable problems. The first, which pits human rights against the supposed interest of the state, is the UK's position as a bolthole for undesirable terrorist suspects who are fighting deportation to countries where their human rights – like the right to a trial untainted by torture and other abuses – are at risk. The second is the Conservative party's increasingly visceral alienation from international institutions, especially those in which the word Europe occurs. Tory leaders were frequently instrumental in establishing these institutions and conventions in the postwar era, yet today's Tory party and press increasingly dreams of withdrawal from such obligations behind a Little England raised drawbridge. Neither of these problems is new, but they have been given fresh explosive potential by the unresolved Abu Qatada case on the one hand, and by the Eastleigh byelection result on the other. The lurch to UKIP at Eastleigh last week has caused Tory leaders to raise the stakes on immigration from Romania and Bulgaria as well by suggesting forceful unilateral measures against international human rights laws in the next Tory election manifesto. It has also, by weakening David Cameron, tempted ministers with leadership ambitions into the open. Lord Neuberger gave his interview before both Chris Grayling and Theresa May trailed their coats in the media at the weekend. But his words will inevitably be seen as a rebuff to them and as a warning to ministers in general about where things could now be heading. Lord Neuberger's words may be intended to calm the current mood, but there is a real danger they will provoke it still further.

In the end, Parliament makes our laws and the judges interpret them. But it is against principle and the national interest to withdraw from the European convention on human rights or from epochal UN treaties against torture and other abuses. It is shameful that so few Tories except Kenneth Clarke now speak up for universal rights. But Tory politicians are living in a fantasy land if they think that lawmaking in their Little England would be able to ignore international human rights. The rule of law and human rights, thank goodness, are bigger than the Conservative party.

6 MARCH

From El Salvador to Iraq: Washington's man behind brutal police squads

MONA MAHMOOD, MAGGIE O'KANE, CHAVALA MADLENA, TERESA SMITH, BEN FERGUSON, PATRICK FARRELLY, GUY GRANDJEAN, JOSH STRAUSS, ROISIN GLYNN, IRENE BAQUE, MARCUS MORGAN, JAKE ZERVUDACHI AND JOSHUA BOSWELL

An exclusive golf course backs on to a spacious two-storey house. A coiled green garden hose lies on the lawn. The grey-slatted wooden shutters are closed. And, like the other deserted luxury houses in this gated community near Bryan, Texas, nothing moves.

Retired Colonel Jim Steele, whose military decorations include the Silver Star, the Defence Distinguished Service Medal, four Legions of Merit, three Bronze Stars and the Purple Heart, is not at home. Nor is he at his office headquarters in Geneva, where he is listed as the chief executive officer of Buchanan Renewables, an energy company. Similar efforts to track him down at his company's office in Monrovia are futile. Messages are left. He doesn't call back.

For over a year the *Guardian* has been trying to contact Steele, 68, to ask him about his role as US defence secretary Donald Rumsfeld's personal envoy to Iraq's Special Police Commandos: a fearsome paramilitary force that ran a secret network of detention centres across the country where those suspected of rebelling against the US-led invasion were tortured for information.

On the 10th anniversary of the Iraq invasion the allegations of American links to the units that eventually accelerated Iraq's descent into civil war cast the US occupation in a new and even more controversial light. The investigation was sparked over a year ago by millions of classified US military documents dumped on to the internet and their mysterious references to US soldiers ordered to ignore torture. Private Bradley Manning, 25, is facing a 20-year sentence, accused of leaking military secrets. Steele's contribution was pivotal. He was the covert US figure behind the intelligence gathering of the new commando units. The aim: to halt a nascent Sunni insurgency in its tracks by extracting information from detainees.

It was a role made for Steele. The veteran had made his name in El Salvador almost 20 years earlier as head of a US group of special forces advisers who were training and funding the Salvadoran military to fight the FNLM (Farabundo Martí National Liberation Front) guerrilla insurgency. These government units developed a fearsome international reputation for their death-squad activities. Steele's own biography describes his work there as the 'training of the best counterinsurgency force' in El Salvador.

Of his El Salvador experience in 1986, Steele told Dr Max Manwaring, the author of *El Salvador at War: An Oral History*: 'When I arrived here there was a tendency to focus on technical indicators – but in an insurgency the focus has to be on human aspects. That means getting people to talk to you.'

But the arming of one side of the conflict by the US hastened the country's descent into a civil war in which 75,000 people died and 1 million out of a population of 6 million became refugees.

Celerino Castillo, a Senior Drug Enforcement Administration special agent who worked alongside Steele in El Salvador, says: 'I first heard about Colonel James Steele going to Iraq and I said, "They're going to implement what is known as the Salvadoran Option in Iraq" and that's exactly what happened. And I was devastated because I knew the atrocities that were going to occur in Iraq which we knew had occurred in El Salvador.'

It was in El Salvador that Steele first came in to close contact with the man who would eventually command US operations in Iraq: David Petraeus. Then a young major, Petraeus visited El Salvador in 1986 and reportedly even stayed with Steele at his house. But while Petraeus headed for the top, Steele's career hit an unexpected buffer when he was embroiled in the Iran-Contra affair [a scandal during the Ronald Reagan era which saw senior officials facilitating the sale of arms to Iran in spite of an embargo and supplying weapons to Nicaraguan rebels]. A helicopter pilot, who also had a licence to fly jets, he ran the airport from where the American advisers illegally ran guns to right-wing Contra guerrillas in Nicaragua. While the congressional inquiry that followed put an end to Steele's military ambitions, it won him the admiration of then congressman Dick Cheney who sat on the committee and admired Steele's efforts fighting leftists in both Nicaragua and El Salvador.

In late 1989, Cheney was in charge of the US invasion of Panama to overthrow their once favoured son, General Manuel Noriega. Cheney picked Steele to take charge of organising a new police force in Panama and be the chief liaison between the new government and the US military.

Todd Greentree, who worked in the US embassy in El Salvador and knew Steele, was not surprised at the way he resurfaced in other conflict zones. 'It's not called 'dirty war' for nothing; so it's no surprise to see individuals who are associated and sort of know the ins-and-outs of that kind of war reappear at different points in these conflicts,' he says.

A generation later, and half the world away, America's war in Iraq was going from bad to worse. It was 2004 – the neo-cons had dismantled the Ba'athist party apparatus, and that had fostered anarchy. A mainly Sunni uprising was gaining ground and causing major problems in Fallujah and Mosul. There was a violent backlash against the US occupation that was claiming over 50 American lives a month by 2004. The US Army was facing an unconventional, guerrilla insurgency in a country it knew little about. There was already talk in Washington DC of using the Salvador option in Iraq and the man who would spearhead that strategy was already in place.

Soon after the invasion in March 2003, Jim Steele was in Baghdad as one of the White House's most important 'consultants', sending back reports to Rumsfeld. His memos were so valued that Rumsfeld passed them on to George W. Bush and Cheney. Rumsfeld spoke of him in glowing terms. 'We had discussion with General

Petraeus yesterday and I had a briefing today from a man named Steele who's been out there working with the security forces and been doing a wonderful job as a civilian as a matter of fact.'

In June 2004, Petraeus arrived in Baghdad with the brief to train a new Iraqi police force with an emphasis on counterinsurgency. Steele and serving US colonel James Coffman introduced Petraeus to a small hardened group of police commandos, many of them among the toughest survivors of the old regime, including General Adnan Thabit, sentenced to death for a failed plot against Saddam but saved by the US invasion. Thabit, selected by the Americans to run the Special Police Commandos, developed a close relationship with the new advisers. 'They became my friends. My advisers, James Steele and Colonel Coffman, were all from special forces, so I benefited from their experience, but the main person I used to contact was David Petraeus.'

With Steele and Coffman as his point men, Petraeus began pouring money from a multimillion dollar fund into what would become the Special Police Commandos. According to the US Government Accounts Office, they received a share of an $8.2 billion (£5.4 billion) fund paid for by the US taxpayer. The exact amount they received is classified.

With Petraeus's almost unlimited access to money and weapons, and Steele's field expertise in counterinsurgency, the stage was set for the commandos to emerge as a terrifying force. One more element would complete the picture. The US had barred members of the violent Shia militias such as the Badr Brigade and the Mahdi Army from joining the security forces, but by the summer of 2004 they had lifted the ban. Shia militia members from all over the country arrived in Baghdad 'by the lorry-load' to join the new commandos. These men were eager to fight the Sunnis: many sought revenge for decades of Sunni-supported, brutal Saddam rule, and a chance to hit back at the violent insurgents and the indiscriminate terror of al-Qaida.

Petraeus and Steele would unleash this local force on the Sunni population as well as the insurgents and their supporters and anyone else who was unlucky enough to get in the way. It was classic counterinsurgency. It was also letting a lethal, sectarian genie out of the bottle. The consequences for Iraqi society would be catastrophic. At the height of the civil war two years later 3,000 bodies a month were turning up on the streets of Iraq – many of them innocent civilians.

But it was the actions of the commandos inside the detention centres that raises the most troubling questions for their American masters. Desperate for information, the commandos set up a network of secret detention centres where insurgents could be brought and information extracted from them. The commandos used the most brutal methods to make detainees talk. There is no evidence that Steele or Coffman took part in these torture sessions, but General Muntadher al Samari, a former general in the Iraqi army, who worked after the invasion with the US to rebuild the police force, claims that they knew exactly what was going on and were supplying the commandos with lists of people they wanted brought in. He says he tried to stop the torture, but failed and fled the country. 'We were having lunch. Col Steele, Col Coffman, and the door opened and Captain Jabr was there torturing a prisoner. He [the victim] was hanging upside down and Steele got up and just closed the door, he didn't say anything – it was just normal for him.'

He says there were 13 or 14 secret prisons in Baghdad under the control of the interior ministry and used by the Special Police Commandos. He alleges that Steele and Coffman had access to all these prisons and that he visited one in Baghdad with both men. 'They were secret, never declared. But the American top brass and the Iraqi leadership knew all about these prisons. The things that went on there: drilling, murder, torture. The ugliest sort of torture I've ever seen.'

According to one soldier with the 69th Armoured Regiment who was deployed in Samarra in 2005 but who doesn't want to be identified: 'It was like the Nazis ... like the Gestapo basically. They [the commandos] would essentially torture anybody that they had good reason to suspect, knew something, or was part of the insurgency ... or supporting it, and people knew about that.'

The *Guardian* interviewed six torture victims as part of this investigation. One, a man who says he was held for 20 days, said: 'There was no sleep. From the sunset, the torture would start on me and on the other prisoners. They wanted confessions. They'd say: "Confess to what have you done." When you say: "I have done nothing. Shall I confess about something I have not done?", they said: "Yes, this is our way. The Americans told us to bring as many detainees as possible in order to keep them frightened."'

'I did not confess about anything, although I was tortured and [they] took off my toenails.'

Neil Smith, a 20-year-old medic who was based in Samarra, remembers what low-ranking US soldiers in the canteen said. 'What was pretty widely known in our battalion, definitely in our platoon, was that they were pretty violent with their interrogations. That they would beat people, shock them with electrical shock, stab them, I don't know what else ... it sounds like pretty awful things. If you sent a guy there he was going to get tortured and perhaps raped or whatever, humiliated and brutalised by the special commandos in order for them to get whatever information they wanted.' He now lives in Detroit and is a born-again Christian. He spoke to the *Guardian* because he said he now considered it his religious duty to speak out about what he saw. 'I don't think folks back home in America had any idea what

American soldiers were involved in over there, the torture and all kinds of stuff.'

Through Facebook, Twitter and social media the *Guardian* managed to make contact with three soldiers who confirmed they were handing over detainees to be tortured by the special commandos, but none except Smith were prepared to go on camera. 'If somebody gets arrested and we hand them over to MoI they're going to get their balls hooked, electrocuted or they're going to get beaten or raped up the ass with a coke bottle or something like that,' one said. He left the army in September 2006. Now 28, he works with refugees from the Arab world in Detroit teaching recent arrivals, including Iraqis, English.

'I suppose it is my way of saying sorry,' he said.

When the *Guardian*/BBC Arabic posed questions to Petraeus about torture and his relationship with Steele it received in reply a statement from an official close to the general saying:

General (Ret) Petraeus's record, which includes instructions to his own soldiers reflects his clear opposition to any form of torture.

Colonel (Ret) Steele was one of thousands of advisers to Iraqi units, working in the area of the Iraqi police. There was no set frequency for Colonel Steele's meetings with General Petraeus, although General Petraeus did see him on a number of occasions during the establishment and initial deployments of the special police, in which Colonel Steele played a significant role.

But Peter Maass, then reporting for the *New York Times*, and who has interviewed both men, remembers the relationship differently: 'I talked to both of them about each other and it was very clear that they were very close to each other in terms of their command relationship and also in terms of their ideas and ideology of what needed to be done. Everybody knew that he was Petraeus's man. Even Steele defined himself as Petraeus's man.'

Maass and photographer Gilles Peress gained a unique audience with Steele at a library-turned-detention-centre in Samarra. 'What I heard is prisoners screaming all night long,' Peress said, '... at which point you had a young US captain telling his soldiers, don't, just don't come near this.'

Two men from Samarra who were imprisoned at the library spoke to the *Guardian* investigation team. 'We'd be tied to a spit or we'd be hung from the ceiling by our hands and our shoulders would be dislocated,' one told us. The second said: 'They electrocuted me. They hung me up from the ceiling. They were pulling at my ears with pliers, stamping on my head, asking me about my wife, saying they would bring her here.'

According to Maass in an interview for the investigation: 'The interrogation centre was the only place in the mini green-zone in Samarra that I was not allowed to visit. However, one day, Jim Steele said to me, 'Hey, they've just captured a Saudi jihadi. Would you like to interview him?'

'I'm taken not into the main area, the kind of main hall – although out the corner of my eye I can see that there were a lot of prisoners in there with their hands tied behind their backs – I was taken to a side office where the Saudi was brought in, and there was actually blood dripping down the side of this desk in the office.'

Peress picks up the story: 'We were in a room in the library interviewing Steele and I look around and I see blood everywhere, you know. He (Steele) hears the scream from the other guy who's being tortured as we speak, there's the blood stains in the corner of the desk in front of him.'

Maass says: 'And while this interview was going on with this Saudi with Jim Steele also in the room, there were these terrible screams, somebody shouting "Allah Allah Allah!" But it wasn't kind of religious ecstasy or something like that, these were screams of pain and terror.'

One of the torture survivors remembers how Adnan Thabit 'came into the library and he told Captain Dorade and Captain Ali, "Go easy on the prisoners. Don't dislocate their shoulders." This was because people were having to undergo surgery when they were released from the library.'

General Muntadher fled after two close colleagues were killed after they were summoned to the ministry, their bodies found on a rubbish tip. He got out of Iraq and went to Jordan. In less than a month, he says, Steele contacted him. Steele was anxious to meet and suggested he come to the luxury Sheraton hotel in Amman where Steele was staying. They met in the lobby at 8 p.m.and Steele kept him talking for nearly two hours. 'He was asking me about the prisons. I was surprised by the questions and I reminded him that these were the same prisons where we both used to work. I reminded him of the incident where he had opened the door and Captain Jabr was torturing one of the prisoners and how he didn't do anything. Steele said: "But I remember that I told the officer off." So I said to him: "No, you didn't ... you didn't tell the officer off. You didn't even tell General Adnan Thabit that this officer was committing human rights abuses against these prisoners." And he was silent. He didn't comment or answer. I was surprised by this.'

According to General Muntadher: 'He wanted to know specifically: did I have any information about him, James Steele? Did I have evidence against him? Photographs, documents: things which proved he committed things in Iraq; things he was worried I might reveal. This was the purpose of his visit.'

'I am prepared to go to the international court and stand in front of them and swear that high-ranking officials such as James

Steele witnessed crimes against human rights in Iraq. They didn't stop it happening and they didn't punish the perpetrators.'

Steele, the man, remains an enigma. He left Iraq in September 2005 and has since pursued energy interests, joining the group of companies of Texas oilman Robert Mosbacher. Until now he has stayed where he likes to be: far from the media spotlight. Were it not for Bradley Manning's leaking of millions of US military logs to Wikileaks, which lifted the lid on alleged abuses by the US in Iraq, there he may well have remained. Footage and images of him are rare. One video clip just 12 seconds long features in the hour-long TV investigation into his work. It captures Steele, then a 58-year-old veteran in Iraq, hesitating, looking uncomfortable when he spots a passing camera. He draws back from the lens, watching warily out of the side of his eye and then pulls himself out of sight.

13 MARCH

Pope Francis: faithful left dazed and amazed in St Peter's Square

LIZZY DAVIES

'Oh mamma mia! Oh la la! The light is on in the loggia! Habemus papam!' cried Sister Walburga, a polyglot nun from Germany who almost ran out of languages in her excitement as a shadow formed behind the curtain on the balcony.

When, minutes later, the new pope stepped forward, he was greeted with a huge roar that echoed around St Peter's Square and befitted his new status as the 266th infallible leader of the Roman Catholic church. But his first words could hardly have been less grand, or less distant. 'Dear brothers and sisters,' he said, simply. 'Good evening.'

With his head tilted slightly to the side and a smile that seemed almost apologetic, Jorge Mario Bergoglio, the Buenos Aires-born son of a railway worker from Turin, seemed almost as dazed as everyone else as he appeared before the cheering masses. 'You know the work of the conclave is to give a bishop to Rome,' he said, and then laughing: 'It seems as if my brother cardinals went to find him from the end of the earth. But here we are. Thank you for the welcome.'

Of course, the crowd welcomed him in style. They would not have done anything else. They waved their handkerchiefs, flew their flags, chanted 'long live the pope'. Once his papal name had been announced, they chanted that, too, in its Italian form of Francesco.

Those from Bergoglio's home continent, particularly, went wild with enthusiasm. 'A Latin American pope!' cried Rafael Duno, a 22-year-old student from Venezuela wrapped in his national flag. 'I hope it'll be a good change for the church, a chance for another reality. And even if we don't know him too well we will do soon.'

But if many in the crowd appeared confused, it was perhaps because they did not know quite what to make of the 'great news' given to them at 8.12 p.m.by the French cardinal whose duty it was to pronounce 'Habemus Papam'. Such had been the speculation surrounding Angelo Scola, the archbishop of Milan, and the Brazilian, Pedro Odilo Scherer, that when the name was given, many brows were left furrowed.

'It was the first time I'd heard of him; the first time I'd heard his name,' said one 31-year-old priest. Sister Walburga did not know who he was. Jean Tonglet, a Belgian, did know who he was and did know that he had a reputation for supporting the poor. But he also knew, with a note of regret, that the 76-year-old was 'not too young'. 'We'll see. We'll soon discover,' he said.

Others, though, had already seen enough. 'Bellissimo, bellis-simo,' repeated Riccardo, an Italian public sector worker, while Francis I introduced himself to his 1.2 billion-strong flock. 'His face is very beautiful.' And, when the new pope asked for the people's blessing before he gave them his, Riccardo gave his solemn verdict: 'A great.' He had been impressed, he said, by the new pontiff's appearance of 'humility, like a pastor'.

He wasn't the only one. Federica Perotta and her mother Giuliana Leone were instantly won over by Bergoglio's simple style. 'Good evening! He said "good evening!"' said Perotta, as if she could hardly believe their luck. 'Wonderful. It was like he was a relative. He seemed very close to us. And the closer he is to us, the closer we are to God.' Leone said. 'He was the pope we'd been looking for,' she said. 'I hope he'll be able to renew the world with faith. And I think he'll manage it because he has a paternal face. '

Thousands of people – the young and old, believers and non-believers, Americans, Italians, Latin Americans – had been waiting in the square for the new pope for hours. In the relentless rain, they stood beneath umbrellas singing, praying and keeping their eyes transfixed on the large television screens showing the chimney of the Sistine chapel. Toddlers were placed on stools by their mothers; the elderly were warmed by their relatives. For one woman, 76-year-old Am Nguyen from Vietnam, it was the experience of a lifetime – quite literally. 'My mother wanted to see the pope before she dies,' said her daughter. 'Now, she says, she's very, very happy.'

For many the new papacy was a chance for a new era, a line in the sand after Benedict XVI's fraught eight years of trouble and scandal. 'We are so happy,' said Raffaele Esposita, an Italian brick-layer. 'Now we hope for a good pope and a strong pope – most of all strong. It doesn't matter where he's from – Italian, white, Asian, whatever. What matters is that there is renewal.'

Two priests from Kerala, standing in the rain, alluded to the scandals that had dogged his predecessor. Bergoglio needed to 'guide the church efficiently'. 'This is not the time to speak about [scandals],' one said. 'This is a time of joy.'

19 MARCH

It's duty, not money, that's made me move back north

HELEN PIDD

When it was announced that I was moving to Manchester to become the *Guardian*'s northern editor, the reaction of certain friends and colleagues was illuminating. 'Did you, erm, want that job?' asked more than one, as if being dispatched up the M6 was tantamount to being sent to a Siberian gulag. Others, clearly struggling to think of something positive to say about what they obviously considered a hardship posting, fell back on a fail-safe pleasantry: well, they said, at least you'll live like a princess up there.

Money. That's what it all-too-often comes down to. How much is your rent? (About half of what it would be in an equivalent area of London). Do you have a spare bedroom? (Yes, and a room to dry my washing, the decadence!). Do you have to pay to park? (Not outside my house, no). Sometimes they ask about the weather, but mostly they just want to know how much stuff costs. They love the story about the time I went into a bakery in Rotherham during the byelection before Christmas and was astonished to be charged just 50p for a slice of homemade victoria sponge. I couldn't help myself, and told the lady she should demand at least £3. Her reply was chastening. 'I couldn't, love.'

I don't want to be that wally from London who struts around with her wallet open, telling people I could swap my one-bedroom flat for the manor house. Not everything is cheaper here, incidentally: petrol at my local garage in Chorlton is a penny more expensive per litre than it was in Clapton, not that I owned a car in London. Getting the bus from my parents' house into Lancaster, their nearest town, is twice the price of a single journey the breadth of the capital on a London bus.

But I didn't just move back because my money would go further. As pompous as it may sound, there was also a sense of duty. I felt compelled to ensure that a prophecy made by my predecessor, the beloved Martin Wainwright, would not come true: that his memoirs would be entitled *The Last Northern Editor*. David Ward, northern correspondent for 34 years, once told me that when he joined the paper in 1974, there were 95 journalists working from the Manchester office. When Martin leaves next week, after 37 years' inimitable service to the *Guardian*, I will be the only staff reporter in the north.

I was more than 20 years off existence when the *Guardian* lost its Manchester prefix in 1959. And though a Lancastrian by birth, I have been exiled in Edinburgh, London, Berlin and Delhi for the past 14 years. But I always defined myself as a northerner, secretly proud when my first *Guardian* editor once claimed to not understand my 'northern patois'. A joke, yes, but with a London-born mum I was always the one with the 'posh' accent in the playground, and so I was glad my flat vowels had been noted down south.

Even after all this time away, I always felt the *Guardian* – despite the tireless efforts of my gallant predecessors – was not terribly good at speaking to its readers beyond the tube map. Whenever the *Guardian* ran a trend piece about how 'we' are all now watching *The Wire*/eating baba ganoush/wearing harem pants, I always thought to myself: in north London maybe. No wonder the media, particularly the so-called 'quality' press, misses important shifts happening among the majority of people in the UK, who do not live within the M25.

A year ago, covering a colleague's sabbatical from the Manchester office, I received unwarranted plaudits from my peers for correctly suggesting that George Galloway had a chance of winning the Bradford West byelection. 'How did you know?' I was asked in the *Guardian*'s morning conference, a few days after the Respect MP won a 10,000 majority. It wasn't rocket science, I said: I was there. Or, perhaps more accurately: I had bothered to go. The prevailing wisdom from Westminster was that Galloway was a spent force and the seat would be an easy hold for Labour. But an hour on the stump with Galloway told a different story, and I wrote as much. I was rewarded with an email from a Labour lord chastising me for my prediction, and another from my colleague, Michael White, counselling me that it was a rite of passage to be dazzled by Gorgeous George, but that he surely had no chance (Mike later apologised in a typically generous piece).

Most weeks bring a new egregious example of London-centricity. In January, the route of the first three stages of the 2014 Tour de France had just been revealed. It was a red letter day for Yorkshire, which had been chosen to host not just the *Grand Départ* but also stage two; the result of a magisterial lobbying campaign by the marketing wallahs of God's Own County. And yet the headline on the first BBC online piece trumpeted the fact that the Tour was coming 'to London' – which was true, at the end of stage three, when the peloton will speed into the Olympic park. But it missed the point.

When people back in London ask me about house prices and parking permits and the going rate for a pint, I get it. I just sometimes wish they would ask about the Manchester International festival, which those in the know consider superior to its Edinburgh cousin. Or the brine pool in Nantwich, which knocks your urban lidos into a cocked hat. Or the fact that the next Labour cabinet are almost all serving their time in northern constituencies. But they are more interested in whether I have a garden.

21 MARCH

How Brown Moses exposed Syrian arms trafficking from his front room

MATTHEW WEAVER

Eliot Higgins has no need for a flak jacket, nor does he carry himself with the bravado of a war reporter. As an unemployed finance and admin worker his expertise lies in compiling spreadsheets, not dodging bullets. He has never been near a war zone. But all that hasn't stopped him from breaking some of the most important stories on the Syrian conflict in the last year.

His work on analysing Syrian weapons, which began as a hobby, is now frequently cited by human rights groups and has led to questions in parliament. Higgins' latest discovery of a new batch of Croatian weapons in the hands of Syrian rebels appears to have blown the lid on a covert international operation to arm the opposition. And he's done it all, largely unpaid, from a laptop more than 3,000 miles away from Damascus, in his front room in a Leicester suburb.

Behind the tulip-patterned lace curtains, among the discarded toys belonging to his toddler daughter, a new video has just popped into his inbox. It appears to show Croatian weapons, believed to have been smuggled to Syria with the collusion of the West, in the hands of jihadi fighters, who are increasingly leading the fight against Bashar al-Assad's government.

Higgins' weapons-spotting eye is immediately drawn to two tubes next to a large gun. The detail suggests that any US attempts to vet which groups get such arms are failing. Pointing at the screen, Higgins says: 'Those are rocket pods for the M79 Osa Croatian rocket launcher. And what's even more interesting is this YouTube channel belongs to Ansar al-Islam, which is a jihadi organisation. That group shouldn't be getting those weapons.'

Higgins, 34, has no training in weapons, human rights research or journalism – he dropped out of a media studies course at university. But his work is being taken up by everyone from Amnesty International to the *New York Times*. He is amused to be referred to as a weapons expert. 'Journalists assume I've worked in the arms trade,' he says, 'But before the Arab spring I knew no more about weapons that the average Xbox owner. I had no knowledge beyond what I'd learned from Arnold Schwarzenegger and Rambo.'

Higgins initially operated on chatrooms and comment threads under the pseudonym Brown Moses. His online avatar – taken from one of Francis Bacon's paintings of a screaming pope – was often the first to appear in the comments section on the *Guardian*'s daily Middle East live blog. Each day he would do verbal battle below the line with online trolls, conspiracy theorists and fellow Arab spring obsessives. The name Brown Moses, taken from a Frank Zappa song, has led to confusion about his identity. 'It makes some people think I'm black and Jewish – I've even been racially abused. I've been accused of all sorts of things online: CIA, MI5, MI6, Mossad, Bilderberg group.' Partly to avoid such suspicions, he no longer conceals his identity and has emerged into the open, where he is being hailed as something of a pioneer.

The conflict in Syria has been extremely difficult and dangerous for conventional media organisations to cover. But the slew of YouTube footage from citizen journalists has opened up a new way of monitoring what's happening for those such as Higgins who are dedicated and meticulous enough to sift through it.

'Brown Moses is among the best out there when it comes to weapons monitoring in Syria,' says Peter Bouckaert, emergencies director at Human Rights Watch, who worked with Higgins to document the use of cluster bombs in Syria. He represents an important development in arms monitoring, which used to be the domain of a few secretive specialists with access to the required and often classified reference materials. 'He'd be the first to admit that he is obsessive compulsive in his attention to details. He gets his facts right, and has become an indispensable resource.'

The *New York Times* veteran war reporter C. J. Chivers, author of *The Gun: the story of the AK47*, says fellow journalists should be more honest about the debt they owe to Higgins' Brown Moses blog. 'Many people, whether they admit or not, have been relying on that blog's daily labour to cull the uncountable videos that circulate from the conflict,' he says. Chivers acknowledged that Higgins was on to the Croatian arms story weeks before the *New York Times*. He and Higgins then worked together to develop the story, with Chivers rooting out extra details about how the weapons were financed. In a blogpost about the genesis of the report, Chivers wrote: 'Thank you, Eliot, for your patience, and your fine eye, and for creating an opportunity for merging new and old forms of reporting into a fresh look at recent events.'

Higgins goes through about 450 YouTube channels from Syria every evening. The list includes uploaded footage from activists, rebel brigades and Islamist groups, as well as from

Spring

IDS should try living on £53 a week. Even minimum wage opened my eyes

POLLY TOYNBEE

Can IDS [Iain Duncan Smith] live on £53 a week, as an online petition is calling for him to do? Perhaps he can just, for a short time,
with increasing difficulty every day and sudden nasty shocks. Is
there any point in trying? Yes there is, and he should.

There is a common fantasy among the well-heeled that the poor
are hopeless with money. If only they'd eat healthy lentils and not
all that frightful frozen stuff, say smug emails I get all the time.
But the opposite is true. The poor only survive at all by obsessive
penny-counting and price comparing. Go shopping with a mother
on a low income to watch the skill and discipline it takes.

For my book *Hard Work* I rented a council flat (available in a
block being renovated) and I took minimum-wage jobs from the
jobcentre, when they were plentiful: care home assistant, hospital
porter, cake packer, call-centre operator, dinner lady and nursery
assistant. I could afford some buses but walked mostly long
distances to jobs that meant being on your feet all day. I calculated the cost of every meal: rice, lentils and potato, an orange
as a treat. Furnishing a flat depended on a furniture charity, but
I never got curtains. I calculated the furnishing cost from what
I would have received as a social fund crisis loan: as of this week
that vital source of emergency loans is abolished, replaced with
food vouchers instead. So I could never have bought light bulbs:

THE BEDSIDE GUARDIAN 2013

as it was I was only ever able to afford three. Without a crisis loan I'd have had to survive some weeks penniless, waiting a month until payday for some jobs.

Instead of doing this myself I could have interviewed people and followed families around. But the purpose was to show people like those who send the 'feckless' emails that however careful you are, even the minimum wage, let alone benefits, doesn't provide a living standard that is adequate, decent or fair. How much worse if I'd had children with me, wanting and needing things. Shocks came regularly, reminding me how clueless I was. With a bad headache at work in the hospital, I went out at lunch to buy painkillers – forgetting it would take me over my daily budget. I needed comfortable shoes: that was a purse-crippling blow, even the cheapest I could find. This is a life with no break, no treat, no movie ever, no drink. Free public places are a wonder – libraries, museums, parks, all now under threat – but lack of bus money limits where you can go.

Let IDS try it, but a week isn't long enough. What starts as a challenge and a puzzle soon settles into a bleak greyness. I did this only to do the sums, to calculate each penny you earn and spend in minimum-wage jobs. I didn't pretend I ever knew what it was like to be poor. I can't know how it feels to be genuinely insecure, to have nothing to fall back on in sickness or emergencies, always one step from disaster and out of phone credit, with no one to ask for help. That remained an imaginative leap too far: I can only guess.

Most of the poor are those 'hard-working strivers who do the right thing' in essential jobs, grossly underpaid. As they get by, keeping their heads above water, I doubt many identify with Osborne's 'aspiration nation'. Now he is pressing them yet harder by shrinking tax credits, council tax benefit and other supports. The Resolution Foundation exposes his pretence that raising the tax threshold compensates low paid workers for his cuts: most low-to-middle earners will lose out, again.

I am, like IDS, untouched by austerity. Osborne asks no sacrifice of me, no crisis tax for the well-paid. If IDS tried living on that £53, after rent and heat, he might admit the colossal gap that yawns between the lives of MPs at Westminster or London journalists and the millions earning the minimum wage or less. They strive, but the gap still grows. The minimum wage has fallen in value to 2004 levels – and now Osborne threatens to cut it again.

6 APRIL

From Snoop Dogg to Snoop Lion: the reinvention of a gangster rapper

SIMON HATTENSTONE

Snoop appears, as if by magic, in a puff of his own smoke. The rapper, actor, gangster and stoner extraordinaire has reinvented himself as a reggae-singing messenger of hope.

Snoop Dogg is dead, long live Snoop Lion.

We meet in his management office in Los Angeles, an enormous warehouse dedicated to all things Snoop. On the walls are huge Snoop posters, to the left is the Snoop television studio, where two near-naked women are chatting, and to my right is an old-fashioned video with a stack of Snoop VHSs lined up alongside it. He slopes in, long and loping, in a white T-shirt, dark jeans and jacket, trainers and shades, blingtastic lion medallion hanging down his chest, patchy Rasta beard, and surprisingly beautiful. He shakes hands, asks one of his homies why there is no oil in his ganja pipe, flicks on the huge flatscreen TV in front of us and starts watching a bit of Snoop history. He is instantly engrossed. No sooner has he sat down than he is up and dancing. 'Baby if you want me ...'

Snoop has just made a documentary that charts his path from gun-toting gangsta-rapper to the peace-and-love Rastafarian who claims to have been reincarnated (the name of both the film and his new album). I tell him I like the film. 'Thank you, man. It's from the heart and soul.' He talks about how he has changed as a man, a husband, a father of three. 'When you allow evolution to happen, that's when it becomes the greatest thing it could possibly be.' He's still staring at the screen and comes to a sudden stop. 'Who is that? Is that Rachel from Black Entertainment Television? Well, whoever she is, she fine as a motherfucker. She pregnant, too. That is Rachel! You bitch, you. Jamaican Rastafari. Yeah, man.'

Snoop Lion still has a fair bit of the Dogg in him. But then Snoop Doggy Dogg, as he was first known, was never afraid of embracing his contradictions. He emerged in 1993 with the hugely successful album *Doggystyle*, and set the pattern for 20 years of guns, gangsters and misogyny. His voice was rich and seductive. His raps were X-rated, yet the kids loved him. He wrote about pimping and dealing on the streets of underclass black America, yet the white middle classes adored him (even the upper classes: Princes William and Harry are fans). Despite the bleak violence he portrayed, there was an innocence to his world – the video to one of his early hits 'Gin & Juice' showed partying kids panicking as the parents arrive back early. Only Snoop could dare to write 'Ain't No Fun (If The Homies Can't Have None)', which critics have described as a paean to gang rape, as a love song 'for the ladies'. He worships the free market, having endorsed every-thing from Pepsi Max to Norton Anti-Virus Software, and is now worth an estimated $110 million. Yet he is a staunch Democrat.

Snoop is one of life's great survivors. Twenty years on, he is still successful when many of his contemporaries are dead. As a young man he was in and out of prison for drug dealing; in 1993 he was charged with being an accessory to murder, though he was eventually cleared; a decade ago he combined his successful recording career with pimping (until it put too much stress on his marriage) and in 2006 he was barred from entering the UK after he and his entourage went tonto at Heathrow airport.

Yet there is something endearing about Snoop – after all, Calvin Cordozar Broadus Jr originally got his nickname because he looked like Snoopy and he still bears a passing resemblance. In 2006, *Rolling Stone* magazine featured him on its cover under the headline 'America's most lovable pimp'.

The metamorphosis into Snoop Lion seems pretty radical. What brought about the change? 'I wanted to make songs about the life I'm living now as a father and as a 41-year-old man, as opposed to always talking about my childhood and my upbringing.'

Couldn't he have done that as a rapper? 'I don't think it could have worked through rap because of my branding.' Like many rappers, Snoop is a good businessman. 'I branded Snoop Dogg to be what he is, and it's too late to change the brand.' What is that brand? 'Gangsta. West coast, from the hood. Speaking for the lost generation – the gangstas, the drug dealers. And I did it 21 years straight, faithfully, till I couldn't do it any more.'

He couldn't do it any more, he says, for the simple reason that it would be dishonest to – this hasn't been his life for a long time. 'Finally I'm able to say I'm comfortable with doing what I do. And I love doing it. And I'm going to keep doing it. If I don't make another rap record for the next year or two or three, or however long it takes, it don't bother me because I'm trying to make music that feels good.'

But, typical Snoop, he makes no bones about the fact that Lion is just an extension of the Dogg brand. The two will happily coexist. Sometimes he will tour as Snoop Dogg, sometimes as Snoop Lion, sometimes as a bit of both.

He offers me his spliff. Though to call it a spliff is an insult really – it's a professionally rolled cigar of pure ganja. An object of beauty, I say.

'You think so?' he says sweetly.

Have you got your own spliff factory?

'I got a couple of homies that do it. We ain't got no factory. But we move like a machine.' He speaks slowly, sensually.

I haven't smoked dope for 20-odd years, but to refuse Snoop seems churlish. 'You gotta have one hit,' he says. I tell him I might make an exception. I inhale. 'Welcome to California,' he says. It tastes gorgeous – mellow, sweet, lovely. So I have another go. Woosh! Within seconds my head's spinning, I'm spluttering and talking in a falsetto. He grins.

I tell Snoop some of his early videos remind me of the television series *Happy Days*. He turns away from the giant flatscreen. 'The Fonz! And Chachi! That's how life was! We lived like that. We were gangstas, but we were having fun.' But those days of innocence didn't last long. By the mid-nineties there was civil war between the west and east coast, and rap was becoming a blood bath. By March 1997, two of the greatest rappers – Tupac Shakur and Biggie Smalls – had been killed within six months of each other.

How did things go so wrong? 'Drugs came into our neighbourhood,' he says. 'And once the drugs became part of our life, guns were introduced to us, and once you introduce the guns and drugs, it becomes jealousy and protect your neighbourhood, and before you know it somebody gets shot at, and you do shooting. And it just goes on and on. And once somebody gets killed it seems like it's never gonna stop because we are trying to even it out. Homies was getting shot every other night, then one of my family members got killed. And when that happens it's a horrible feeling. You never want to feel that.'

Calvin Cordozar Broadus Jr was born in Long Beach, California, in 1971. He took his step-father's name – when he was three months old his biological father walked out on the family, though they have since been reconciled. He sang and played piano in the church choir, but gave up the piano when he finished second in a contest. 'I was like, I don't want to do this no more, I don't like being second.' Was he competitive as a kid? 'I hate losing. Even to this day, I'm a sore loser.'

By his teens, Snoop was a member of the Rollin' 20s Crips, a notorious Long Beach gang. The funny thing is, he says, people now expect him to look back on his early life with regret, and they couldn't be more wrong. 'I wanted to be a gangsta my whole life. Even when I came home from church, we'd see all the gang-stas and that was more appealing to me, so when I finally got a chance to live it, to do it, I rapped about it. I was like, I'm going to do it like nobody's ever done it before because my shit is going to be 100 per cent authentic because I come from it and I am it.' Being a gangster was a way of transcending poverty; then rapping about life as a gangster became a way of transcending the gangs.

Did being a gangster live up to expectations? 'Well hell, yeah, I loved every minute of it. When you ask for it, you've got to be ready to receive it. I knew the job was dangerous when I took it.' Was he a good gangster? For once, he pauses. 'I don't think there are no good ones,' he eventually says.

How surprised is he today to see 41? 'Mmm. I did some things that could have cut my days short.'

Did he think he would go down when he was charged with being an accessory to murder? 'I did. I thought I was going to go down for that. Every day of my life I thought it was my last day on the streets. When you're in court, you have no real sense of vibe and what is going to be until they read it off. You're in there trying to be on your best behaviour, they're tearing your character down, they're bringing up pictures of you with guns, and the kind of person you was when you was that person, and saying you're still that person, and you're on that witness stand and you can't even say anything.'

After he was acquitted, he released his second album, *Tha DoggFather*, which led to accusations that he was glorying in his gangster status: the intro started with a commentary that he was now more famous for his murder charge than his music. Twenty years on, he has written 'No Guns Allowed', which he sings with his 13-year-old daughter Cori B. Is it strange for him to be singing an anti-gun song? No, he says, it makes perfect sense. 'We keep hearing about schools getting shot up, venues being shot up, public places being shot up, and we have to address that. Who better to do it than me because I come from the gangsta lifestyle, carrying a gun every day of the week lifestyle?'

He talks about the other ways Rastafarianism has changed him. 'I used to answer hate with hate. Like if you hate me, I hate you more. But now I answer hate with love.' What about your attitude to women? Was there hate in the lyrics of early songs, the bitches and the hos? 'Yeah, because I was making music for me, speaking from my perspective. I was taught that a bitch is a ho and a ho was a bitch, so my music represented that, until I got to the point where I wanted to show love and appreciation for the woman.'

He's staring at the screen again. 'She is fine. She got tush. You know when they got body? If you go to Taco Bell, right, order something to eat, and the bitch looks good in them slacks,

29 NOVEMBER 2012

Rebekah Brooks, former chief executive officer of News International, leaves Westminster magistrates court after a preliminary hearing on charges of bribing public officials. SEAN SMITH

13 DECEMBER 2012

Trees in Belmont, Lancashire, cloaked in hoar frost – a moment of beauty during the UK's grindingly long winter. Summer more than made up for it. CHRIS THOMOND

21 FEBRUARY 2013

The slum district of Madanpur Khadar in New Delhi, India – a centre for concern about girls missing out on education. DAVID LEVENE

27 FEBRUARY 2013

Blokeish Nigel Farage chats to the head of the Monster Raving Loony party, Alan 'Howlin' Laud' Hope, at the Eastleigh byelection where UKIP pushed the Tories into third place. SEAN SMITH

18 MARCH 2013

Royal Ballet principal dancer Edward Watson prepares to dance the role of Gregor Samsa, who turns into a beetle in Kafka's *The Metamorphosis*. LINDA NYLIND

8 APRIL 2013

One of many ways of remembering Lady Thatcher. Mugs at the Grantham Museum in her Lincolnshire birthplace. DAVID SILLITOE

How the UK has changed since Margaret Thatcher came to power in 1979.

CHRIS CLARKE, ALEX BREUER AND JAMES BALL

Thatcher's Britain

What changed, what stayed the same, and what it means for Britain today

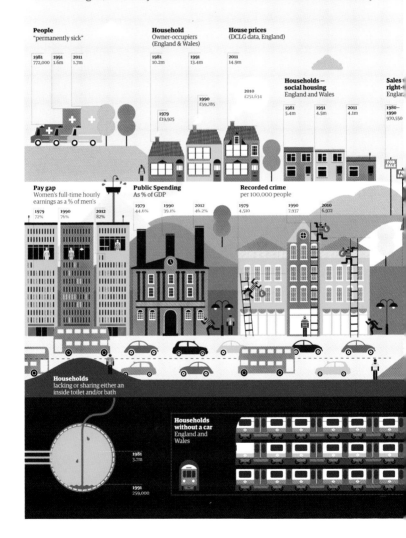

People
"permanently sick"

1981	1991	2011
772,000	1.6m	1.7m

Household
Owner-occupiers
(England & Wales)

1981	1991	2011
10.2m	13.4m	14.9m

House prices
(DCLG data, England)

2011
14.9m

2010
£251,634

1990
£59,785

1979
£19,925

**Households –
social housing**
England and Wales

1981	1991	2011
5.4m	4.5m	4.1m

**Sales
right-**
Englar.

1980–
1990
970,550

Pay gap
Women's full-time hourly
earnings as a % of men's

1979	1990	2012
72%	76%	82%

Public Spending
As % of GDP

1979	1990	2012
44.6%	39.1%	46.2%

Recorded crime
per 100,000 people

1979	1990	2010
4,510	7,937	6,972

Households
lacking or sharing either an
inside toilet and/or bath

**Households
without a car**
England and
Wales

1981
3.7m

1991
259,000

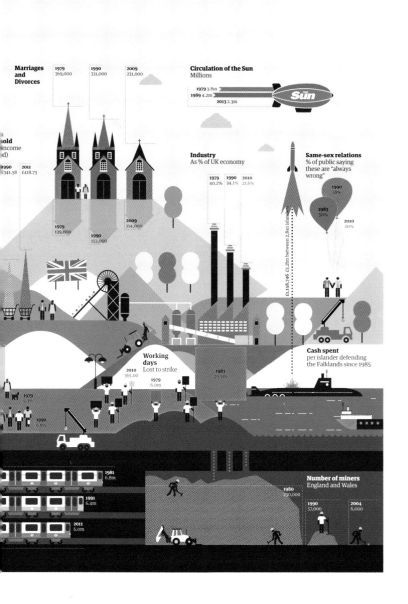

Marriages and Divorces

	1979	1990	2009
	369,000	331,000	231,000

	1979	1990	2009
	139,000	153,000	114,000

...old ...ncome ...d)

1990	2011
£341.58	£418.73

Circulation of the Sun
Millions

1979 3.8m
1989 4.2m
2013 2.3m

Industry
As % of UK economy

1979	1990	2010
40.2%	34.1%	21.6%

Same-sex relations
% of public saying these are "always wrong"

1990 58%
1983 50%
2010 20%

£1,158,746 £1.2bn between 2,841 islanders

Cash spent
per islander defending the Falklands since 1985

Working days
Lost to strike

2010 365.00
1979 6.0m
1983 29.5m

1979 5.7%
1990 6.9%

1981 6.8m
1991 6.4m
2011 6.0m

Number of miners
England and Wales

1980 230,000
1990 57,000
2004 6,000

26 APRIL 2013

Standing on a mound of dirt and stone on the edge of Za'atari camp, groups of Syrian refugees hold their cellphones in the air to try to catch a signal for news of their villages and loved ones. GREGORY BEALS via GuardianWitness

22 MAY 2013

Reader Kate Halls wrote: 'My dad travelled to meet his grandson, Freddie – first time out of his nursing home in many years; captured on a camera phone.' DARREN YOUNG via GuardianWitness

5 JULY 2012

Rider Cody Allred clings on at the Days of the Old West Rodeo on 4 July at Hailey, Idaho. He fell moments later but was unharmed. DAVID LEVENE

27 JULY 2013

Teenage singer Chloe Howl, one of Glastonbury's big successes with her 'steak and kidney' pop. LINDA NYLIND

7 AUGUST 2013

Shellfisher David Cowpenthwaite from Flookburgh on the Foulnaze cockle beds near Blackpool, newly reopened with strict regulations after the Morecambe Bay tragedy in 2004. CHRIS THOMOND

30 AUGUST 2013

Groundbreaking violinist Nigel Kennedy rehearsing at the BBC's Maida Vale Studios before the Last Night of the Proms, the first in 118 years to be conducted by a woman. SARAH LEE

imagine what she going to look like when you put her in a skirt.'
I'm beginning to feel as if I'm in a Tarantino movie.

The more Snoop smokes and the more he focuses on the screen, the easier his words come. Blimey, I say, how many of these do you smoke a day? 'Today is a bad day.' Does that mean lots? 'That means I'm going low. Because I keep getting asked questions so I got to make sure I'm on point. On a bad day five to ten. On a good day 25 to 30.'

Is it true that he smokes with his older son who's 18? 'Yeah, he deserve it.' Isn't he a good sportsman? 'No. He's a good smoker. His brother's a good sportsman. He took on my smoke side, his brother took on my sport side.' He turns back to the TV. 'Hey, that's Sheila Frazier. Super Fly's girl. Sheila Frazier! Show that bathtub scene!'

As he talks, I notice the semi-clad girls at the back of the room. 'Snoop,' I say, 'the ladies here don't have many clothes on.'

He bursts out laughing. 'The ladies here don't have many clothes on!' he shouts to his homies in a fey English accent. 'That's what the interviewer said! I'm loving it! They're my weather girls. They work for my news network.' Snoop's network records its shows from here.

It's amazing how much you get away with, I say. I tell him about an article by the feminist writer Julie Bindel, in which she admitted that, despite despising everything Snoop stood for, she adored him. Why does she forgive you? He turns away from the TV. Now this subject really does interest him. 'It's not even forgiving, it's you connected to me.' He talks about me to illustrate his point: 'I might not like the way you dress, but I like the way you talk, so I'll fuck with you.' Thanks, I say. I had picked out my jeans, striped top and brothel creepers especially. 'You know, for the benefit of the doubt, your outfit ain't really together, but your conversation is sharp. And that's what it is about me.

Sometimes it ain't what I say, it's how I say it. So she may appreciate the delivery more than the particular words. It may tickle her fancy. So I'm going to shoot her a shout-out. Julie Bindel, I just want to let you know that we really love and appreciate everything about you. And what I want to know is how could you hate my lyrics so much and love me as a person? Please let me know. I would love to know so that way we can get a better connection. Appreciate you.' The words drip from his tongue.

One of the many surprises about Snoop is that he has been with his wife, Shante Taylor, since they were childhood sweethearts – though, it has to be said, not exclusively. He filed for divorce in 2004, but they renewed their wedding vows in 2008 on his reality show *Snoop Dogg's Father Hood*

Didn't she go berserk when he wrote all those songs about bitches and hos? 'No, she played her position. At the time she was my girlfriend and she became my wife. I made her my wife because I loved her and I loved everything about what she stood for, as far as being there for me, having my kids, and just being a down-ass woman. And when I say I'm going to marry you that means you gotta take the good, the bad and the ugly. And she took everything. She took it when I was doing it this way, doing it that way. She knew.'

I ask if that is a reference to his pimping days, when he was already a superstar. Now he gives me a filthy look, as if this time I've really disrespected him. 'I mean you make it sound like a game or something. It's for real. You know what I mean? To pimp a bitch is a craft. You couldn't pimp a bitch if I put you in a room with a hundred hos. It's a craft. Some have it, and some don't.'

Perhaps his attitude to women hasn't changed so radically. What about homosexuality? 'I don't have a problem with gay people. I got some gay homies.' He looks round the room and laughs. 'Yeah, for real. People who were gay used to get beat up.

It was cool to beat up on gay people back then. But in the nineties and 2000s, gay is a way of life. Just regular people with jobs. Now they are accepted, not classified. They just went through the same things we went through as black.'

He recently spoke out in support of gay marriage in America. Does he think that Frank Ocean coming out is a sign of progress in the rap world? 'Frank Ocean ain't no rapper. He's a singer. It's acceptable in the singing world, but in the rap world I don't know if it will ever be acceptable because rap is so masculine. It's like a football team. You can't be in a locker room full of motherfucking tough-ass dudes, then all of a sudden say, "Hey, man, I like you." You know, that's going to be tough.'

Some people have been sceptical about the genesis of Snoop Lion. In the film *Reincarnated*, reggae legend Bunny Wailer welcomes Snoop to the fold, but he has recently said he feels betrayed; that Snoop's a fake who has let down the Rastafarian community. What does Snoop think he means? 'I don't know, you would have to ask him.' Does it upset him? 'Either you going to roll with or you roll against. I don't roll against what I love. I love what I love. So even if he's shooting negative energy at me, I can't do nothing but match him with my love.'

It's not hard to guess what upset many Rastafarians. The title *Reincarnated* refers to Snoop's statement that he is the reincarnation of Bob Marley. Does he really believe that? He looks me in the eyes and raps. 'Bob Marley reincarnated, pupils dilated, emancipated, concentrated, debated, rated many times, you defy how I made it? Huh?' It is me.' I don't know it then, but he's quoting 'It Blows My Mind', a song he wrote in 2007.

Snoop's minder Killer tells us time is up. But Snoop isn't quite done. 'I wanna shoot a shout-out to my homeboys in London: the princes, Harry and William. You know I raised them on this music of mine. They were groomed on me. How you think the

Queen like that?' I think she'd hate it, I say. 'Goddamn right,' Snoops says, 'but I'm a part of their revolt. They were at that age when my music spoke to them.'

On my way out, I ask if he's still a big fan of Obama. His face breaks out into a huge smile. 'Yeah, I love Obama. How could I not love him? This motherfucker got three states smoking weed legally now. And they talk about getting Texas, too. If we can get Texas, goddamn it, it's a wrap. That's what our president did for us.'

Did he ever think there would be a black president in his lifetime? 'I thought Jesse Jackson could win one time in the late eighties. "You can win Jesse, you can win." Then Jesse bullshitted, and fell back in and took the money. Then I had no hope. Ain't no nigga ever going to win, and if the nigga do win, they gonna kill him as soon as he get in office. But this president was different. He was sharp, he had the swagger of a real player but he had the conversation the other people related to, so he wasn't just talking to black people. He made everybody feel he was their guy, and now he's in office doing his thang, he's our guy.' Once he starts his Obama love-in, there's no stopping him. 'More niggas have been in that White House in the past four years than the entire amount of years that motherfucker was built. And I ain't just talking about sports teams, I'm talking about barbecues, bingo nights, all kinds of shit. Obama cleared out all the music when he got in there. He was like, hold on, clean that music system, get that bullshit outta here. Get some hip-hop, get some motherfuckin' old-time Motown. The refrigerator, he redid all that; get that bullshit out, get some ribs in here.' He passes me the spliff. 'Hit it one more time. He had some of that in there, too. In the Oval Office. You think he didn't?'

Would Snoop ever go into politics? 'Probably,' he says casually. 'Probably as an old man. If I could make a difference.'

But you'd have to cut down on the smoking, I say. 'Sheeeeeit. Why? How d'you know politicians ain't smokin' like a mother-fucker now?'

It would mean another radical change, but I wouldn't put it past him. Snoop President – the ultimate brand.

9 APRIL

My top five prison tips for Chris Huhne

ERIC ALLISON

Do not be surprised that Chris Huhne, the former energy secre-tary, jailed last month for perverting the course of justice, has told former cabinet minister Jonathan Aitken he finds imprison-ment 'fascinating'. As a former journalist, Huhne ought to be a student of human nature, in which case he will be finding prison a fertile ground for study. To use the now defunct *News of the World*'s motto, 'all human life is there'.

As well as writing to Huhne, Aitken has sent him a book of psalms to help him through his penal journey. Aitken, of course, is himself an ex-con, jailed in 1999, also for perverting the course of justice. (As was Jeffrey Archer. It seems the crime of choice for politicos.) This ex-old lag can also offer a few, perhaps more practical, tips to Huhne.

1. If he hasn't already done so, he should find himself a 'minder'. Not for protection from physical attack – that was never likely. He needs someone more like a Fletcher, of *Porridge* fame; an old sweat who has run the course and distance a few times and can point Huhne in the right direction.

2. He should remember to show humility. Prisons are full of massive egos and there is no shortage of cons wanting to take them down a peg or two. Politicians are an opinionated lot, used to making themselves heard. Huhne should try to keep his views to himself and listen and learn.

3. He should not be afraid to join in some of the 'scams' that are part and parcel of prison life. Jails are run on rules, most of them pointless, and successful breaches add lustre to what are usually long, dull days. I am not suggesting he takes any of the drugs or alcohol, which will certainly be on offer at Leyhill, the open nick where he has landed. But participation in minor infringements will be appreciated by his fellow travellers and make him feel like one of the boys.

4. As a literate man, Huhne will almost certainly find himself in demand as a letter-writer/form-filler-in. A large percentage of prisoners have a reading and writing level below that of a child of 10. Much of my time in jail was spent helping such people and it stood me in good stead. Perhaps Huhne could become a mentor on the reading programme, run by the Shannon Trust, which has taught thousands of prisoners to read and write?

5. Last, but not least, Huhne will observe serious breaches of prison rules – and indeed criminal laws – on a daily basis. He should hear all, see all and say nowt. The number one rule for a successful stay in prison is 'Thou shalt not grass'.

9 April

Marking Margaret Thatcher's passing: a battle over Britain's present and future

JONATHAN FREEDLAND

After a life in politics, now comes the politics of death. Underneath the protestations of decorum, the insistence that now is not the time for such things, that our thoughts should only be of condolence and tribute, something intensely political is under way: a society wrestling over the memory of its most towering recent figure. And make no mistake, this debate over how to remember Margaret Thatcher – whether on the streets, on Twitter or at next Wednesday's funeral – is not about the past. It is a contest over Britain's present and future.

Politics infuses every aspect of it. In the absence of a visible family – her son and daughter reportedly returned to the country on Tuesday – and with the role of deathbed confidant at the Ritz taken by her former foreign policy adviser, Charles Powell, this has felt like a public occasion from the start.

The politics has hardly seemed an intrusion. Indeed, Lord Powell said on Tuesday that the Lady would have been rather disappointed if there had not been demonstrations celebrating her death. Only too willing to oblige, the organisers of street parties and 'happenings' in Brixton or Glasgow vented their long-held urge to dance on the former prime minister's grave. Like-minded activists are now campaigning to make a chart hit of Judy Garland's 'Ding Dong! the Witch is Dead'.

But the more serious, if subtler, effort is happening on the other side. The wider Tory tribe seems determined to use the nine-day limbo between her passing and her funeral to define Thatcher in death in a way that would have seemed impossible, if not outright absurd, in life: as above and beyond politics, as a national rather than partisan figure, as an incontestable and uncontested part of our collective inheritance.

The Tory papers have led the charge, both the Mail and Telegraph devoting their front pages to the same, semi-regal portrait: backlit, bestowing on the golden visage of the onetime leader a kind of halo. Page after page lavished praise on this latter-day Gloriana, accompanied by images of her as if in battle, riding in that tank, urging us to 'rejoice!', dancing with her fellow cold war warrior, Ronald Reagan.

On the front of the Mail, the words 'The woman who saved Britain.' Inside, a declaration that she belongs in the pantheon of Britain's greatest ever leaders, alongside Pitt the Younger, Gladstone, Disraeli, Lloyd George and Churchill. Search for a picture of, say, the miners' strike and you search in vain.

The Mail is not content to leave its intentions implicit. It has mounted a campaign for a full state funeral for Thatcher, granting her parity with Churchill. Such an occasion would ensure Thatcher's transformation is complete, magically recasting the woman who once divided the nation into a consensual figure from an undisputed past – no more controversial than Pitt or Churchill.

The Mail's in-house firebreather, Simon Heffer, has not been placated by Downing Street's reassurance that the ceremony will be 'all but' a state funeral. '"All but": those two words harbour the resentment of the left at her unquestioned triumph as a leader, visionary and statesman,' Heffer wrote. 'The left will not forgive her for proving them wrong.' If you thought Downing Street and Buckingham Palace were safely out of the hands of 'the left', you'd be wrong. Those institutions, insisted Heffer, have been cowed by fear of 'the left' into denying Thatcher her due.

This attack on the government from the right has obscured the more remarkable truth. Which is that Buckingham Palace has indeed broken with recent precedent in granting Thatcher the treatment it gave none of her postwar predecessors. She will get full military honours, on a par with the Queen Mother. In eloquent confirmation of the fact that the institutions of the state are to be deployed in the service of a party political figure, the Ministry of Defence's codename for the army's ceremonial work next week is Operation True Blue. The Queen herself – who stayed away from the funerals of Eden, Macmillan, Douglas-Home, Heath, Callaghan and her reputed favourite, Wilson – will be among the mourners.

The only reason it won't be called a state funeral is that an event of that status requires a vote of parliament, in order to disburse public money. Palace and government have clearly decided that such a debate of MPs – with the likely voicing of dissent – is best avoided, the better to maintain the illusion that the funeral itself will project: that Thatcher's cherished place in our collective memory is now a matter of consensus. As the Labour MP and historian Tristram Hunt puts it, by their decision 'the palace is sanctioning her beatification'.

All of this recalls the send-off granted to Thatcher's beloved ally across the water, Ronald Reagan. Before his funeral in 2004, he was still an object of controversy, his small-state, free-market crusade an ongoing matter of furious debate. But by the end of six days of solemn devotions and ceremony, a kind of sorcery had been performed. Reagan was no longer the Republican president who had enraged his domestic opponents but a national icon, fit to be mentioned alongside Roosevelt and Kennedy, if not Washington and Lincoln. Not content that the national airport in the capital was renamed Reagan, his followers set about renaming roads and public buildings after him, an effort which continues to this day.

'He was hailed as a secular saint,' says Jonathan Martin, a reporter for *Politico*. After his death, the focus became not his ideological programme but 'his optimism, smile and the way he exuded a mom-and-apple-pie American spirit', says Martin. The end result was to reforge Reagan into 'an apolitical marble man', a national monument rather than political flesh and blood.

Nearly a decade later, something similar seems to be at work now with Reagan's former dance partner. Just as the Reagan eulogies omitted his sacking of 11,000 air traffic controllers and fostering of a greed-is-good culture, so today's partisan obituarists for Thatcher have pushed to the edges the devastated pit villages or the hollowing out of the country's industrial base, focusing instead on the easier, feelgood achievements – restoring national confidence, putting the great back into Great Britain and the like. If Thatcher is remembered that way, then why shouldn't she be seen as an unambiguous national treasure?

For those demanding such treatment the hope, surely, is that if Thatcher is commemorated like that, then so too will be Thatcherism. In the US, it has become harder to attack Reaganism, partly because of that intense week of mourning for Reagan. There is no reason why the same process could not happen here.

Especially because the opposition are, inadvertently perhaps, colluding in it. Determined not to be slammed as lacking decorum and good taste, Labour moved fast to button its lip, senior figures taking to Twitter to instruct all supporters to 'respond with dignity'. From the leader on down, the party's statements have expressed nothing but respect, even if qualified by an unspecified reference to 'disagreement'.

The trouble is, that's left the loudest dissent to the likes of George Galloway and the idiots who put out a banner declaring:

The Bitch is Dead. Nothing could have delighted the right more, their papers clearing space to condemn every last Thatcher-loathing placard or tweet. Such outbursts confirmed their thesis: that Thatcher spoke for the whole nation, those who disagree confined to the wild and lunatic fringes. (Any fact which might shatter that illusion – such as the low ratings for the Thatcher tributes on TV, all of them trounced on Monday night by the drama serial *Broadchurch* and by *Coronation Street* – has been deemed too inconvenient to get much of a mention.)

Through that lens, even the archive images of past battles have looked different: the faces of Arthur Scargill, Brenda Dean, Michael Foot and others suddenly appearing archaic and eccentric, as irrelevant and unrepresentative as the current crop of Brixton demonstrators – even though they were nothing of the sort. But by the silence of the mainstream left – broken only by respectful, nuanced tributes – the impression goes unchallenged.

This is how history gets rewritten, the winners presented as inevitable and incontestable, those who opposed them deluded and doomed. It did not feel like that at the time. Back then, it felt as if Britain was divided fairly evenly.

It felt, to recall a song of the time, like two tribes gone to war. Strangely, it feels like that again now – two tribes battling over the memory of the fiercest warrior they ever knew.

11 APRIL

IVF pioneer Robert Edwards will never be forgotten by those he helped

KATE BRIAN

For someone who transformed the lives of so many, Sir Robert Edwards, who passed away yesterday, was a remarkably modest and unassuming man. It was the pioneering work he carried out along with his colleague Patrick Steptoe that had allowed me to have my own two children, both conceived by IVF, so when I was sent to interview him I was daunted at the prospect of coming face-to-face with the man who contributed so much to my own happiness.

What was immediately apparent on meeting Edwards was the empathy that he had for those with fertility problems. It's not easy to understand how devastating infertility can be unless you have had difficulty conceiving yourself, but although he was in his early eighties at the time, he was still passionate about helping infertile couples to have families of their own.

If you ask most parents to imagine life without their children, they'd probably joke about having more time, or more money or more sleep – but Edwards appreciated just how precious children really are to their parents. A kind and generous man, he was very aware of the difference his work could make to those who were trying unsuccessfully to conceive. He felt that everyone should have access to the treatment that might allow them to have a child of their own, and told me it made him angry that the postcode lottery in the UK was denying many people the opportunity to have NHS-funded IVF.

The aspect of his work I'd never really appreciated until meeting him was what a lonely business it had been in the early days: when Edwards began trying to fertilise human eggs in the laboratory, his attempts were not greeted with enthusiasm. He and his colleague, the gynaecologist Dr Patrick Steptoe, endured years of criticism as they attempted to develop the technique of in vitro fertilisation. They faced the disapproval not just of the media, the church and a sceptical public, but were also attacked by many of their fellow scientists, who denounced their work as potentially dangerous and unethical. They were refused funding by the Medical Research Council, and it was only their resolve and strength of character that enabled them to carry on. Edwards said that he had felt 'quite alone' at the time, but that he'd been carried by his absolute certainty that eventually he would be proved right. It was that certainty and his determination that so many of us have to thank for our families today.

Even after the birth of the first IVF baby, Louise Brown, in 1978, Edwards and Steptoe were still regarded with some suspicion, but couples who couldn't conceive began flocking to their fertility clinic at Bourn, Cambridge, to try this amazing new treatment. Scientists across the world learnt from them and were soon successfully performing IVF, and offering hope to thousands of couples with fertility problems.

Infertility has an impact on every aspect of your life when you are trying unsuccessfully to conceive. It affects your friendships, your work and your well-being; it makes you feel powerless, angry and guilty; you put your life on hold, waiting for something that might never happen; you become isolated, depressed and lonely, blaming yourself for being a failure. I know I didn't realise quite how much infertility had changed me, how much it had soured my outlook on life, until I finally got pregnant after my second attempt at IVF. It was as if someone had lifted a grey veil I'd been looking through for years, and suddenly the world was full of colour again.

My first IVF baby is now 16, and his younger sister is 12. There's not a day that passes that I don't have cause to remember how very lucky I am to have them, and I will be forever indebted to Edwards for battling against adversity for what he believed in, and for bringing such joy into my life.

It always seemed strange to me that a man who had done so much for so many didn't gain the accolades he truly deserved until relatively recently, receiving a Nobel prize in 2010 and a knighthood in 2011. Edwards may not receive the pomp and circumstance of a ceremonial funeral, but he will be remembered forever in the hearts of those of us who have benefited from his work, and he has an extraordinary legacy with the birth of an estimated 5 million IVF babies across the world.

17 April

Who is Amanda Thatcher?

PASSNOTES

Margaret Thatcher's 19-year-old granddaughter has become the inadvertent star of the former PM's funeral

AGE: 19

APPEARANCE: Suddenly, into our lives.

Listen, as long as it's nothing to do with George Osborne crying at the funeral, I'm all ears. No, it's not.

Because seriously, I'm still scrubbing it out of my memory banks. If you make me think of it again, I shall vomit myself inside out. I'm this far from plunging my entire brain into a bucket of undiluted bleach. Relax.

Or about Sam Cam's pussycat bow. I've got very difficult feelings about that too. Keep it strictly on Thatcher's granddaughter, please. I promise.

Good. I thought she did rather well. It's not every 19-year-old who could deliver an emotional yet poised reading at her beloved grandmother's funeral in front of serried ranks of heads of state, watching millions and the Queen. Though if any could, she would probably be a close relative of the Iron Lady.

True. Got a way with words too. What do you mean?

All that putting on the whole armour of God that ye may be able to stand against the wiles of the devil – brilliant! Ah …

And 'For we wrestle not against flesh and blood, but against principalities, against powers, against the rulers of the darkness of this world...' I mean, it's cracking stuff, isn't it! She should copyright it before it goes viral. She didn't actually write that. It's *Ephesians* 6: 10–18

Is he an Old Etonian? He's very good, whoever he is. It's a book of the Bible.

Oh. I see. Does everyone know this? Yes.

Why has she got so much attention if she didn't even write the bleedin' thing herself? Oh, you sweet, naive thing. It's because she was the most photogenic thing for miles around. Blond, American, sporting an appropriate yet fetching black suit and hat.

You mean she basically Pippa Middletonned the funeral? Inadvertently – remember neither public celebrants, or mourners get to decide what pops in the public mind.

Wow. I wonder what's next for her then? Free lifetime entry to Chinawhite? A book deal from Penguin on how to organise semi-state funerals? Endorsing a line of celebrity graveside-wear? Anything is possible. God help us.

DO SAY: 'You did your grandma proud, kid.'

DON'T SAY: 'Have you ever thought of going into politics?'

18 April

Hillsborough campaigner Anne Williams dies aged 62

DAVID CONN

Anne Williams, who has died at the age of 62, suffered the loss of her beloved 15-year-old son Kevin in the Hillsborough disaster of 1989, then dedicated her life to challenging flawed medical evidence accepted at the inquest, and its verdict of accidental death.

A mother of three from Formby, who worked part-time in a newsagents, she tracked down witnesses, obtained medical opinions about Kevin's death from some of England's most eminent doctors and levelled repeated legal attacks at the Hillsborough inquest.

With other families of the 96 people who died at Hillsborough, the worst stadium-related disaster in British history, she was refused a judicial review of the coroner's rulings in 1993, then had three applications to the attorney general turned down. In 2009 an application to the European court of human rights was rejected as out of time.

But finally, on 12 September last year, Williams lived to see the truth about the disaster fully established, with the report of the Hillsborough independent panel, chaired by James Jones, the bishop of Liverpool. It confirmed the facts she had known all along and refused to see denied.

The Sheffield coroner, Dr Stefan Popper, had ruled that all the victims had received irreversible crush injuries and were dead or could not have been revived by 3.15 p.m. on the day of the disaster. The ruling meant that no evidence was heard about the chaotic and failed emergency response by South Yorkshire police and ambulance service to the suffering of so many people.

The panel's report, so many years later, established incontrovertibly that the medical evidence was wrong, that many of the victims were alive after 3.15 p.m. and that, with a decent medical response, up to 58 might have been saved. Asked by the *Guardian* then if she would be seeking the painful truth about whether Kevin was one of the 58, Williams replied: 'I have known for all these years that the inquest evidence was wrong and Kevin could have been saved, so I don't need to ask.'

Yet after that 12 September vindication of her 23-year fight, with almost unbelievably cruel timing, Williams was diagnosed with terminal cancer. She always said she would never give up campaigning for justice and had told friends that, once that fight was won, as she always believed it would be, she had 'promised herself a bit of a life again.'

Williams had two other children, Michael and Sara, and three grandchildren, and knew how much the disaster affected the siblings and wider family. She went to live in a hospice before moving in with her brother, Danny, and his wife Sandra, for whose care she told friends she was very grateful.

She lived long enough to savour the day the inquest was quashed, in a damning judgment of the high court on 19 December, including the ruling that the 3.15 p.m. cut-off was 'not sustainable'. Stricken by the cancer, pale and frail, Williams was determined to be at the Strand, where she arrived at the court in a wheelchair, accompanied by Danny.

Afterwards, speaking softly from the wheelchair on the street outside, Williams told the *Guardian*: 'This is what I fought for. I was never going to give up.'

She always rejected the inquest's 3.15 p.m. evidence 'cut-off' because she discovered that Kevin had died in the arms of a special police constable, Debra Martin, at 4 p.m. Martin had testified that Kevin had a pulse and that, just before he died, breathed a final word: 'Mum'.

Martin's statement, and that of another witness, off-duty police officer Derek Bruder, were later changed following visits from the West Midlands police, the investigating force into Hillsborough, to suggest there were no signs of life after 3.15 p.m. Martin has since claimed she was pressured to change her statement, Bruder officially complained that his evidence was not presented properly to the inquest.

Williams sought medical opinions about how Kevin died from some of the country's most senior experts, including Dr Iain West, consultant forensic pathologist at Guy's hospital. West contested the inquest finding that Kevin had died from traumatic asphyxia, arguing that he died from neck injuries and could have been treated and possibly saved. Yet Williams could find no court prepared to accept her appeal or that any of the evidence in that inquest was faulty.

It has finally been accepted, following the panel's report, that the portrayal of the Hillsborough families and campaigners as whingeing Scousers was a misrepresentation almost as foul as the stories that South Yorkshire police peddled to shift the blame on to the supporters. Williams and the other families fought with remarkable implacability and unity that police campaign, the flawed inquest and other legal processes that left not one person or organisation accountable for 96 people dying at a football match.

It is now accepted that the families fought this battle, with no glimpse of vindication for so long, only out of love for their relatives. So, at the end of her life, Williams, with other Hillsborough families, was recognised not as part of some Liverpool rabble but as a shining example: an everyday person embodying the extraordinary power and depth of human love.

At Monday's memorial service to mark 24 years since the disaster, the Everton football club chairman, Bill Kenwright, said the two greatest words in the English language were 'my mum'. He paid tribute to the families' fight, and to the solidarity with which the people of Liverpool supported it, saying: 'They picked on the wrong city – and they picked on the wrong mums.'

Williams had defied medical advice to attend, and watched quietly from her wheelchair. Three days later, she died. She was proved right by the end of a life's mission, and was greatly and widely admired. Like her son Kevin, for whose good name and memory she fought so indomitably, she will be deeply missed.

19 APRIL

Inside Camp Farah: the making of marathon man Mo

SEAN INGLE

It's the smile you notice first. Even on this groggy-grey Oregon morning; a Saturday where the sun has forgotten to set its alarm and the wind is blunt enough to redden ears and chafe lips, Mo Farah is beaming. There is a football at his feet, a crimson shirt with 'MOBOT 10' on his back. Before training he watched Arsenal, his team, beat Norwich on cable TV: now he is relishing the 18 hard miles ahead. He rubs his hands, chuckles. And says, in an accent as broad as the Thames: 'Bit nippy today, isn't it?'

Happiness comes to him easily; especially here in the Pacific Northwest, 5,000 miles away from the paparazzi's long lenses and the incessant do-you-mind requests to grin at strangers' phones.

He has all he needs. His wife Tania and daughters Rihanna, Aisha and Amani. His friend and training partner, Galen Rupp, the American who took silver behind Farah's gold in the 10,000 metres at the London Olympics. Alberto Salazar, the hall of fame coach whose methods have made him the best distance runner on the planet. And anonymity. Sweet, blessed anonymity.

With his return to London, to run the first 13 miles of Sunday's marathon, Farah re-enters the vortex. He insists he is not coming just for the money, and admits he is 'a bit annoyed' with the *Daily Mail*, in particular, for suggesting otherwise (as well as bringing up his extended family's history), although he sounds more exasperated than angry. His words are a low rumble not a full-scale eruption, and he moves on quickly: why waste time on the carpers and little Englanders?

Instead, he says, the trip is about reconnaissance: a tentative toe on the tarmac before a first tilt at the full 26.2-mile distance in 2014. 'London is one of the biggest marathon races in the world,' he says. 'It's special. It's quite exciting as I saw a lot of great athletes running it when I was a kid. And after the Olympics it will be good to give something back to those who come out and watch.'

He is speaking two days before Boston; the bombs and the deaths and the amputations. From a different time; when the marathon was mainly about joy and charity and men dressed as bananas being interviewed on Tower Bridge.

'When I was 15, I ran the mini-marathon – a mile and a half race for different age groups,' he says. 'I ran for my club and won a little trophy. It was a great feeling and I've always wanted to do the full marathon. We went past the high street on the way home and I was on TV. I was like: 'I'm on TV! I'm on TV!' It was very exciting.'

Could Farah, 30, live in London now? He deflates his cheeks. 'I don't think so,' he says. 'I'm spending hours training, so I need to rest a lot. In Britain, there is always something; when you are taking the kids to the park, or with people taking pictures. You want to be able to give them your time but it's not easy.'

Rupp puts it more starkly. 'Mo tells me what it's like for him in the UK and it sounds crazy,' he says. 'People always following you wherever you go, always wanting a picture.'

This Sunday will be more procession than race for Farah: a breezy morning amble before he drops out at halfway. As Salazar says: 'Mo ran a half-marathon in 61 minutes recently and he is in much better shape now. He will run 62 minute 30 seconds to keep with the pace in London. That will be easy for him.'

The tough miles are instead done on his treadmill at home, where he sticks 2Pac or Dizzee Rascal on his iPod and lets the provocative beats distract his mind, or – more often – on the grass track or 2.2-mile wood-chipped trail that encircles Nike's worldwide HQ in Beaverton. It is not uncommon for company employees, out on their lunchtime jog, to experience the thrill of being left for dust by a double Olympic champion.

He rarely runs on the road. 'It is the worst thing for runners,' Salazar says. 'It pounds their body and kills their speed. Mo and Galen will use a treadmill before they run on tarmac.'

Few outsiders are invited to witness Project Oregon, as Salazar's elite running group of 10 athletes are known. Nike's campus has buildings named after the company's greatest stars, such as Tiger Woods and John McEnroe, and there are dozens of wooden statues of sponsored athletes on the way to the main sports centre, lined up like stations of the cross.

As we watch, Farah and Rupp begin a three-mile jog to warm up. Limbs are then stretched and contorted, ligaments loosened and lubricated. Then a final routine, not found in any sports science textbook: head tennis. 'They try to convince me it is good for their warm-up,' Salazar says, smiling. 'We see how often they can keep the ball in the air. Their record is 42 touches.'

'This place just works for me,' says Farah later. 'When I came here in 2010 my aim was to get close to a medal in London [2012]. Without coming I don't think I would have achieved that. My family are really enjoying it too.' He hesitates, disclosing: 'My eldest daughter has an American accent now,' then laughs.

Portland has other benefits too. The air is so pure it tickles the lungs. It is liberal, chilled out. And its inhabitants rarely have eyes for the Olympic champion in their midst. 'Only people within Nike recognise me,' Farah says. 'I go down to the supermarket and nobody knows who I am.'

How does he cope with the lack of sleep, given he has new-born twins? 'We have a nanny and I've got my wife and they take care of everything,' he says matter-of-factly. 'My training comes first. If I didn't put the effort in I wouldn't have achieved what I have. It's important to know that. As much as you want to have fun, you have to know this: if you don't train you are going to get beat.'

It has been over 18 months since Farah's colours were lowered. He won all his races in 2012, and 13 out of 16 in 2011, but until he joined Salazar he was consistently a notch below the super elite. He finished sixth in the 5,000 metres at the 2007 World Championships and seventh in the same event in 2009. Not bad but not exceptional. That year his agent, Ricky Simms, suggested he move up to the marathon. Dave Bedford, then race director of the London Marathon, agreed. They sought out Salazar, a former world record holder in the event, believing he would persuade Farah. But Salazar reckoned Farah's future was still on the track – if not entirely on track.

Salazar was also asked to coach Farah but couldn't: he worked for Nike; Farah was sponsored by Adidas. In 2010 Farah's Adidas contract ended and he went for a trial with Salazar and got the nod. He was in.

'It's kind of like the mafia,' Salazar says. 'The chemistry of the group is critical. You have to be voted in. We turned down Tariku Bekele [who came third in the 10,000 metres at London 2012]. But everybody wanted Mo.'

Rupp remembers Farah making an instant impression. 'We had good chemistry from the start. He was struggling because of the travelling but he was adamant that he would lead as much as he could. He tapped me on the shoulder and said: 'If you want, I will get out of your way because I'm not feeling good today.' Right there he showed me what kind of person he is. He's very unselfish. We are competitive for sure but he's not scared to be humble and do things a great team-mate does.'

Farah remembers thinking: this is the perfect group – I have to move here. 'Alberto said that if he was going to coach me, he couldn't come to England. I had to move to Portland. So that's what I did. Looking back, it was a no-brainer.'

He was always lean but now he is sculpted. He has upped his mileage since joining Salazar – during an average week he will run 120 miles – but it is the weight room where there has been the most radical shifting of plates and mindset. His strength and conditioning coach David McHenry has introduced him to power-lifting: traditionally the preserve of strong men and bodybuilders wanting their muscles to pop out like melons. He can squat 200 lb (one and a half times his bodyweight), for four to six reps. He also flings and swings a kettlebell, a device that looks like a cannonball with a handle, to order. And there is a relish to his combinations on the boxing pads, part of a long core workout, even if he does leave his chin hanging in the breeze.

'I was a lot weaker before,' Farah says. 'All the core stuff, all the weights? I couldn't lift anything. I just used to run and do a bit of core but I never did specific stuff. That's been the difference for sure.'

Salazar goes further. 'He was flitting around before joining us. His training was haphazard. He was all over the place. He did no weight training. He would jog and do five minutes of drills with no stretching afterwards. And technically, Mo tended to over-stride towards the end of races. That's why he lost at the 2011 World Championships in Daegu.'

'Now he is not just a skinny guy, he's a strong wiry guy,' he adds, pride evident. 'And he's not gained more than a pound or two despite lifting heavy weights for power. People have always thought distance runners should lift light. Don't you believe it.'

Farah has a slight labral tear in his hip which can lead to over-compensation and stiffness in his groin. Three sessions a week where McHenry works to twist and tighten and torment his core have helped, along with specific exercises for his hip flexors.

'We train them at a level that keeps them healthy and we do it smart,' Salazar says. 'There's the core work. The massage. The chiropractor. Everything else. Mo and Galen are not just a pair of lungs with legs. We want them to be complete athletes.'

Last year, Farah missed only one week of running due to injury, in March: a minor bump on the road to London 2012. He arrived at the Games fitter than ever. But while the rest of the country was engrossed in the daily drama he was training or resting or trying to relax.

'There was pressure but we were away in training camp so we didn't have the TV on. The only thing I watched was the opening ceremony. It was only two days before my first race that I came into the athletes' village.'

Looking back, he says winning the 5,000 metres was 'definitely better because I was so tired after the 10,000 metres'. He was not sure he could recover in time. 'After winning the 5 km, it was like: "What? I've won?" I couldn't believe it. It was the best feeling ever. To win your home Olympics – it can't be any better than that.'

To speed up Farah's recovery between those races, Salazar ensured his training group's $50,000 cryosauna, which uses nitrogen gas to lower skin surface to 30°F, was shipped to London. 'We had a mobile van,' Salazar says. 'It would visit Mo one day and Galen the other day. It's noticeable how quickly it helps them recover. It's particularly good for inflammation at the end of the season.'

Could Farah improve further in the next two or three years? Sure, Salazar says. He is stronger now. He runs barefoot twice a week which also helps. And he and Rupp have recently started going to Los Angeles to train with the sprint coach John Smith. This is not about shaving tenths of seconds off their flying finish: it's more fundamental than that. Salazar is using the state-of-the-art foot-sensing software at Smith's camp to shift the way Farah and Rupp run. He wants their feet to be in contact with the ground less often – in effect, to run more like sprinters.

'A lot of people will say: it's not broke, don't try to fix it,' Rupp says. 'But that's never been Alberto's attitude. Until it's the most efficient, the most powerful, the most perfect way to do something he says you should always strive to improve.'

In Portland, their routine starts with Farah and Rupp running 12 miles on grass before they jog to a running track that seems to have been dropped from 30,000 feet into the woods. From the start line only the home straight is visible; the rest of the track is hidden by thick trees. If Hansel and Gretel were runners, this would be their playground. Sometimes a herd of deer arrive to watch.

As the pair scamper past, Salazar points out that Farah's arms rock less than they used to. 'If I'd got him when he was younger I'd have tried to make him be even stiller, to conserve his energy like Galen,' he says. 'But what are you going to do? Mo is the best in the world.'

Farah's plan is to double up again in Moscow at this year's World Championships, take on the marathon in 2014 and then pick his targets for the 2016 Olympics in Rio. He will either double up at the 5,000 metres and 10,000 metres again or attempt 10,000 metres and marathon, depending on Salazar's guidance. 'He's the boss,' Farah says. 'I just do what he tells me.'

Salazar quickly returns the compliment, marvelling at just how versatile Farah has become. 'Mo is one of the most intuitive runners around. He knows how to race. He won't ever lead until he has to. He's faster than everyone; he will kill them on the kick. But sometimes he will go with two to three laps remaining because he knows he is both very strong and very fast. He's a monster tactician.'

At this point Farah and Rupp, who are 14 miles into their workout, finish an 800 metre interval in 1 minute 58 seconds. After a 400 metre recovery run at seven-minute-mile pace, they have one more fast lap remaining. 'Fifty-five seconds for this 400 metres,' shouts Salazar, who swats aside Farah's half-hearted pleas for a 51-second interval, even though he later confides he knows he could do it.

Salazar cocks his stopwatch. The pair crouch, pause: fully engage. Then Farah playfully thumps Rupp on his back and shouts 'Goonmyson!', and they are away: glowing spirits bounding into the distance.

A female conductor at the Last Night of the Proms is worth waving a flag for

ELIZABETH DAVIS

It's taken 22 conductors, 118 years and almost as many renditions of 'Land of Hope and Glory' to get here. But on 7 September 2013, Marin Alsop will become the first female conductor to wield the baton at the Last Night of the Proms.

I should be shocked it's taken so long. But actually I can't say I'm surprised.

The number of women who hold top-level conducting posts around the world can be counted on one hand. Besides Alsop, there's JoAnn Falletta, principal conductor at the Ulster orchestra, Jane Glover, head of opera at the Royal Academy of Music, Xian Zhang – who also appears at this year's BBC Proms – and precious few others.

Announcing the Proms programme this week, its director, Roger Wright mentioned the 'weight of history', the traditional division of family roles and the system of training conductors as three reasons women haven't made an impact on the podium. And it is true that it's a career that puts an almost impossible strain on family life. The world's best conductors have to live a nomadic life, constantly travelling across continents and producing a steady stream of dazzling performances and brilliant recordings.

But there must be more to it than that – after all, one of the other stars of the 2013 Last Night of the Proms will be mezzo-soprano Joyce DiDonato, the epitome of an international opera superstar, who appears in New York one week and London the next. So why are there so few female conducting superstars to match the Barenboims, Elders and Rattles of this world?

It's no longer true to say that the concert hall is dominated by men when artists like violinist Nicola Benedetti, trumpeter Alison Balsom, cellist Alisa Weilerstein, pianist Mitsuko Uchida and soprano Renée Fleming can sell out venues. And they're in good company – the list of female soloists at the top of the classical world stretches on and on, and orchestral musicians are just as likely to be women as men (with the notable exception of the Vienna Philharmonic). And yet, the person at the front remains, by and large, male.

Perhaps the world of business – another sector in which men still outnumber women at the top – is a useful parallel. Like CEOs, conductors have to be excellent people managers. I spoke to one (male) conductor recently who said managing the fiery personalities of his orchestra took up at least 50 per cent of his time. Conductors have to bend a roomful of musicians to their particular interpretation of a piece of music. And that's a role that, like it or not, musicians, audiences and critics are more used to seeing filled by a man, an impression that's been formed largely by the mythical maestros of the 20th century – Sir Georg Solti, Arturo Toscanini, Wilhelm Furtwängler. The job itself is no more biased towards men than that of CEO is: but while the perception of the male maestro remains, so will the inequality.

Of course, I'd prefer not to be writing this, I'd rather female conductors were the norm. But they are emphatically not, and this is no time for gender-blindness. Nadia Boulanger, the great teacher and composer, was once asked about being a female conductor to which she witheringly replied: 'I've been a woman a little over 50 years and have gotten over my initial astonishment.' Which is brilliant. But it's not going to get more women on the podium.

Nor is the argument that more women will gradually filter through the system. Time may eventually bring about equality – but I'm not prepared to wait for that. Concert halls need to engage more women, orchestras need to employ them, festivals need to invite them and – crucially – the media has to cover them. Changing audience perception has to be a joint effort.

And that's why the BBC Proms's decision to hand the Last Night over to a woman is so historic. All of the festival's concerts are broadcast on Radio 3 and many are filmed – but only the Last Night, with its star soloists, classical favourites and traditional tunes, attracts viewers in their millions. Alsop isn't conducting any old Prom, she's conducting the most high-profile event of the classical music calendar and one of the few events at which the conductor is also expected to give a speech.

Yes, Alsop is the first in far too long and, yes, only five out of 50 Proms conductors this year are women. But in September millions will tune in to see her conduct works by both men and women. And that is something worth waving a flag for.

19 APRIL

Why the Boston terrorist plot is the least successful in living memory

MARINA HYDE

It's an early call, but the Boston marathon bombing may well be the least successful terrorist plot in living memory. I doubt the realisation dawned on the suspect now lying dead in a hospital morgue, his last breaths taken as medical staff battled unquestioningly to save him as they would any other patient. But if the effect of your supreme act of cynicism is to slough away cynicism, then you are a stunning failure, and so is what we'll flatter absurdly as your 'ideology'.

A week ago, many might well have remarked that Sunday's London marathon was probably only a year off being rebranded the McDonald's London marathon. Even more might have confessed to that slight reflexive dread as another sponsorship request pinged in. Anyone who denies that a certain degree of ennui has accrued around such events must ask themselves why so many charity marathon runners feel the need to begin their emails with regretful second-guessing. 'I hope you don't mind ...', 'Sorry for another request ...'

As Boston has reminded the world: DON'T YOU DARE APOLOGISE.

It's just a hunch, but I bet viewing figures for the London marathon are stonking. Just as the Olympics felt like a cavalcade of aspirational and inspirational stories, so those same aspects of the marathon have been newly exposed again. A week ago I might have scanned that tumult of charity runners and rolled my eyes at someone in a comedy ostrich costume. Thanks to the Boston bombers' moronic masterplan, I will now see something else entirely. I will look at those seas of bobbing heads and imagine thousands of vicarious brushes or head-on collisions with tragedy or pain or deprivation, and thousands of people knackering their arses to do something about it.

In telescoping their act of murderous imbecility on the finishing line of an event in which the overwhelming majority of participants are ordinary people putting themselves through the wringer in the cause of other ordinary people, the Boston bombers served only to remind the world that marathons are something in which we all have a stake. Not everyone in the UK knows someone running in Sunday's marathon, but you could imagine everyone knowing someone who knows someone running in it. Have you got a someone? It's not too late to get a someone.

My someone in this year's marathon is called William Sherwood, and he's the surgeon who saved my newborn son last August, operating on him when he was three days old in a procedure I'll paraphrase as 'rearranging his insides'. I had spent what felt like a couple of decades – but was in fact only a couple of days – asking everyone from doctors to nurses to cleaners to random people in corridors whether my baby was going to die, and been only answered with what felt like an increasingly tentative 'Look, he's in the best place ...'

Will was the first person to say 'No'. No, he wasn't going to die, because he was going to operate on him later that day. I still don't know the precise details of what went on during those hours because I was too gibberingly fearful to ask in full, let alone go anywhere near the internet for information. When we were out of the worst woods, my Google outings were limited to search terms such as 'possible to actually fall in actual love with surgeon and for husband to also fall in actual love with surgeon'. I obviously resolved to marry Will to one of my sisters, and was most put out during one of the night vigils with the brilliant nurses when one of them confided that he was spoken for. 'What a surprise,' I hissed over the nest of tubes. 'He's young, good-looking, and his job is SAVING BABIES. I literally can't believe he's not single.' (You'll note it wasn't all surgical wins for us: my sarcasmectomy was unsuccessful.)

On Sunday, Will is running for Chelsea and Westminster hospital's Pluto appeal, a drive by the Children's Hospital Trust Fund to raise cash for a surgical robot. This is a spectacular piece of kit – let's call it RoboDoc – that enables surgeons to perform intricate operations on children and even the tiniest babies with greater precision than the human hand allows. There's currently only one children's surgical robot in the UK, based in Leeds (there are 300 in the US).

So, if you haven't a sponsorship interest in Sunday's marathon, might I respectfully suggest a flutter on Will? He's at justgiving. com/william-sherwood, and at the time of writing he had not reached his sponsorship target, probably because he fritters his time away saving lives as opposed to sending out those aforementioned dreaded sponsorship emails. Or pick someone else. Back a mate or a comedy ostrich. Consider it a wondrous human Grand National on which we can all have a flutter.

And it is the ultimate flutter, if you think about it, because you never know when you or yours might need to collect on the communal winnings their charitable efforts produce. Maybe some of the medical equipment that saved those injured in the Boston blasts was, by some circuitous route, funded by Bostonians running in previous marathons. Maybe the work of the medical staff who battled to save the bombing suspect was in part made possible by past donations from ordinary people doing this extraordinary, mad, 26-mile thing. If it was, I can't think of an irony more sublimely illustrative of who's on the side of humanity and right. Go on. Have a punt.

Rod Stewart: 'I thought songwriting had left me'

MICHAEL HANN

We are talking about soul music. Rod Stewart is telling me what a disaster his 2009 covers album *Soulbook* was. 'It was a cock-up,' he says, his raspy voice made raspier still by a developing cold, 'simply because you can't beat the originals. You'll never beat the originals, because they're still on the airwaves.'

He didn't hear Cliff Richard's soul abum from 2011, then?

Stewart looks a little astonished. 'He didn't do a soul abum ...'

He did.

Revue-style live show, too, with Percy Sledge and Freda Payne and James Ingram up on stage with him.

Stewart looks even more astonished. 'Really?'

Yup. He looked a bit out of his depth, to be honest.

'Oh, bless him.'

At 68, hair still spiky and sandy, skin the colour of antique furniture, Stewart remains a musician, then. If he is better known for countless things that have nothing to do with music – a list of statuesque, blonde partners (including three wives) longer than that of Cyprus's creditors; a selection of myths and legends ranging from him having been an apprentice professional foot-baller, to his stomach having been pumped clean of semen after he performed fellatio on a bar's worth of sailors in San Diego, to his having invented a way of taking cocaine anally – then it should be remembered that no one would know any of those stories if the music hadn't captured the public imagination in the first place.

The couple of albums he made with the Jeff Beck Group in the late sixties laid down the template that was then developed and coloured by Led Zeppelin. The solo albums he made for Mercury in the early seventies were perfect fusions of his musical loves – soul, folk, rock'n'roll – and the second side of his 1971 album *Every Picture Tells a Story* is as perfect a 20 minutes as rock has produced. The Faces, the group that ran concurrently with those albums – and with whom he would be delighted to reunite next year after everyone's schedules are clear – developed a reputation, through the booze fumes, as the surest guarantee of a good time that live music had to offer.

The problem for many listeners lies in the 40 or so years since. Which is an awfully long time, even if they have been punctuated with the occasional gem. Never mind that *Every Picture* and its attendant single 'Maggie May' both topped the US and UK charts simultaneously – Stewart never seemed afraid to lower his standards in search of hits. And so we got the critic Greil Marcus's famous assessment: 'Rarely has a singer had as full and unique a talent as Rod Stewart; rarely has anyone betrayed his talent so completely. Once the most compassionate presence in music, he has become a bilious self-parody – and sells more records than ever.' And that was written 33 years ago. Chances are, Marcus hasn't changed his mind since, especially since Stewart's *Great American Songbook* series of albums became the most commercially successful of his career.

But you know what? He gets a free pass, because most singers don't even manage his few years of near perfection – even if he doesn't seem too fussed about his art. It's perhaps telling that he seems more interested in talking about football, north-London property prices and our respective children than he is about *Time*, his new album – and the first on which he has contributed song-writing since 1998's *When We Were the New Boys*, a misfiring effort that also featured him covering Oasis and Primal Scream.

He is known less as a writer, though, than as an interpreter of other people's songs, and at his absolute best he deserves to be treated as rock's Sinatra – a superlative interpreter of superlative songs. He gets lots of Identikit Rod submissions, all swirling bagpipes and roaming in the gloaming, but he ignores them. But when he hears the right song, he looks for the way to make it a Rod Stewart song. 'For instance, I'm sure Tom Waits wouldn't mind me saying this – Tom's "Downtown Train", I realised there was a melody there in the chorus, and it's beautiful, but he barely gets up and barely gets down to the lower notes, so I took it to the extreme. That was a case where I brought the chorus alive and there have been a couple like that.'

He says he's a better singer now than in his youth, despite his voice having lowered half a tone after his throat cancer in 2000. 'I've got much better pitch, much better control, much better understanding of a song. I've always been able to get inside a song really easily, and if it's my song I can make it seem honest.'

What happened to his writing? Why did he stop?

'Ayeayeayeayeaye. A combination of the *Great American Songbook* albums, being somewhat lazy, and certain remarks made by a high-flying executive at a record company saying that my songs were shit and didn't sound like nothing new. Songwriting's never been a natural art for me; it's always been a bit of a struggle. I just thought it had got up and left me. I'd done the best I could and maybe I'd got nothing to write about any more.'

He puts writing lyrics off until the last minute, 'when the song's got a hook. The way I do it is hum and hah along while the band are playing. I sing whatever comes into my head and nine times out of 10 that will be the title of the song. Either that or I'd just write down a good title – like "Young Turks" or "Baby Jane" – and wait until the right vehicle comes along for it.'

But some of the lyrics on those Faces and early solo albums are wonderful – a unique combination of picaresque tales, music-hall bawdiness and reminiscence. 'You really think so? Bless you. I always thought they were … Well, they're just black and white. I tell stories. I can't do that wonderful thing that Tom Waits and Bob Dylan do – to do imagery. I'm not good at that. I just write from the heart.'

He only started writing again because his friend Jim Cregan forced him into it on a visit to Stewart's Essex mansion (he splits his time between there and LA). 'He comes round for Sunday dinner when I'm in the country and always brings his guitar. I watch him come up the drive and … "Oh, fucking hell, he's brought his guitar again." He's always pushing me to write a song. So he says: "Come on, siddown, let's have a go." I said: "No, I wanna have a little lie down. Just had Sunday dinner." So he said: "Come on, have a little go." So I started singing, and he took it home, worked on the track a little bit, added a couple more guitars, and that was "Brighton Beach".'

That's one of the semi-autobiographical songs on the album, reflecting on his weekend beatnik days, hanging out under the pier with his girlfriend and his acoustic guitar in the early sixties; it's complemented by songs about his kids, his dad, his divorce. It's all very pleasant, though those who love *Every Picture* are unlikely to be putting it on constant rotation, despite the acoustic guitars and mandolins and fiddles being a presence again.

The critics, the sneerers, perhaps despair of Stewart because he has never been remotely apologetic about his success and its trappings: he's always happy to show off his latest car, blonde, house. 'I've always put myself out there for ridicule,' he says. 'And the rewards are just wonderful, so I'll take any stick the press can throw at me.'

Among the rewards were the string of women Stewart couldn't keep his hands off. Large chunks of his autobiography, published last year, are devoted to his efforts to keep his various girlfriends separate from one another, or from the press, before he chose fidelity in 1990 with his second wife, Rachel Hunter (they parted in 1999, divorcing in 2006). 'There was a lot of smoke and mirrors in those days,' he agrees. 'It was like a Brian Rix comedy. One door slams, someone runs out in their brassiere, another door slams and someone comes out with their trousers round their ankles. It was very much like that.'

Did he never think: Is this really worth the effort? 'Nah,' he says, sounding rather wistful, despite his evidently devoted marriage to wife number three, Penny Lancaster-Stewart. 'It was lovely. The only time it was getting sad was probably late eighties, when we had this "Long Hot Summer" – me and one of my best mates were down in the south of France [he was making a video with Tina Turner]. And the girls were just coming in and out, from all over Europe. It was wonderfully easy, but there was a sadness about it, a shallow emptiness. Once you'd got your leg over, that was it.'

Ah, the Long Hot Summer. In the book, he describes sleeping with a roll call of women.

'Let me say it was a minimum of three. It wasn't like one every night, coming in and going. It wasn't that bad! Jesus Christ! Three would be the number. Probably a maximum of four. I dunno how I got away with it. I was never ever a good-looking guy, but I knew I had a certain amount of charm, and most importantly I was the singer in a rock group. And I had a couple of bob. That's what turned the key in the door for me.'

Did it make it harder to find The Right Woman when the choices open to him were so wide? Because he – in his prime, at least – could probably pull more women even than me. Probably.

He looks shocked.

'Than you?'

Than me.

There's silence for a couple of beats, then a rattle of outrageous laughter. 'I thought you were serious. I'm a ROCK SINGER! It's dead easy. That was always my downfall. There's always someone prettier or better looking. Maybe I believed something magical was going to happen. And it did eventually.'

The women aren't a myth. Some of the other things are. Stewart was never a grave-digger ('I just measured up the graves') nor an apprentice footballer ('I didn't even get close. I was good but I wasn't good enough'). He made those stories up to make himself more interesting in interviews. And he claims a publicist made up the one about the sailors and the stomach pump. 'He had an evil streak in him. But you won't find, so far as I know, any written material on that anywhere. It was purely done through the grapevine. And I think the same thing happened to Richard Gere with a small rodent.'

But the anal ingestion of cocaine is true. After his Faces band-mate Ronnie Wood discovered a hole in his septum, the pair decided to eschew the nasal route – which also helped Stewart protect his voice ('It dries all the membranes out. What it does to your nose, it does to your throat as well, cos it'll all go down the back of your throat as well') – and pack their coke into emptied aspirin capsules to take in suppository form. There was a problem, though: 'It didn't have the same thrill as putting it up your nose, you know?'

And presumably it removes some of the social element from the ritual of taking drugs.

'No, you can't go in the toilet with the lads and lay one out.' He hoots with laughter.

We part, and I mention I'd been playing my kids his old albums in the car.

'Did they like them?'

Sorry, no. But you know the maxim: Spare the Rod, spoil the child.

'Spare the Rod, spoil the child,' he laughs delightedly. 'Exactly!'

26 APRIL

Damascus, the city where everything's for sale but no one's buying

IAN BLACK

Damer's ice-cream shop has delighted Damascenes for decades with its exquisite lemon and chocolate flavours, French patisserie and milky puddings garnished with almonds and green Aleppo pistachio nuts. Nowadays, though, trade is sluggish and falls away sharply by mid-evening.

'We used to stay open till 1 a.m.,' said a gloomy Faez Mutaim, whose family owns the business on Maysaloon Street in the heart of Syria's capital. 'Now we finish by nine and are closed by ten. People are short of money and don't want to go out any more. It's too tense. And it's hard to get here because so many roads are closed.'

In a city that lives in fear of car bombings and to a soundtrack of artillery salvoes and air strikes against rebel positions, night-life is a thing of the past. Damascus was once famous for its clubs, restaurants and tourist attractions. Now they are struggling to survive a crisis that is crippling the economy as well as killing and displacing Syrians.

Khawali, one of the finest restaurants in town, has closed down. Naranj, where Bashar al-Assad hosted Vladimir Putin, shuts early, its morose waiters serving barely a handful of diners. The district of Jebel Qassioun, where restaurants have stunning views across the ancient city, is a closed military zone. 'It's grim, but you have to find ways to survive,' reflects Mina, a thirtysomething professional. 'Now we eat out in friends' homes at 6 p.m. and leave early.'

By dusk the streets are almost deserted. Cars speed home to get through checkpoints before nightfall. Cinemas have shut. Lavish weddings are still held in big hotels where dancing masks the sounds of war – though one faced a problem the other day when the florists' van was not allowed past the blast barrier outside.

For all the talk of a looming battle for the city, central Damascus has not seen the kind of fighting that has ravaged Aleppo and Homs. But it is alarmingly close, and the effect is devastating. Factories in the surrounding region have been closed, damaged and looted. Shops and companies have shut and jobs have gone with them. 'I know many young people who are having to live off their fathers' pensions,' said Zeina, a student. 'And everyone knows that worse is coming.'

Obtaining supplies has become harder and costlier. Damer's used to get its milk from Douma and Daraya in the Damascus countryside but many farms no longer function because of the fighting. Sugar and butter are more expensive. The price of tomatoes has doubled, rice tripled. It's the same for cooking gas and heating oil. The hardest hit are those who have to survive on government salaries, which have not gone up.

Khaled, a pro-regime industrialist, owns a factory in Sbeineh that was hit by mortar fire. 'It suffered $2 million worth of damage,' he said. 'Who is going to compensate me?' Sami's factory in Qaddam is inaccessible, stuck in no man's land between the army and the rebels.

Economic indicators are disastrous across the board – from soaring prices and unemployment to a lira that has lost half its value. Hard currency deposits and foreign investment have disappeared, as has tourism. Estimates of losses since the crisis began range from $48 to $80 billion. Sanctions have halted international financial transactions. Credit cards cannot be used.

Petrol is scarce, resulting in queues of ill-tempered drivers outside filling stations. Damascus airport is closed to most international flights. The only safe way in is by road from Beirut: another sign of the worsening crisis can be seen at the Lebanese border, where scores of long-distance trucks are backed up because the Gulf route via Deraa and Jordan is unsafe.

The death of tourism is painfully obvious. Travel agents sit glumly in silent offices. Apart from the odd journalist, there are no foreigners in the precincts of the magnificent Umayyad mosque. On the Via Recta in the old city no one is buying; everything from tacky souvenirs and aromatic spices to gorgeous hand-crafted inlaid wood and mother-of-pearl furniture sit unsold.

'We are living on our savings and everything is more expensive,' said shopkeeper Hassan Abu Assali. 'Rents are high and raw materials are getting hard to find, some of them because of the sanctions. Twenty per cent of the shops here have already closed. If the situation continues like this until the end of the year all of them will close. And even if the crisis does end, prices are never going to go back to what they were before.'

In the store next door, Osama al-Shahaf, proud of his traditional swords of tempered Damascene steel, tells a similar story but chooses his words carefully. 'I'm not saying that things were ideal before the crisis,' he said. 'But there is bad and worse, and this is worse.'

It is the poor who suffer most. Umm Mohammad, originally from Deir al-Zor in the north, was forced by fighting to abandon her home in the southern Damascus suburb of Tadamon last July with her husband and baby son – some of the 3.8 million Syrians who have been displaced internally. Now they are renting in nearby, and relatively safe, Jaramana, its original Christian and Druze population swollen by Sunni refugees like themselves.

'It's a lot harder now,' she said. 'My husband works in the market from morning till night and only earns 1,400 [£13] a day. The rent is 7,000 a week. Prices are terrible. Oil, fat and everything is going up. Damascus was safer than Deir al-Zor and there were more jobs – until now. All of Syria has become a war zone.'

Beggars on the streets are another sign of the deepening crisis. Rumour has it that the secret police are turning a blind eye to them in exchange for information about any suspicious activity. 'Please help me,' beseeched a little girl, pigtailed and grimy. 'We are immigrants and we are living the park.' Another child, a scrawny boy of seven, said: 'Sir, sir I don't want money, but I can work.'

Naji, a stateless Palestinian born and raised in the Yarmouk refugee camp, has been living with friends since his house was shelled in clashes between the army and rebel fighters. Every few weeks he braves the Syrian and Lebanese bureaucracy to pay an expensive visit to his wife and baby son in Beirut. Rami also left Yarmouk for an outlying town last November: his eight-year-old daughter hasn't been to school since and he has a tense and sometime dangerous two-hour commute to work in the city centre.

Many Damascenes admit to wondering what to do: should they stay or should they go? 'It's hard to decide,' admits Talal, who works in a pharmacy, one of the few businesses that are still doing OK. 'Things have got so much worse in the last few months.'

Samir, an engineer, has abandoned Damascus for Turkey. 'Some of my friends went to Beirut and thought they would be back in two or three months,' he said. 'That was last year and most of them have started to arrange their lives on the basis that they will be away for a long time – whether the regime stays or falls.'

Perched by the till as Damer's last customers disappeared into the twilight with their ice-cream, Faez Mutaim reflected on the hard choices he and so many others face: tension and danger at home, harsh coonditions in the refugee camps in Jordan or impossibly high prices in Lebanon. 'If we go abroad we will end up begging,' he concluded. 'It's better to stay put.'

30 APRIL

Harry Whewell: northern editor of the *Guardian* who was proud of being a 'Manchester man'

JAMES LEWIS

Harry Whewell, who has died aged 90, was a long-serving news editor of the *Guardian* – and previously of the *Manchester Guardian*. He was one of a loyal team who saw the paper through lean financial years and played an invaluable part in maintaining the efficiency of its news operation during the paper's move to London.

Rather to his surprise, in 1957 Whewell was appointed news editor of the *Manchester Guardian* by Alastair Hetherington. Following his own appointment as the paper's editor the previous year, Hetherington set about transforming its situation. In 1959 came the change of name; in 1961, printing in London as well as Manchester; and in 1964, the transfer of the editor and major departments to the capital. Before becoming news editor,

Whewell had been a reporter with the paper for seven years, most of them spent covering the northern industrial scene. Much of Manchester's life then still revolved around cotton and he was the last correspondent dedicated to the subject.

Hetherington and Whewell began making an annual trawl of the older universities in search of writing talent. Those who joined Whewell's newsroom in this way included Michael Frayn, Neal Ascherson, David Marquand, Benedict Nightingale and many others who went on to forge reputations elsewhere.

These recruits rubbed shoulders in Cross Street with such established figures as Brian Redhead, Anthony Howard, Richard West and W. J. Weatherby. This talented cast were encouraged by Whewell to pursue often outlandish stories that gave them freedom and space envied by their colleagues on other papers.

They were given to understand that it was better to come back from an assignment empty-handed than with a story contrived to justify the journey. Young reporters, and some older ones, found that it was a sensible policy to join Whewell for a lunchtime drink in one of the city-centre pubs, where many newsworthy projects were dreamed up. The abstemious Hetherington frowned on those who frequented 'ale houses', but accepted that his paper's air of somewhat detached academe needed to change.

The quality and even-handedness of the paper's coverage of the Northern Ireland Troubles were due in no small measure to Whewell's determination to make the complexities of Irish politics understandable to its readers. And he was solid in his backing of the reporters – Simon Winchester, Simon Hoggart, Derek Brown and others – whom he sent to work in Belfast in what were, initially, unenviable conditions.

In the early days of the Troubles, Winchester worried that his dutiful daily accounts of Ireland's factional strife might not be making their intended mark on the readers. Whewell told him:

'I don't care if the readers do think it's boring. You report it all, every day – we'll get it through to them in time – it's a duty.'

News editors seldom expect to be popular, but Whewell was well-liked by most of those who wrote for him. He revelled in his reputation for mild eccentricity and disdained anything that smacked of order or regimentation. Even by the standards of news desks, his was conspicuously untidy. Order was boring; only ideas mattered.

He was an excellent raconteur, and his infectious laughter could be heard over long distances. His quick and shrewd wit was appreciated on television and he was a popular presenter of *What the Papers Say*. And he enjoyed his occasional appearances as a TV games panellist and broadcaster on local radio.

From 1961, Whewell's role became that of northern news editor, and he fought his corner to see that the paper's columns continued to reflect the nature and distinctive colour of life outside London and the south-east. He was, and remained, a 'Manchester man' who never wanted to be anywhere else except, perhaps, beachcombing near his Anglesey cottage and collecting curious objects to add to his office clutter.

Born in Stretford, to the south-west of Manchester, Harry was the youngest child – he had two older sisters – of the unassuming but determined Ada Whewell and her dustman husband Walter. Harry recalled that while he had aspirations to be a vet, his father wanted him to become a sanitary inspector.

A scholarship took him to Stretford Grammar school and in his teens he took part in productions by Joan Littlewood's Theatre Union, the forerunner to the Theatre Workshop. Between leaving school at the age of 16 and volunteering for the RAF in the Second World War, during which he reached the rank of flight lieutenant, he worked for the local council. While based in north Wales, he met Esther Rose, stationed nearby as a Wren, and in December

1945 they got married. She went on to work for the *News Chronicle* and *Daily Express*, and was then the long-serving story editor of Granada's *Coronation Street*.

Following some months in Ceylon (Sri Lanka) as an education officer, Whewell was demobilised in 1946 and took a degree in modern history and economics at Manchester University. There he encountered the historian Lewis Namier, who, as a former adviser to Chaim Weizmann, helped to stimulate Whewell's fascination with Israel.

In his later years with the *Guardian*, from 1975 until his retirement in 1988, Whewell was the paper's northern editor. This allowed him time to write a quirky, tongue-in-cheek column that older readers readily identified with. He wrote with a disarmingly light touch, but the words never came easily. Nor was he ever entirely at ease with a typewriter. Almost to the end his thoughts were recorded on a seemingly endless supply of yellowing, lined foolscap. In 1987 he was appointed OBE.

Esther died in 1986 and Whewell is survived by his son, Tim, now a correspondent with BBC's *Newsnight*.

MARTIN WAINWRIGHT WRITES:

Harry Whewell's impish spirit inspired his successors in Manchester and helped to keep us cheerful in hard times. As the last northern editor with real resources at his command, he was an oracle of wise advice to the end of his long, rich life, but above all a source of boundless fun.

Brimming with enthusiasm even in the frailty of old age, he would conjure up extraordinary scenes from the *Manchester Guardian*'s past, including the night that a circus elephant stayed in the company garage and pub sessions where he and colleagues would apply for unlikely jobs advertised in the paper. The one that lingers was governor of Bermuda as a job share with a night subeditor.

Harry took a similar sideways view of his own trials in old age. Widowed, recovering from ill-health and struggling to cope without a spin-dryer, he followed a neighbour's advice to dry his laundry by spreading it over the shrubs in his garden. The job was just finished when a woman from social services arrived to check that he was managing. His description over a pint of the look in her eyes matched the undying gleam in his own.

James Lewis worked with Harry Whewell for many years and wrote this piece in readiness for the inevitable. He died in 2002.

6 MAY

In praise of ...
Yorkshire solidarity

GUARDIAN LEADER

No Yorkshireman should want to see Barnsley, stalwarts of second-tier football for a century, shunted southwards; and yet for Huddersfield Town, with an even more illustrious past, as the first club to win the top tier thrice in a row – that initially looked like the only way to stay in the Championship on Saturday. In minute 82, James Vaughan shot the equaliser, which was all the terriers required, and despair hit the Barnsley end. But it gave way to joy as word came that Crystal Palace had knocked in an 89th-minute goal that condemned Peterborough to the drop instead. Described by Engels as the most handsome town in the north, Huddersfield displayed all its nobility both on the pitch, by allowing the Barnsley keeper to dribble his ball around his box unchallenged, and off it – fans at both ends chanted 'Yorkshire!' in unison. After Richard III was rescued from under that Leicester car park, just maybe the House of York is ready to rise as one again.

7 MAY

TV Preview: *The Apprentice*

JULIA RAESIDE

Hark, can you hear Prokofiev's 'Dance of the Knobheads'? It must be time for another enervating parade of go-getters and their bad personalities to bore on about their passion for business to Lord Sugar and co. Like a grinning herd of lemmings pretending they can't see the carcasses of their predecessors at the bottom of the cliff, over they go, spouting bollock-speak as they hurtle towards the rocks. For their first task, the teams must sell a shipping container full of tat. The second episode follows tomorrow.

8 MAY

Sir Alex Ferguson: the eulogy, the apology and the thank you

DANIEL TAYLOR

On Sunday, when Manchester United take on Swansea City, a 58-year-old man by the name of Pete Molyneux will lift up an old bed-sheet just as he did, infamously, in December 1989 when Alex Ferguson's back was pressed against a cold, unforgiving wall and the mood inside Old Trafford was of brooding discontent.

The message back then was short and to the point. 'Three years of excuses and we're still crap, ta-ra Fergie,' the banner read. It has gone down in history, the nadir of Ferguson's reign, and now the man with the paintbrush and the tin of black emulsion plans to makes an updated version. This time it will come, in part, as an apology. Mostly, it will come as a thank you.

Pete, like a lot of United supporters, expects to be holding back the tears during Ferguson's 1,500th – and last – game in charge. His banner will read: 'Twenty-three years of silver and we're still top, ta-ra Fergie.'

Ta-ra, indeed. Busby closed his reign at Old Trafford when he was 62. Shankly left Liverpool at the age of 60. Paisley lasted at Anfield until he was 64. Clough was 58 when he bowed out. Ferguson is 71, with a pacemaker in his chest and a hip replacement on the calendar, yet the first reaction is still near disbelief and a sense of wonder.

The Man Who Can't Retire, one newspaper used to call him. And there he was, after the latest championship, cracking jokes, full of levity and humour, talking effusively about working next season and beyond. Someone asked whether we should take it for granted he would still be in charge and he talked about the 'magic pills' still working. He always was particularly skilled at spinning a line, Fergie.

His legacy is as solid as the stadium where his statue – long overcoat, match-face, strict side-parting (it was always a side-parting, even in the seventies when football went shaggy) – now rises behind the stand they named after him. Thirteen league titles for United, two European Cups, two Intercontinental World

Cups, one European Cup-Winners' Cup, five FA Cups, four League Cups. Does the Community Shield count? There were 10 of them.

Add in those years at Aberdeen, when he set about dismantling the Old Firm's dominance, and the trophy count is 49. Manager of the year? Ten times. Manager of the month? Twenty-seven. It's bordering on ridiculous: has there ever been another manager whose silverware has to be totted up like a maths problem?

Nobody has ever done it with so much competitive courage. Nobody has beaten the system like he has. Ferguson has outlasted 24 different managers at Real Madrid, 19 at Internazionale, 18 at Chelsea and 14 at Manchester City. He has seen off prime ministers Thatcher, Major, Blair and Brown and most of us probably expected Cameron would be added to that list rather than joining in the tributes in the House of Commons.

Ferguson's latest title, United's 20th in total, brings him personally level with Arsenal, the third most successful club in the country. It is not strictly true that he knocked Liverpool off their perch but he has certainly done a fine job of helping to make sure they did not clamber back. Liverpool have won the title 18 times. If Ferguson were a younger man – maybe 10 years or so – you would have fancied him to catch and overhaul them, too.

When Ferguson took over on 6 November 1986 United were 19th in the old First Division and had not won the league for nearly two decades. Fuji had just launched the world's first disposable camera. Mike Tyson was a couple of weeks away from his first world title. Nick Berry was at number one in the charts with 'Every Loser Wins'. It was the year of Crocodile Dundee and Top Gun, Andrew marrying Sarah, Charlene marrying Scott, 'Freddie Starr Ate My Hamster' and Wayne Rooney's first birthday.

Ferguson's team for his first game, at Oxford United, was: Turner, Duxbury, McGrath, Moran, Albiston, Hogg, Blackmore, Moses, Stapleton, Davenport, Barnes. Ferguson, determined to get his first team-talk right, managed to call Peter Davenport 'Nigel' by mistake. They lost 2–0.

Twenty-six years on, we probably have a better idea why he could not bring himself to face the media after that defeat to Real Madrid in the Champions League in March and the shattering effects it must have had on him, knowing as he did that it would be his last stab at the trophy he has always coveted the most.

We can imagine how much he will have craved the perfect ending: trophy number 50 at Wembley on 25 May. And it is a strange, almost unnerving feeling knowing that he will not be in the dugout next August. We always knew he was going to have to cut himself free one day but it still comes at you like a mallet. 'He's like a seat in the stadium, the grass on the pitch,' Roberto Mancini said recently. 'He is a part of United.'

He is also unique and it is probably only now, and in the future, that his achievements will fully get the recognition they deserve.

At the same time, it is difficult not to think how he will cope without the daily fix. Football has been the thing that has made the most sense in his life and the journalists who have travelled round the world on his coat tails are well accustomed with his usual reaction to any talk of retirement. Apprehension, mostly. At other times, he would treat the question like an affront and, suddenly, you might be in that wind tunnel as he leant in and unleashed all that anger.

But there were other occasions, too, when Ferguson really opened up and the impression he left was of someone who considered life as the former manager of Manchester United might be shapeless and unattractive, scary even. 'The big fear is what you would do with yourself,' he once said. 'There are too many examples of people who retire and are in their box soon after. You're taking away the very thing that makes you alive, that keeps you alive.

'I remember my dad had his 65th birthday and the Fairfields shipyard gave him a dinner in Glasgow with 400 people there. The next week my mother phones and says: "Your dad's going in for an X-ray, he has pains in his chest." I said: "It'll be emotion." Well, it was cancer. A week. One week.'

Ferguson regarded retirement as something, in an ideal world, he could just file away in a drawer.

How will he make his retreat? We know he is staying on as a board member but that 6 a.m. routine, into the training ground, a slice of buttered toast and then the 'bloody mountain of paper-work' on his desk is going to be a desperately hard routine to shift. More time for the horses, you might think. He has a large, extended family, with a small fleet of grandchildren and no doubt they will all be on the pitch on Sunday when he takes the microphone for the last time. Ferguson always wanted to teach himself to play the piano. He keeps wine and loves to read, always taking in new information. Yet football – or, specifically, football management – is his addiction and it is not going to be an easy habit to kick. Even Ferguson, with that powerful clarity of mind, could be forgiven for experiencing the odd moment of insecurity.

The tributes during the day reflect the sadness that most people feel, because this is not just the retirement of a great manager. It is the departure of the last of his kind: the old-school manager.

No doubt there will always be some who cannot get past the caricature and will not be able to marry all the tributes with their own memories of how Ferguson has behaved to his own rules. Ferguson, let's not sugarcoat it, could be terribly ruthless. He could be cold, vindictive, with little thought about how his actions impinge on others. His press conferences could be tense, joyless affairs. The 'hairdryer', that blast of full-on rage whenever he felt affronted, was a remarkable thing to witness and there is no point being hypocritical here: there were moments when he could be, in the vernacular of the business, a proper bastard.

Alternatively, there is a different Ferguson, one that is not seen enough, and maybe we will get to know more about when he is removed from the frontline of his industry.

There were acts of great kindness, for example. Not many people know of the video message Ferguson sent to Paul Hunter, a couple of weeks before his death, telling the former Masters snooker champion he should be proud of everything he has achieved and praising him for his bravery and dignity fighting his cancer. Few column inches were devoted to the fact Ferguson felt compelled to get in touch with the parents of Josh Furber, a student killed on holiday in Australia, after hearing that he was a United supporter. Nor are these isolated cases. Ferguson will go out of his way to attend the funeral of a loyal supporter, an unsung member of staff or one of his many acquaintances.

Yes, there were times when his relationship with the media was fraught and it felt like he was at war with the industry. Yet that has been overplayed, too.

Some of Ferguson's oldest friends have been football writers. He has been known to ring newspaper offices and demand to be put straight through to the editor after hearing that one of the reporters on his patch might be made redundant.

David Meek, the former *Manchester Evening News* correspondent, always remembers the incredible kindness Ferguson showed him when he was diagnosed with cancer in 2003. Meek's phone rang one day and the message at the other end simply growled: 'The Scottish beast is on his way.' Ferguson was at Meek's front door 20 minutes later. Meek, who has been Ferguson's ghostwriter of choice for many years, remembers how Ferguson looked him in the eye and told him exactly what he had wanted to hear: 'You can handle it.'

Even then, there is a delicious irony that Meek put together Ferguson's last set of programme notes for the game against Chelsea without any idea that he, along with everybody else, was being had. The standout line was this: 'I certainly don't have any plans at the moment to walk away from what I believe will be something special and worth being around for all to see.' Classic Ferguson, right to the end.

28 MAY

My iPhone thief: why I shook his hand

STUART JEFFRIES

At ten to five one Saturday afternoon last year, I was walking up the Hornsey Road in London with a tin of rhubarb from Tesco, checking the football results on my iPhone after a lovely day at Kew Gardens. The phone replaced the BlackBerry I'd destroyed a month earlier by running into the sea to save my daughter from drowning.

Behind me on the pavement I heard a motorbike and, thinking the rider was going to park, carried on holding the phone in my left hand and scrolling with my right index finger – that fey, give-away gesture of iPhone users. Over my shoulder the right arm of the bike's pillion passenger appeared and snatched the phone. The bike was 200 yards away before I composed myself enough to look for the registration plate or think about clubbing the thieves with canned fruit – it was a seamless snatch from a soft target. And a common one. The *Guardian* reported last year that in my borough (Islington) there was a 400 per cent-plus increase in phone snatches between 2010 and 2011. Detective Inspector Karen Gilmour, head of Islington police's robbery unit, was quoted in the local paper recently saying: 'It seems to me they can make an assessment very quickly as to whether the person they're looking at has got the sort of phone they want.' She said that most stolen phones are immediately switched off, the sim card removed, and the phone passed on to handlers who ship them abroad for as much as £600.

Of all the minor unpleasant incidents I've suffered – bus stop shovings, that time I unwisely confronted a disturbed dog owner about letting his pit bulls run wild in the toddlers' sandpit, the interview during which Robert de Niro called me a 'fucking wise guy' – none had as intense a physical, nor as enduring an emotional, effect. I felt winded even though I hadn't been touched. I plodded home hyperventilating, thinking grimly about my neighbourhood – drug busts in the park, a fatal stabbing outside the chip shop, my partner's sister beaten black and blue on this same street the year before by three boys for whom punching a woman until she lay flat on the pavement was a summer evening's entertainment.

At home, I called the phone company, whimpered to my partner, and my seven-year-old made a collage of autumn leaves with the inscription: 'To Daddy, love Juliet. P.S. I am sorry about your phoun [sic]'. Meanwhile, the kids who had stolen my phone had crashed their bike during a police chase and the driver had been arrested. Later police caught the boy who had snatched my phone, conspicuous because his jeans were ripped from the crash and he was wearing only one trainer.

My partner's phone rang half an hour after the theft. 'We've got your phone,' a sergeant told me. 'Think yourself lucky. Hardly ever happens.' A few days later I picked it up from a police station covered in finger-print dust.

Six months later, I was on a train to meet the boy. In March, after pleading guilty to several counts of theft and robbery, the boy was given a youth rehabilitation order, one of whose conditions bans him from London for six months. What did I want from the meeting? I wanted to see the thief. I spent a lot of time imagining the woeful life that would lead him to become so adept a thief. I was a victim certainly, but a privileged one. Even if I hadn't got my phone back, I'd have been able to buy another; moreover, I now feel more circumspect in my neighbourhood – in that, the theft was a usefully chastening experience.

At the Youth Offending Team offices in Chatham, Kent, I shook the hand that had snatched my phone. A 16-year-old black British boy in hoodie and jeans, uncomfortably hot in this airless room. He told me he was a boxer, whose mum had aspirations for him to make it as a heavyweight. What if I'd held on to my phone? Would he and his mate have beat me up? If so, doubtless, I wouldn't be feeling so benign now.

What did he want from the meeting? 'To say sorry,' he said. This, said the victim liaison officer who arranged the appointment, was a 'restorative justice meeting' at which the victim could say how the crime had made them feel and the criminal express regret to the victim for what they had done. None of his other victims wanted a face-to-face meeting, least of all, perhaps, the 34-year-old woman who had hung on to her phone, was knocked to the ground and dragged along the pavement suffering scrapes and bruises before she finally gave it up. Did she feel, as I do, like a privileged victim? Unlikely.

We (him, his case worker, a victim liaison officer, me) sat down and turned off our phones. 'This is the one you stole from me,' I laughed. 'I am sorry,' he said. He said so repeatedly. I complimented him on the professionalism of the theft. But what if it had gone wrong? 'I never thought about it at the time. But I should have – we crashed a few minutes later.' What about hurting his victims? 'I didn't set out to hurt anyone.'

Why did he do it, I asked. He told me that since his parents had split up he had felt as though he had to be the man of the family and provide for his mother, who lives on benefits. I said that sounded like a story he might tell afterwards to feel nobler about robbing people in the street.

If his dad had been at home rather than living with a new wife outside London, he said, he probably wouldn't have become a criminal. It was his dad who laid down the law. It's a huge social problem, I said, only later thinking – what do I know of it? I'm not from a broken home. At 16, I was revising for O-levels, not meeting my crime victims with school years a wasteland behind me.

Diane Abbott MP asked during a Commons speech last year about black and ethnic minority achievement: 'Why do black children fail?' The answer, she said, 'is partly to do with poverty in an absolute sense, although all the research shows ... black children systematically do less well than children of other ethnicities. There is no question but that poverty is an issue. Nowadays there is also increasing peer-group pressure.' Such peer pressure was a factor in this case. Earlier that day, the boy told me, he had two choices – go to boxing training or go on the rob with his friend as he had done before. He chose the latter.

Peer pressure isn't the whole story. Abbott spoke of black boys 'who throughout their education have engaged only with women and have never seen a man as an educational role model. More male teachers are important.' He told me he hadn't done well at school, couldn't concentrate – again hardly a surprise. Abbott said: 'If we abandon a cross-section of the community in our inner cities, they have a way of bringing themselves back into the political narrative – a way that is not good for them or for society.' That, maybe, is what happened one dismal evening on the Hornsey Road.

The victim liaison officer asked how I felt after the theft. Wary, I said, careful not to use my phone in a dodgy neighbourhood (such as, it turns out, the one in which I live). 'You shouldn't have to think like that,' said the boy, shaking his head. 'You should feel OK using an expensive phone in the street.' But thanks to him I'm not. It was about the only time during the interview where I got cross. I think he was disappointed that I wasn't more angry during our hour together. If so, good – I didn't want to give him the satisfaction.

Rather, I wanted to give him something worse, crueller even – pity. He suffered much more than me, I said repeatedly. I showed him my daughter's drawing as if to stress how loving and solid a family I have. A low blow. He told me about his family – how furious his mother had been, that his dad was so angry he wouldn't visit him in jail, how his nan was ashamed of him. He told his nephew that the thing he has around his leg is a hi-tech watch – just so he doesn't learn his uncle's a tagged criminal. I felt sorry for his mum, who couldn't come to the meeting, for his dad, who wouldn't, and – a little – for their son.

The order bans him from going inside the M25 for six months. It means he can't see his mother, unless accompanied by his case worker. He now lives with his dad in Kent.

At court, he readily accepted the terms of the order rather than go back to Feltham Young Offenders' Institution, where he'd already spent a month, to serve an 18-month sentence. In Feltham, he said, he was OK because he knew gang members who could protect him. But their protection was a double-edged sword – it meant he would still associate with people who might lure him back into committing crimes. The order, then, gives him a chance to remake his life in a way that jail may not have. He's away from gangs, away, perhaps, from greater risks of recidivism. He attends boxing training and in September goes to college to train as plumber or mechanic.

As the case worker drove him back to his dad's house to fulfil his curfew, I returned to the city from which he is banned, thinking about this boy, both victim and perpetrator of the crime. He said he would write to me and when he does, I hope he'll tell me he's doing something worthwhile with his life, because it doesn't do either of us any good for him to remain what he is to me now, an object of pity.

4 JUNE

The Crown

CAROL ANN DUFFY

A new poem for the 60th anniversary of the coronation by the poet laureate

The crown translates a woman to a Queen –
endless gold, circling itself, an O like a well,
fathomless, for the years to drown in – history's bride,
anointed, blessed, for a crowning. One head alone
can know its weight, on throne, in pageantry,
and feel it still, in private space, when it's lifted:
not a hollow thing, but a measuring; no halo,
treasure, but a valuing; decades and duty. Time-gifted,
the crown is old light, journeying from skulls of kings
to living Queen.
Its jewels glow, virtues; loyalty's ruby, blood-
deep; sapphire's ice resilience; emerald evergreen;
the shy pearl, humility. *My whole life, whether it be long
or short, devoted to your service.* Not lightly worn.

10 JUNE

Edward Snowden: the whistleblower behind the NSA surveillance revelations

GLENN GREENWALD, EWEN MACASKILL
AND LAURA POITRAS

The individual responsible for one of the most significant leaks in US political history is Edward Snowden, a 29-year-old former technical assistant for the CIA and current employee of the defence contractor Booz Allen Hamilton. Snowden has been working at the National Security Agency for the last four years as an employee of various outside contractors, including Booz Allen and Dell.

The *Guardian*, after several days of interviews, is revealing his identity at his request. From the moment he decided to disclose numerous top-secret documents to the public, he was determined not to opt for the protection of anonymity. 'I have no intention of hiding who I am because I know I have done nothing wrong,' he said.

Snowden will go down in history as one of America's most consequential whistleblowers, alongside Daniel Ellsberg and Bradley Manning. He is responsible for handing over material from one of the world's most secretive organisations – the National Security Agency. In a note accompanying the first set of documents he provided, he wrote: 'I understand that I will be made to suffer for my actions,' but 'I will be satisfied if the federation of secret law, unequal pardon and irresistible executive powers that rule the world that I love are revealed even for an instant.'

Despite his determination to be publicly unveiled, he repeatedly insisted that he wants to avoid the media spotlight. 'I don't want public attention because I don't want the story to be about me. I want it to be about what the US government is doing.' He does not fear the consequences of going public, he said, only that doing so will distract attention from the issues raised by his disclosures. 'I know the media likes to personalise political debates, and I know the government will demonise me.'

Despite these fears, he remained hopeful his outing will not divert attention from the substance of his disclosures. 'I really want the focus to be on these documents and the debate which I hope this will trigger among citizens around the globe about what kind of world we want to live in.' He added: 'My sole motive is to inform the public as to that which is done in their name and that which is done against them.'

He has had 'a very comfortable life' that included a salary of roughly $200,000, a girlfriend with whom he shared a home in Hawaii, a stable career, and a family he loves. 'I'm willing to sacrifice all of that because I can't in good conscience allow the US government to destroy privacy, internet freedom and basic liberties for people around the world with this massive surveillance machine they're secretly building.'

Three weeks ago, Snowden made final preparations that resulted in last week's series of blockbuster news stories. At the NSA office in Hawaii where he was working, he copied the last set of documents he intended to disclose. He then advised his NSA supervisor that he needed to be away from work for 'a couple of weeks' in order to receive treatment for epilepsy, a condition he learned he suffers from after a series of seizures last year. As he packed his bags, he told his girlfriend that he had to be away for a few weeks, though he said he was vague about the reason. 'That is not an uncommon occurrence for someone who has spent the last decade working in the intelligence world.'

On 20 May, he boarded a flight to Hong Kong, where he has remained ever since. He chose the city because 'they have a spirited commitment to free speech and the right of political dissent', and because he believed that it was one of the few places in the world that both could and would resist the dictates of the US government. In the three weeks since he arrived, he has been ensconced in a hotel room. 'I've left the room maybe a total of three times during my entire stay,' he said. It is a plush hotel and, what with eating meals in his room too, he has run up big bills.

He is deeply worried about being spied on. He lines the door of his hotel room with pillows to prevent eavesdropping. He puts a large red hood over his head and laptop when entering his passwords to prevent any hidden cameras from detecting them. Though that may sound like paranoia to some, Snowden has good reason for such fears. He worked in the US intelligence world for almost a decade. He knows that the biggest and most secretive surveillance organisation in America, the NSA, along with the most powerful government on the planet, is looking for him.

Since the disclosures began to emerge, he has watched television and monitored the internet, hearing all the threats and vows of prosecution emanating from Washington. And he knows only too well the sophisticated technology available to them and how easy it will be for them to find him. The NSA police and other law enforcement officers have twice visited his home in Hawaii and already contacted his girlfriend, though he believes that may have been prompted by his absence from work, and not because of suspicions of any connection to the leaks.

'All my options are bad,' he said. The US could begin extradition proceedings against him, a potentially problematic, lengthy and unpredictable course for Washington. Or the Chinese government might whisk him away for questioning, viewing him as a useful source of information. Or he might end up being grabbed and bundled into a plane bound for US territory. 'Yes, I could be rendered by the CIA. I could have people come after me. Or any of the third-party partners. They work closely with a number of other nations. Or they could pay off the Triads. Any of their agents or assets,' he said. 'We have got a CIA station just up the road – the consulate here in Hong Kong – and I am sure they are going to be busy for the next week. And that is a concern I will live with for the rest of my life, however long that happens to be.'

Having watched the Obama administration prosecute whistleblowers at a historically unprecedented rate, he fully expects the US government to attempt to use all its weight to punish him. 'I am not afraid,' he said calmly, 'because this is the choice I've made.' He predicts the government will launch an investigation and 'say I have broken the Espionage Act and helped our enemies, but that can be used against anyone who points out how massive and invasive the system has become'.

The only time he became emotional during the many hours of interviews was when he pondered the impact his choices would have on his family, many of whom work for the US government. 'The only thing I fear is the harmful effects on my family, who I won't be able to help any more. That's what keeps me up at night,' he said, his eyes welling up with tears.

Snowden did not always believe the US government posed a threat to his political values. He was brought up originally in Elizabeth City, North Carolina. His family moved later to Maryland, near the NSA headquarters in Fort Meade. By his own admission, he was not a stellar student. In order to get the credits necessary to obtain a high school diploma, he attended a community college in Maryland, studying computing, but never completed the coursework. (He later obtained his GED.) In 2003, he enlisted in the US army and began a training program to join the Special Forces. Invoking the same principles that he now cites to justify his leaks, he said: 'I wanted to fight in the Iraq war because I felt like I had an obligation as a human being to help free people from oppression'. He recounted how his beliefs about the war's purpose were quickly dispelled. 'Most of the people training us seemed pumped up about killing Arabs, not helping anyone,' he said. After he broke both his legs in a training accident, he was discharged.

After that, he got his first job in an NSA facility, working as a security guard for one of the agency's covert facilities at the University of Maryland. From there, he went to the CIA, where he worked on IT security. His understanding of the internet and his talent for computer programming enabled him to rise fairly quickly for someone who lacked even a high school diploma. By 2007, the CIA stationed him with diplomatic cover in Geneva, Switzerland. His responsibility for maintaining computer network security meant he had clearance to access a wide array of classified documents. That access, along with the almost three years he spent around CIA officers, led him to begin seriously questioning the rightness of what he saw.

He described as formative an incident in which he claimed CIA operatives were attempting to recruit a Swiss banker to obtain secret banking information. Snowden said they achieved this by purposely getting the banker drunk and encouraging him to drive home in his car. When the banker was arrested for drunk driving, the undercover agent seeking to befriend him offered to help, and a bond was formed that led to successful recruitment. 'Much of what I saw in Geneva really disillusioned me about how my government functions and what its impact is in the world,' he says. 'I realised that I was part of something that was doing far more harm than good.'

He said it was during his CIA stint in Geneva that he thought for the first time about exposing government secrets. But, at the time, he chose not to for two reasons. First, he said: 'Most of the secrets the CIA has are about people, not machines and systems, so I didn't feel comfortable with disclosures that I thought could endanger anyone'. Secondly, the election of Barack Obama in 2008 gave him hope that there would be real reforms, rendering disclosures unnecessary.

He left the CIA in 2009 in order to take his first job working for a private contractor that assigned him to a functioning NSA facility, stationed on a military base in Japan. It was then, he said, that he 'watched as Obama advanced the very policies that I thought would be reined in', and as a result, 'I got hardened.' The primary lesson from this experience was that 'you can't wait around for someone else to act. I had been looking for leaders, but I realised that leadership is about being the first to act.'

Over the next three years, he learned just how all-consuming the NSA's surveillance activities were, claiming 'they are intent on making every conversation and every form of behaviour in the world known to them'. He described how he once viewed the internet as 'the most important invention in all of human history'. As an adolescent, he spent days at a time 'speaking to people with all sorts of views that I would never have encoun-tered on my own'. But he believed that the value of the internet, along with basic privacy, is being rapidly destroyed by ubiquitous surveillance. 'I don't see myself as a hero,' he said, 'because what I'm doing is self-interested: I don't want to live in a world where there's no privacy and therefore no room for intellectual explo-ration and creativity.' Once he reached the conclusion that the NSA's surveillance net would soon be irrevocable, he said it was just a matter of time before he chose to act. 'What they're doing' poses 'an existential threat to democracy', he said.

As strong as those beliefs are, there still remains the question: why did he do it? Giving up his freedom and a privileged lifestyle? 'There are more important things than money. If I were motivated by money, I could have sold these documents to any number of countries and gotten very rich.' For him, it is a matter of principle. 'The government has granted itself power it is not entitled to. There is no public oversight. The result is people like myself have the latitude to go further than they are allowed to,' he said.

His allegiance to internet freedom is reflected in the stickers on his laptop: 'I support Online Rights: Electronic Frontier Foundation,' reads one. Another hails the online organisation offering anonymity, the Tor Project. Asked by reporters to establish his authenticity to ensure he is not some fantasist, he laid bare, without hesitation, his personal details, from his social security number to his CIA ID and his expired diplomatic passport. There is no shiftiness. Ask him about anything in his personal life and he will answer. He is quiet, smart, easy-going and self-effacing. A master on computers, he seemed happiest when talking about the technical side of surveillance, at a level of detail comprehensible probably only to fellow communication specialists. But he showed intense passion when talking about the value of privacy and how he felt it was being steadily eroded by the behaviour of the intelligence services.

His manner was calm and relaxed but he has been understandably twitchy since he went into hiding, waiting for the knock on the hotel door. A fire alarm goes off. 'That has not happened before,' he said, betraying anxiety wondering if was real, a test or a CIA ploy to get him out onto the street. Strewn about the side of his bed are his suitcase, a plate with the remains of room-service breakfast, and a copy of *Angler*, the biography of former vice-president Dick Cheney.

Ever since last week's news stories began to appear in the *Guardian*, Snowden has vigilantly watched TV and read the internet to see the effects of his choices. He seemed satisfied that the debate he longed to provoke was finally taking place. He lay, propped up against pillows, watching CNN's Wolf Blitzer ask a discussion panel about government intrusion if they had any idea who the leaker was. From 8,000 miles away, the leaker looked on impassively, not even indulging in a wry smile.

Snowden said that he admires both Ellsberg and Manning, but argues that there is one important distinction between himself and the army private, whose trial coincidentally began the week Snowden's leaks began to make news. 'I carefully evaluated every single document I disclosed to ensure that each was legitimately in the public interest,' he said. 'There are all sorts of documents that would have made a big impact that I didn't turn over, because harming people isn't my goal. Transparency is.' He purposely chose, he said, to give the documents to journalists whose judgment he trusted about what should be public and what should remain concealed.

As for his future, he is vague. He hoped the publicity the leaks have generated will offer him some protection, making it 'harder for them to get dirty'. He views his best hope as the possibility of asylum, with Iceland – with its reputation of a champion of internet freedom – at the top of his list. He knows that may prove a wish unfulfilled. But after the intense political controversy he has already created with just the first week's haul of stories, 'I feel satisfied that this was all worth it. I have no regrets.'

This was the most-read article of the year on the Guardian *website.*

10 JUNE

Parkour life:
Iranian women get physical

AZADEH MOAVENI

On any given Friday, groups of young women across Iran can be seen jumping from rooftops, scaling the graffitied walls of apartment blocks, and catapulting themselves over stairways. They are not being chased by riot police, but merely practising their parkour moves, especially the ground roll, tricky to execute while wearing a headscarf.

Parkour's popularity among young women in Iran is soaring, despite the bulkier clothing and head coverings Islamic dress codes require them to wear. The outdoor sport, a fast-paced hybrid of gymnastics and martial arts, seems designed to get you out of a fix quickly, which perhaps explains its appeal to young Iranians, whose social lives in the strict Islamic republic often require considerable agility. Iran's female practitioners are running their own threads on Persian-language forums and posting films online to showcase their skills. Unlike the men's scene, with its heavy rap culture overtones and emphasis on group rivalries, the girls' movement comes across as more athletic and purposeful, despite the greater challenges women face practising outdoors.

Men hold major parkour tournaments in urban parks and talk openly online about parkour being accepted by local police. Not so for women, whose equal access to sports facilities and public areas for exercise has long been contested by the government. The authorities may tolerate matrons doing aerobics in parks, but young women dashing over obstacles pushes the boundaries of acceptability. One young woman, hiding behind oversize sunglasses, says in a YouTube clip: 'It's become quite acceptable for guys, but because we're girls, when we're out practising, they sometimes hassle us.'

What's striking about parkour's appeal among Iranian women is the sheer breadth of the trend. It's not being led by the reed-thin, Fendi-clad women of north Tehran, but girls in trainers and practical headscarves (maghnaeh) from Lahijan to Shiraz. Parkour's punchiness seems to resonate among Iranian women, who in recent years have also taken up martial arts in record numbers. The context is the bullying culture and street violence that women face under the country's Islamic government, whose discriminatory laws make seeking legal recourse for domestic violence almost pointless.

Women in Iran, who make up 60 per cent of graduates, have never had so much to feel angry about, with the state increasing gender segregation at university, among other changes. Nooshin, a councillor for Iran's welfare organisation in the city of Hamedan, says she has seen women's awareness of their own physical capabilities shifting. 'Do you think it's coincidence that more women are taking karate and kung-fu classes? Women, especially young women, are learning about their rights and fighting back.' Even in the rebellious milieu of Iran's parkour scene, where you encounter endless clips set to edgy Persian hip-hop and would expect to find more progressive social mores among men, women's involvement has met with criticism. One young man questioned on the national parkour website whether the sport was in line with women's 'modesty and chastity'. But in film clips online there are also scenes of men standing by to aid women doing air somersaults, clearly enjoying their role as helpers.

As one student from a Tehran parkour clan says: 'It gives us courage and helps us release our pent-up energy. It's great to feel that nothing can stand in your way.'

10 JUNE

Pilloried as a 'conchie' after serving in Kenya, I now feel vindicated

LETTER

I doubt if all the secrets of the Kikuyu uprising will ever be known. Young soldiers were brainwashed into believing they were fighting in Kenya for our glorious empire. Sixty years ago I was there as a 19-year-old national service officer. I am delighted that the government has given some token compensation for Kenyans who suffered torture. I still suffer from memories of the British apartheid system there and numerous instances of arbitrary killing and brutality by British forces, Kenya police and Kenyan African Rifles. In reality we protected land-grabbing British farmers and enriched UK companies.

Young troops were encouraged to shoot any African on sight in certain areas. Prize money was offered by senior officers for every death. The brains of one young black lad I shot with no warning (by orders) landed on my chest. He had no weapons, only a piece of the Bible and part of an English-language primer in his pocket. Before I burned his body near the farm where he had been working, I was ordered to cut off his hands, which I did, and put them in my ammunition pouches, as we'd run out of fingerprinting kits. Of course, he was recorded as 'a terrorist'. I was told to shoot down unarmed women in the jungle because they were carrying food to the so-called 'Mau Mau' – a word they never called themselves.

The whole of this Kenyan tragedy was predictable. Although Kenyan black troops had fought for the British in the Second World War, they were rewarded with their land being taken away, no press- or trade union freedom, suppression of political movements and slave-like conditions of work, which I witnessed. Yes, some black Kenyans did turn on others for not rising up against such indignities. But many of those who were killed were local chiefs and their supporters, who had co-operated with hugely rich white farmers. However, the revenge killings by the colonial authorities were totally disproportionate – with bombing raids, burning of villages and the forced movement of thousands of families onto poorer land, in the name of 'protection'. Very few white people were killed by Africans.

But it wasn't just the black people who suffered. I remember telling my company commander that a young soldier whose medical records showed he was only fit for clerical work should not go on a military exercise. I was laughed at. He was forced to go. After three hours' steep climb through jungle, he died in my arms, probably from a heart attack. Because I remonstrated, I was ordered to take a donkey and carry his body, which kept slipping off, for nearly a week to deposit him at HQ on the other side of the Aberdare mountains. His mother was told he was a hero who'd died on active service.

I was sickened by my experiences. I disobeyed orders and was court-martialled and dismissed from the service. I actually thought I was going to be shot. Stripped of my uniform, I was told to make my own way home. Then I wrote to Bessie Braddock, the Labour MP, and was put back in my uniform to fly home in a RAF plane. After campaigning around the country for Kenyan independence, I received new call-up papers, because I had not finished my national service. I then decided to stand trial and become the first British man allowed to be registered as a conscientious objector against colonial warfare. History has proved me right. With these expressions of 'regret' by our foreign secretary, I now feel vindicated for being pilloried as a 'conchie'.

David Larder
Retford, Nottinghamshire

13 JUNE

L. S. Lowry's rage against the machine

JEANETTE WINTERSON

In 1916, L. S. Lowry had missed his train from Pendlebury, the Salford suburb where he lived, into Manchester. 'It would be about four o'clock and perhaps there was some peculiar condition of the atmosphere or something. But as I got to the top of the steps I saw the Acme Mill; a great square red block with the cottages running in rows right up to it – and suddenly I knew what I had to paint.'

Dickens and Mrs Gaskell had written about Manchester. D. H. Lawrence found a language for the rough beauty of the Derbyshire mines. George Bernard Shaw, J. B. Priestley and George Orwell were fascinated by the culture of the industrial working class: its see-saw alcoholism and tee-totalism; its unrepentant godlessness versus its low-church evangelical fervour; its brawling brutality and sudden gentleness. But no one was painting it.

'My ambition was to put the industrial scene on the map, because nobody had done it – nobody had done it seriously.'

That was his brief; it became his obsession. Lowry, the sensible night-school-trained amateur artist in search of a subject, was overtaken – possessed would be a better word – by an unconscious force far bigger than either the man or his mission-statement. For the rest of his life, he spoke of that moment seeing the Acme Mill in 1916 as his vision. He was as much a mystic as William Blake was with his 'dark satanic mills', or W.B. Yeats's 'foul rag and bone shop of the heart'. Where? In Lancashire.

It is pointless to try to understand Lowry the painter as Lowry the Tory, the rent-collector, the virgin who lived with his mother, the timid voyeur in the buttoned-up mac (the man can't really be an artist, he worked for a living and he never had sex). And it is beside the point to talk about his pictures as belonging, fleetingly, to a vanished world. All of us belong, fleetingly, to a vanishing world. It is fashionable to look back at Warhol and talk about how his repetitions provoked us out of familiarity when he piled up the soup cans and screen printed the Monroes – multiplying two iconic brands; the one glamorous, the other mundane – his genius to recognise that they vibrated on the same cultural wavelength.

Lowry is popular but unfashionable – a deadly combination in the art world, so his critics use his repetitions against him. It is true that one Lowry looks a lot like another, though that seems to me to be a view closer to prophecy than to criticism in our post-Lowry global village of chains and brands. This Lowry same-ness interests me. At the loom, on the assembly line, on the track, the human being must perform the same task in the same way every working hour. The machine does not tire of this repetition, a repetition reinforced by the uniform lines of the mill windows, the identical terraced houses leading down to the factory. Lowry paints his figures as repeats because that is what they are – clones for the industrial machine. Units. The means of production. The machine is the antithesis of the human.

If Lowry had been painting Mao's great leap forward or Stalin's five-year plans, his faceless figures, over-sized factories, underfed bodies and drab housing would have been celebrated as critical commentary on the de-humanising evils of Communism (whose 1848 Manifesto, don't forget, was written by Marx after he had spent time with his friend Engels in Manchester). As it is, Lowry's pictures unsettle the myth of our land of hope and glory, blowing the cover story of capitalism: freedom and choice. Look at a Lowry and you are looking at a rebuke to that class whose wealth depends upon the ceaseless labour of others. These are also the people rich enough to buy art.

Lowry would have laughed at this analysis. He voted Tory all his life and worked all his life as a rent collector, bagging the pounds, shillings and pence from families who would never own their own home. Lowry's world was a week away from destitution. The weekly wage went on the weekly rent, on the weekly food, on medicine, on booze. Yet Lowry's workers, like Lowry, often voted Tory too.

Margaret Thatcher tapped into the British working-class distrust of socialism, a distrust that persuades those whose labour creates our wealth to believe it is safer in the hands of those who manipulate it. Lowry did not intend to be a political painter, but he is one. He painted what was real – the industrial life of the north of England – but he painted it past documentary and into a dialogue of the soul – what happens to a human being when they are forced to couple with the machine?

The demon world of industrialisation forces meaningless repetition. The Industrial Revolution is a story we tell about progress, about the coming of the modern. It is also the story of a collective nervous breakdown – 'I have seen hell and it's white,' Mrs Gaskell on Cottonopolis – the nickname for Manchester. 'The piston of a steam engine worked monotonously up and down like the head of an elephant in melancholy madness,' – Dickens on Manchester.

Agricultural societies and cottage industries work long hours every day, but no matter how poor and backbreaking, it is not repetitive in the way that factory work is repetitive. The seasons, the weather, the cycle of crops and gestation, all make for variety – not ease of labour, but variety. The imperative behind the Factory Acts and the trade unions' focus on cutting factory hours, happened out of a late understanding that you cannot use the work practices of agriculture as a template for industry.

Look at the famous Lowry figures. There is something static about them even in movement. This has been used to criticise his technique. But have those art critics ever looked at what happens to the human body when its only purpose is to serve the machine? Repetition produces rigidity. The body seizes up in certain positions – it's why professional musicians and athletes spend a fortune on physiotherapy.

Lowry's figures suffer even in their gaiety. The park pictures are the saddest. The bent-over bodies, the thin legs, the bewilderment of those who stand and stare. How did we get here? How did this happen to us? Mental distress is somatised as posture.

Freud recognised that humans go on repeating a trauma as a means of revealing it, with the hidden hope of healing it. Lowry kept painting the trauma. The trauma of industrialisation, the shock to the system that is the machine – until clock-out time, until the whistle blows, until death.

My father worked in a factory from the age of 14 until he was 65, with time off to kill six men with a bayonet at the D-Day landings because the ammunition was only given out to the ranks of sergeant and above. His body held all of that. He was scarred, fit, misshapen, proud. He was a working man. Who was going to paint the likes of him in his machine-stamped life? (A jaunty hat for Saturday sport). Lowry.

The closer I look at the pictures, the more variety I see. Take any of Lowry's industrial scenes and look closely: the urban drab is relieved by a bunch of flowers in an upstairs window, by a figure in a doorway, by a hand stuffed in a pocket in a whistling sort of a way, by somebody waving, by a slash of colour, by a break across the rigidly divided canvas.

Lowry's use of the flat surface of the canvas is both rigid and anarchic. Put a ruler on the picture, see what happens in what section, and where it breaks its own rules of ordered composition. Check out the horse's ears in *Coming Home from the Mill* (1928). Look again. The monotonous palette? The colour is there. Manchester is made of red brick, blackened by soot. Red and black are the colours of the inferno. Lowry takes the red and turns it into defiance and blood. Pride is as important as pain.

Lowry's figures are fighting back; the houses show tiny flares of human resistance against the baleful factory chimneys that stand like arrogant, blasphemous, broken crosses – the hanging beam gone; the hope of redemption gone.

His critics say there is no interiority, no inner world, in Lowry. They say this because his scenes literally happen on the streets, and they say it as a description of what he lacks. As a rent collector, he was a man who stood on doorsteps, not invited in. And his own private world, without passion as he called it, had no glass for self-reflection. Yet it seems to me that the again and again repetition of these scenes of working-class life is more than a surface show.

Where is the inner life when you work a 12-hour day six days a week? It is not found in the cold, cramped back room of your damp terrace, it's in the talk over the fence or fishing with the dog on the canal, or listening to the street preacher and wondering if you believe a word of it. It's saving up for a mouth organ because you want to play a tune. It's the boy – any boy – watching the girl – any girl – and he's Romeo and she's Juliet, and she'll be pushing the pram like the girl behind and he'll be drunk like the man in front, but the machine hasn't broken all the dreams – not yet.

Look at them – art's not for them is it? Art is for the galleries, for the money, champagne, good taste, fancy language, the posh boys at the Courtauld, Christie's, the Tate. No wonder they keep the Lowrys in the basement.

19 JUNE

Cat stands for election in Mexican city

JO TUCKMAN

It started as a joke between friends, but Morris the cat's bid to become mayor of the Mexican city of Xalapa, the capital of the state of Veracruz, has now turned into a social media phenomenon with a serious message about political disenchantment. 'Morris has become an expression of how fed up people are with all the parties and a political system that does not represent us,' said Sergio Chamorro, the owner of the furry black-and-white candidate whose first campaign slogan was: 'Tired of voting for rats? Vote for a cat.'

The Facebook page for the *Candigato* (*gato* means cat in Spanish) now has more than 130,000 'likes' – far more than those accrued by any of the candidates registered to stand in the Xalapa election, and more too than those of Veracruz's current governor. Mexico will hold local elections in around half of the country on 7 July.

Morris's Facebook page and website are filled with artwork, videos and slogans sent in by supporters from all over Mexico and beyond. Spin-off Twitter accounts have sprouted too, beyond

the control of Chamorro and the small group of thirtysomething professionals who have run Morris's campaign since his
popularity took off earlier this month. 'The truth is that Morris
no longer belongs to us. He belongs to his fans,' said Chamorro,
adding that he had even received messages from citizens designated to run the polling stations on election day describing their
plans to ensure the cat's votes are registered and made public,
even if they do not officially count.

Morris has also inspired a number of other animal candidates
in other Mexican cities including a donkey in Ciudad Juárez,
a dog in Oaxaca and a chicken in Tepic. None, however, have
become as popular as the cat, which appears to have politicians
and the authorities genuinely worried.

The head of Veracruz's electoral institute, which organises elections in the state, has urged members of the public not to waste
their votes by spoiling their ballots with support for Morris. 'It is
important to vote for the registered candidates,' Carolina Viveros
said. 'Please.'

The cat's popularity also prompted the well-known columnist
Julio Hernández to claim its candidacy was a front for the incum-
bent Institutional Revolutionary party's efforts to draw votes
away from genuine electoral alternatives. Morris's team insist
their point is precisely that they don't care who wins.

And beyond the election? The current plan is to put the cat's
future public role to a vote of his Facebook friends.

Who wants to serve a billionaire?

AMELIA GENTLEMAN

Terry Gilmore, senior yacht staff trainer, tosses some striped cushions from the white canvas sofa and drops several blue mono-grammed towels on the scrubbed wooden foredeck of the *Latitude* superyacht. He watches as his trainees hasten to restore order.

'What do we always ensure?' he snaps, looking with irritation at the new arrangement. 'That the zip is down.' He rotates several cushions to conceal barely visible zips. In any case, it turns out that the towels should be picked up first, so that they do not soak dampness into the sofas, and the lesson proceeds with detailed instructions on the correct method for rolling a towel, so that the monogram is prominently displayed (not easy). 'Not like that; totally wrong,' he tells a trainee, pointing out in passing that his belt is too long, and the creases on his polo shirt are insufficiently sharp.

As the economy internationally struggles with the fall-out from recession, the lives of the super-rich continue largely unruffled by the constraints of the global downturn. There are few starker examples of pure extravagance than the superyacht. Because a luxury yacht (unlike a Knightsbridge house, say) is less an investment, more a bottomless pit to throw money at, owners of superyachts are not people who worry much about penny-pinching. These are people who are used to getting what they want and, as employers, they tend to be extremely exacting.

The expanding ranks of billionaires worldwide are creating a new market for servants for the super-rich, often providing esoteric services. At the more arcane end of the spectrum are the people who staff superyachts, who need to be equipped with discretion, servility and good ironing skills, and are relatively well-paid for their work (starting salaries of between €1,700 and €2,500 (£1,450 to £2,130) a month, which includes a berth on the yacht and all meals, rising to €4,000 (£3,400) a month for more senior staff).

Sara Vestin Rahmani, founder of London-based Bespoke Bureau, a high-end domestic staff recruitment agency, has this year launched this yacht-staff training course in Antibes with local firm Abacus & March, because she identified a demand from her clients for well-trained staff capable of working on board superyachts (the term for a large yacht, more than 50 metres, or 164ft, long, usually on sale for anything between £30 million and £60 million). Her placement agency has thrived and expanded throughout the economic downturn, and she is also running butlering courses in Norfolk, for the European market, and Chengdu in south-west China, for her clients there. 'We're lucky in the sense that the rich get richer in a recession,' she says.

On board *Latitude*, a vessel occasionally chartered by musicians such as Rihanna, trainees are being instructed in the art of humility and occasional invisibility that should make them attractive to superyacht owners.

Gilmore has spent a career serving members of the Saudi royal family and rich Russians on board their yachts and is well-qualified to pass on his expertise; his fellow trainers have worked on vessels owned by Roman Abramovich and the Emir of Qatar. Students have paid €900 (£770) for the week's course, hopeful that it will help them secure a job on board one of the world's superyachts. In the abstract, the work appears steeped in glamour, but Gilmore is at pains to disabuse his trainees of any starry-eyed notions about the role. A couple of days on Gilmore's training programme stamps out any lingering sense that this might be a desirable job. Staff need to understand they will simply be 'glorified cleaners', he tells them.

Trainees must memorise correct forms of address from a training manual, which informs them that it is unacceptable to ask 'Why?' (it should be substituted with 'May I know the reason?'). The inquiry 'Are you done?' should be replaced with 'May I ask if you have finished?'

Trainees are told that some guests may request that they stand silently on board deck, motionless in the sunshine, waiting for instructions. 'It's stupid, because they could use a buzzer,' Gilmore says, but much of the staffing on yacht businesses is about ostentation and if a motionless steward, standing by on deck is what the owner requests, then staff are not to argue.

He tells trainees they must never wear sunglasses while addressing guests on board a yacht, because guests want to see be able to see their eyes.

'Never stand there and tell them your life story. Never interrupt the guest. Never ask them personal questions,' he says. 'Just say, "Good morning, sir." Don't ignore them, but don't engage.'

A daily list of housekeeping tasks includes polishing the television remote control and checking the towels for stray threads, which need to be chopped off with nail scissors. Students learn that they must monitor the bathrooms and lavatories, and are given guidance on the correct amount of time they should pause before they can scurry in and tidy up after a guest, refolding the end of the loo paper into a pointed V. 'Be aware when people have used the rest rooms. You must be their shadow, but not too close,' Gilmore explains.

The trainees take notes diligently in their notebooks as Gilmore tells them to check the contents of the yacht's sun-cream bottles daily. 'If they are less than half full, you can't have that because it looks cheap.' The bottles that have dropped beneath the 50 per cent mark are discarded. He claims the last yacht he worked on had an annual budget of around £5,000 for sun cream alone.

To own a superyacht such as this one, you need to have a serious chunk of disposable income. If you had a net worth of around £100 million, you would probably be too poor to contemplate taking on the considerable outgoings that staffing and maintaining this kind of extravagance entails. Although some of these vessels exist to be chartered out as a business (at around £200,000 a week), they rarely make money for their owners this way, once the annual docking, licences and engineering costs are factored in. Merely transporting your yacht from the Mediterranean to the Caribbean on a container vessel for the winter season (to avoid damaging it en route) costs around £250,000.

Despite the expense, the superyacht market is expanding. There are 400 new superyachts under construction (and unlike cars, old yachts are repaired rather than scrapped, so this represents an increase in the absolute numbers), which will create work for an estimated 3,500 new crew. At the extreme end of the market, the superyacht is no longer a particularly ostentatious purchase. Three years ago, Abramovich took delivery of the *Eclipse*, a 163-metre (536ft) gigayacht (considerably larger than a super- or a megayacht), and even this massive liner has subsequently been shunted into the second position, by the *Azzam*, at 180 metres (590ft), currently ranked as the world's largest private yacht.

Working for billionaires comes with unique complications. 'The security implications are horrendous. Most of the people who own these boats are people who are security targets – royal family, politicians,' Gilmore explains, warning his students that pictures taken on the ship should never be uploaded on to Facebook or Twitter, to avoid exposing the yacht's owners to security breaches or embarrassment.

Crew members' mobile phones must always be left down-stairs, in the minute cabins assigned to staff. Gilmore relates an alarming story of a junior steward who was serving dinner to guests when her phone rang in her pocket. She was lucky not to lose her job, he says. He tells another cautionary tale of a junior crew member who put a guest's £750 cashmere jumper into the drier, shrank it to the size of a doll's jumper, pressed it, wrapped it in tissue paper (standard presentation for newly laundered clothes), and returned it to the guest's cabin. She, too, was lucky not to lose her job, although this revelation is greeted with aghast horror by a fellow trainer, observing the session, who declares that she would have sacked her.

Very little attention is paid to employment law by yacht owners, partly because of the international nature of the opera-tion; crew members can be fired on a whim. 'You might have an Egyptian owner, a boat registered in the Cayman Islands, based in Monaco, a company registered in Germany, a crew made up of Australians and South Africans. Where are the social secu-rity payments made?' says a representative of an international yacht association, which offers support to yacht staff, who asks not to be named. 'This is probably the most politically incorrect industry in the world. You can get fired because you are not blonde or pretty. It is all about the look and the image.'

Because of concerns over workers' rights, the International Maritime Organisation has recently drawn up the Maritime Labour Convention, which should be introduced from August, and will ensure that crew get three meals a day and proper breaks. Attempts to introduce regulations aimed at improving the size of crew quarters had to be abandoned, though, because larger crew cabins would have cut into the yacht owners' living space. 'Eight guest cabins would have gone down to four cabins. People wouldn't have wanted to own yachts. It would have made the industry obsolete,' says the woman from the yacht association.

A lot of time is spent on discussing the trainees' personal appearance; they are told to make sure they smell fresh, that they should clean their teeth after drinking coffee and they should be clean-shaven. 'That's for girls as well as boys. It's not nice if you are having breakfast to see a girl's hairy legs,' says Gilmore. No nail polish is allowed, in case it chips off in the food. He also warns new recruits that they should be on their guard when the weather turns bad. 'If the sun shines, everyone is happy. If not, they start nitpicking. They will start looking for fault. That's when you get aggro.'

Many of the skills the students learn here could be transferred to work in a domestic setting, Vestin Rahmani says, and over the weekend visit, she is also scouting for butler talent for her London business. She is seeing a rising demand for butlers, she says, and her experience chimes with recent research indicating that there are more servants in Mayfair now than there were 200 years ago, with entourages stretching to maids, part-time chefs, part-time drivers and personal assistants.

The job specifications on recruitment sites like Vestin Rahmani's, and similar businesses such as Greycoat Lumleys, give an insight into the lives of prospective employers, who hope their staff will have everything from 'a high level of technological knowledge and ability to deal with complex electronic control systems for household security systems', to experience in maintaining media rooms and orangeries.

A good butler can expect to earn well over £50,000, but many are paid more; she acknowledges that it is sometimes hard for her richer clients to keep a handle on what average UK salaries are. The expansion in demand for high-end staff has not come from British households, she adds; the reverse has been seen, with many of these households retrenching, cutting back the number of staff they employ. 'I have a lot of Middle Eastern and Russian clients who are hiring butlers. Sometimes it's a statement. It says: "I have a lot of money, and now I have a butler." And then there are some people who genuinely need a butler.'

She appreciates that working for this kind of employer can be challenging. Recently, she heard of two yacht stewardesses who jumped into a jellyfish-infested patch of sea to create a clear swimming channel for one of the boat's guests. 'She was really in the mood to go swimming, so they swam alongside her – they wanted to make sure she didn't get stung. They got stung to bits, and were in a bit of pain the next day. That's sweet, I think. They got a big tip at the end of the week,' she says.

The woman from the yachting association relates a story of a flatmate who worked for Abramovich's first wife, who liked a particular kind of home-made chocolate on board her yacht. Even if her flatmate was busy, she was often asked to make an 80 kilometre round trip to Monaco to buy the chocolates from the only supplier. 'I wonder, if they knew the trouble it caused, whether they wouldn't say: "Actually, don't bother; take the morning off." The chocolates were divine, but they could have had other chocolates,' she says.

Gilmore, 63, retired last year, after 40 years working on yachts, because he was exhausted. 'It is a tiring job, keeping these people happy,' he says. 'It is not a family-friendly business. These people, they like you, but they don't like baggage.'

'Inevitably there are going to be people you won't choose to get on with in life, but it's all about respect,' he says. Part of the course is dedicated to helping staff understand how to react to bullying from their employers. 'They can order you in a way you are not used to,' he says. 'You train people to respond to that kind of abuse. You stand there and let it go in one ear and out of the other.'

Sexual harassment is uncommon (because the relatively confined space on a yacht inhibits it), but not unheard of. Gilmore discusses what to do if an owner pinches a member of staff on the bottom. 'Slap him and you've lost your job,' he points out, advising trainees to remain silent and report the incident to a superior.

In the afternoon, trainees are sent to a villa a few miles inland of Antibes, where they are taught how to make beds, given ironing training, drilled in laying the tables swiftly for 12 guests, and finally practise serving champagne to their trainers (who seem to enjoy the session).

Gilmore is phlegmatic about the joys of yacht ownership, remarking that the appeal still escapes him. 'Personally, I would never own a yacht, even if I had all the money in the world. It is a bottomless pit; you're always putting money into it.'

Gary Robson, who is a recruitment consultant for Abacus & March, is still unsettled by the amount of money he encountered during his career as a chief steward, working first for a Saudi Arabian construction magnate and later for Russian oil oligarch and then a Chinese billionaire who had made his money from casinos and property.

'I'd never met that kind of money before. We are talking the billions. What do you have to do to earn this kind of money? I don't know what is happening to society, but there is such a big divide,' he says during a break from training. Occasionally, the extreme extravagance he witnessed on board overwhelmed him. 'They would say to me, there will be 15 to 20 guests. Everything would be prepped and done – lobster and caviar – and then there are just two people for dinner and it's all wasted. I think some of them have lost their understanding of what it actually is, money. Money, to them, is not what it is to you and me.

'Some of them are not even very keen on yachts,' he adds. 'They get seasick. You wonder why do they buy them? Keeping up with the Joneses?'

The yachts' designs reinforce the division between owner and staff, he says. 'The crew is not seen or heard. We're like rats, I suppose. Just stowed away. I have had some really nice owners, and some who are totally the opposite. It's nice when you get owners who say hello to the crew. Some are rude – grunt, or wave – no eye contact.'

Occasionally, the exposure to this level of wealth rubs off on the staff who find themselves infected with the big-spender mentality, he says. He recalls nights out where he ordered Dom Perignon (which you can buy for €80, or £68, in a shop) for €300– 500 (up to £425) in a bar.

Most of the trainees are excited about having a chance to work for billionaires. Andrew Drysdale, 28, a former cocktail waiter from Newcastle, has been in Antibes for several weeks, looking for yacht work. 'I wouldn't think of myself as a servant,' he says; instead, he hopes the work will become a long-term career. 'I'd like to be working for someone who wants excellence in their service, in their drinks, and food. You want them to care. It's the appreciation of your work you want,' he says.

He doesn't find the extremes of wealth demonstrated in the yacht industry disconcerting. 'You can't even be jealous because it is so out of reach that you are never going to come into it. It doesn't upset me.'

Pavleta Hristova, 28, a trained dentist from Bulgaria, hopes to find work on a yacht because she has not found work at home in dentistry. She would like to join her husband, Anton Hristov, 32, who has been working for a number of years on cruise ships, and has recently shifted to yacht work. The couple listen attentively to Gilmore's instructions on silver service table arrangements, and race obediently to lay an outside table for six people, for a three-course (imaginary) dinner of salad, veal and soufflé.

Anton likes what he has seen of the yacht world. 'These people don't think twice about how they spend their money. If you can afford to have a yacht, why not? People like to have fun and enjoy their privacy.'

Max Hinton, 19, from Kent, has given up his job as assistant manager in a cocktail bar in Manchester, and is paying for the course with his savings. He has been dock-walking for more than a month – pacing the harbours in Antibes and marinas in neighbouring resorts before breakfast, with dozens of other prospective crew members, searching for work – and hopes that the course might improve his employability.

Vestin Rahmani identifies something very pleasing in his demeanour – a mix of eagerness to help and a humble reserve – and says she thinks he will go far in the industry. She takes her work very seriously, but manages to maintain a healthy sense of the peculiarities of the niche world that her company caters for. Brought up in Sweden, she has strong feelings about the proper payment of staff, and it took her a while to acclimatise to the growing ranks of the super-rich in London.

'I appreciate that it is a little bit of a weird market. I am so used to it now, but I can see from the outside it sometimes seems a bit weird,' she says. 'When I first came over from Sweden, I worried that people had so much money. I don't think about it any more. What matters to me is whether or not people are nice.'

24 June

Edward Snowden leaves reporters chasing shadows around an airport

MIRIAM ELDER

As the Aeroflot jet bound for Havana rolled away from the gate at Sheremetyevo airport, the question became: was he ever even really here? For more than 24 hours the sprawling international airport on Moscow's northern outskirts was the site of an intricate game of cat-and-mouse. The target: Edward Snowden, sought by an enraged US, which has charged him with leaking classified documents on US surveillance programmes and warned countries suspected of abetting his escape.

The action culminated at 2 p.m. on Monday outside gate 28, where Snowden was checked in for a flight to Havana, another stopover en route to Venezuela or Ecuador, where he had sought political asylum. Dozens of journalists assembled at the window, hoping to spot the man who had eluded them for endless hours inside Sheremetyevo's winding halls. Hours later, they imagined, they would have Snowden cornered, ready to spill his innermost thoughts as the plane hurtled towards Havana for a full 12 hours.

The news zoomed through the hall – Russian news agencies reported that Snowden and his travelling companion, Sarah Harrison of WikiLeaks, had checked into seats 17A and 17C. Those seated nearby were giddy. As the plane started to board, more than a dozen Aeroflot agents converged on the gate and ushered reporters away from the windows. They threatened to confiscate cameras and telephones, and attempted to block the view. Some journalists said they were ready to hide their telephones in their pants. Anything for a snap of Snowden.

One by one, the journalists got on board – all the world's media, and Russia's too. The line dwindled to a crawl and the Aeroflot agents began to whisper: 'He's not on board.' The gate closed. A detachable staircase pulled away from the aircraft. The Airbus began to roll backward. 'He's not on board,' said Nikolai Sokolov, an Aeroflot gate employee, his eyes wide. 'I was waiting for him myself.' Around two dozen journalists settled in for the 12-hour journey to Havana – a flight on which no alcohol is served, much to the chagrin of the reporters, many of whom aren't used to going half a day without a stiff drink.

And, yet again, Snowden was nowhere to be found.

He was reportedly in Moscow for 21 hours but no photographs or video of him have emerged – no leaks from the Federal Security Service or police, who use the website *Life News* to broadcast the news they want the world to see. Moscow has made its overtures to Snowden obvious, with Vladimir Putin's spokesman, Dmitry Peskov, repeatedly saying the Kremlin would consider an asylum request from the American government, as it would from any other. But the events come amid the worst Russian-US relations since the end of the cold war, with the Kremlin once again making anti-Americanism a central governing pillar. The sight of a US whistleblower, hounded by his own government, being welcomed on Russian soil would be nothing short of a coup.

But was he ever here?

When it emerged on Sunday morning that Snowden had boarded Aeroflot flight SU23 from Hong Kong to Moscow en route to an undisclosed third country, journalists streamed towards the airport. They shoved pictures of Snowden into the faces of disembarking passengers, asking: 'Have you seen this man?'

Most shrugged and pushed on through the crowd. Two Spanish men, transiting through Moscow en route to Madrid, thought that maybe one of them had. It was the first suspected sighting of a man who would become a ghost. Russian news agencies jumped into the story, issuing a host of contradictory information by citing an endless stream of anonymous sources. 'Snowden is in the transit area!' 'Snowden has been examined by an Ecuadorian doctor.' While the Hong Kong-Moscow plane was still in midair, somewhere over the Siberian city of Omsk, the Kremlin's English-language channel, Russia Today, flashed: 'Snowden already in Russia – SOURCE.'

Journalists were not alone in waiting for Snowden. Outside the transit area in terminal F, a grey branch of the airport that remains frozen in Soviet times, plainclothes officers attempted to blend in. As the day wore on, more and more arrived, some following reporters from a distance, others guarding heavy doors that appeared to lead nowhere.

Snowden is believed to have landed in Moscow shortly after 5 p.m. on Sunday. Lacking a Russian visa, and stripped of his US passport anyway, he could not leave the airport. That left the Capsule Hotel, a newly opened site in Sheremetyevo's terminal E, featuring sparse suites with room for little more than a bed. Receptionists there examined photos of Snowden and said they had never seen him.

As evening began to fall, Ecuador's ambassador to Moscow arrived. He too was seeking Snowden (the country's foreign minister later said it had received an asylum request). He did not know where to find Snowden. He was still waiting in the airport, empty of its daytime rush, at 2 a.m. on Monday. It was unclear whether he had, at that point, achieved his goal.

The comparisons began to roll in. It was like that Tom Hanks movie *The Terminal*, about a stateless man stuck in New York's JFK airport. Or like that other Tom Hanks movie, *Catch Me If You Can*. The overtones of *Waiting for Godot*, about expecting the arrival of a man who never arrives, were, perhaps, too obvious.

Nothing like that was to come. Those chasing Snowden resorted to following ridiculous leads – was that group of Russian agents milling around a handicapped people's bathroom hiding Snowden? That airport employee, rolling a tray with three plates, was she about to feed Snowden, Harrison and an unknown third party? That man with the sunglasses, he kind of looks like him, doesn't he?

By 4 p.m. on Monday, after spending 27 consecutive hours inside Sheremetyevo's barely air-conditioned halls, Lidia Kelly, a journalist with Reuters, squinted her eyes in the direction of an overweight senior citizen and asked: 'Wait, is that Julian Assange?'

The hunt for Snowden continues.

25 JUNE

Brian Cox voices the new nationalist mascot: a cartoon terrier called Duggy Dug

SEVERIN CARRELL

Scotland's pro-independence movement has unveiled a new weapon, a laconic cartoon dog called Duggy Dug which – voiced by the veteran actor Brian Cox – will fearlessly 'sniff out fact from fiction while cracking a few jokes'.

The Highland terrier has been recruited by Newsnet Scotland, the vigorously partisan pro-independence news and commentary website, to 'counter the relentless negativity and scaremongering' of the pro-UK campaign. Duggy Dug will be hosting his own website, Twitter feed @duggy_dug, and YouTube channel, from July. The trial run saw Duggy cheerfully promise to 'smell the keech [crap] a mile off'.

Cox, the Shakespearean actor famous as the villainous intelligence chief Ward Abbott in the Bourne film franchise, in Ralph Fiennes' film *Coriolanus* and the TV western series *Deadwood*, has donated voice overs for Duggy's outings after becoming one of the most prominent celebrity faces of the independence movement. Formerly and famously a Labour supporter (he voiced its 2007 general election broadcast), Cox starred at the launch of the Yes Scotland pro-independence campaign in Edinburgh in May 2012, with an impassioned denunciation of new Labour and its shift to the centre during the Tony Blair years.

Newsnet Scotland quoted Cox as saying: 'One of the most effective ways to combat fear is through humour. If we can provide a few laughs, at the same time as showing just how ridiculous some of the anti-independence scare stories actually are, then it can only help. I think Duggy Dug has the potential to inject a bit of fun into the referendum debate, and that's surely good thing.'

Newsnet describes Duggy as 'a scruffy yet likeable old Scottish terrier whose eyesight isn't the best – but who uses his nose to sniff out fact from fiction as he wanders through some of the more controversial areas of the debate, wisecracking along the way.'

Lynda Williamson, Newsnet Scotland's communications officer, said: 'We believe a loveable cartoon character is just the thing to counter the relentless negativity and scaremongering. Duggy Dug isn't just likeable though, he's also knowledgeable, and those watching the cartoons will be taken on an enjoyable yet informative wee journey.'

There's something of the tit for tat going on here, as both sides seize on favourable statistics and information to prove their case or dis their opponents by inventing new propaganda tools. It's a world where sarcasm and facetiousness gains particular currency, and digital graphics software offers each side a more accessible armoury; Wings Over Scotland's *Project Fear* film poster spoof a case in point.

Scottish Labour's deputy leader Anas Sarwar unveiled his party's own debunking campaign at its annual conference in April, a Twitter campaign and website called Truth Team 2014, with a pledge to 'find out the facts and expose the myths'. So far, its public efforts have been modest: in the 65 days since its fanfare launch at conference, it has sent out 37 tweets.

As when the pro-UK campaign Better Together chose a name which had been used before (amongst many iterations, it's a song by folk balladeer Jack Johnson, a social cohesion initiative at Harvard university and a unity campaign by Anglo-Catholics in England), there is a risk of early confusion for the nationalists' new mascot. There is another similarly named evangelist mutt out there called Duggie Dug Dug, a singing and dancing dog which promotes Christian evangelism from his kennel in Epsom, who also has his own website and virtual theme park. The alter ego of a musician called Doug Horley, who is signed to an EMI label, claims a fanbase of 25 million worldwide and has sung for the Billy Graham organisation, Duggie Dug Dug's top track, a winsome MOR ballad heavy on the echo, is 'I Will Love You Now'. That, we can assume, is where the similarities die.

Summer

Young, qualified and jobless: plight of Europe's best-educated generation

JON HENLEY

'All your life,' says Argyro Paraskeva, 'you've been told you're a golden prince. The future awaits: it's bright, it's yours. You have a degree! You'll have a good job, a fine life. And then suddenly you find it's not true.' Or not so suddenly. Paraskeva left Thessaloniki University five years ago with an MSc in molecular biology. Beyond some private tutoring, paid essay writing ('I'm not proud. But a 50-page essay is €150') and a short, unhappy spell in a medical laboratory, she hasn't worked since.

Over cold tea in a sunlit cafe in Greece's second city, Paraskeva says she has written 'literally hundreds of letters'. Every few months, a new round: schools, labs, hospitals, clinics, companies. She delivers them by hand, around the region. She's had three interviews. 'I will go anywhere, really anywhere,' she says. 'I no longer have the luxury of believing I have a choice. If someone wants a teacher, I will go. If they want a secretary, I will go. If they want a lab assistant, I will go.'

So would countless other young Europeans. According to data out on Monday more than 5.5 million under-25s are without work, and the number rises inexorably every month. It's been called the 'lost generation', a legion of young, often highly qual-ified people, entering a so-called job market that offers very few any hope of a job – let alone the kind they have been educated for.

European leaders are rarely without a new initiative. Last week, they pledged to spend €6 billion (£5 billion) over two years to fund job creation, training and apprenticeships for young people in an attempt to counter a scourge that has attained historic proportions. This week, Angela Merkel is convening a jobs summit to address the issue. Yet still the numbers mount up. In Greece, 59.2 per cent of under-25s are out of work. In Spain, youth unemployment stands at 56.5 per cent; in Italy, it hovers around 40 per cent.

Some commentators say the figures overstate the problem: young people in full-time education or training (a large proportion, obviously) are not considered 'economically active' and so in some countries are counted as unemployed. That, they say, produces an exaggerated youth unemployment rate. But others point out Europe's 'economically inactive' now include millions of young people (14 million, according to the French president, François Hollande) not in work, education or training but who, while technically not unemployed, are nonetheless jobless – and have all but given up looking, at least in their own country. Millions more are on low-paying, temporary contracts. By most measures, the situation is dire.

In the words of Enrico Giovannini, Italy's employment minister, this is a disaster all the more shocking because it is hitting Europe's best-educated generation: in Spain, nearly 40 per cent of people in their twenties and early thirties have degrees; in Greece it's 30 per cent; in Italy, more than 20 per cent.

The crisis is even more acute because of its knock-on impact: these are often young people with no pensions, no social security contributions, diminishing networks, limited opportunities for independence. High youth unemployment doesn't just mean social problems and productivity wasted; it means falling birthrates and intergenerational tension between parents and their thirtysomethings still living at home. 'A wholesale destruction,' a Bologna University professor says, 'of human capital'.

In the first three months of last year, Paraskeva earned €300. Then nothing for four months, then €250 more, then nothing again. She spends '€30 a week, max, mostly my parents' money'. She is not entitled to unemployment benefit because what little work she has done has mostly been on the black market. So at 29, she's back living at home with her parents. Her mother has rheumatoid arthritis, her father is on dialysis – but both, thankfully, still have their jobs as teachers. And their health insurance.

As a registered jobseeker, Paraskeva gets a few discounts, and free screenings at Thessaloniki's film festivals. She goes to classes for the jobless: art, fantasy fiction, French. She sees friends (though most of her classmates have gone abroad; she might too, next year, a funded PhD in the United States). She collects her parents' prescriptions. She reads, a lot. 'You have to find a routine,' she says. 'You need a routine. And to meet other people like you, that's really important. To understand that it's not your fault, you've done nothing wrong, that everyone's in the same boat.' But still, some mornings 'you wake up and there's no meaning to getting out of bed'.

Sporadically, this overwhelming frustration boils over into anger on the streets: the *indignados* of Spain, the near-riots that have scarred Athens in recent months, the great movement of Portuguese protesters that forced the government into an embarrassing U-turn last year. This month, thousands marched in Rome to demand action on record unemployment.

But in between times, young people are just as likely to respond to their predicament with a mixture of gloom and resignation. Vasilis Stolis, 27, has a master's in political science and – apart from odd evenings playing the bouzouki in restaurants until the work dried up – has been unemployed since 2010. 'Sometimes,

I'm not going to lie, it feels really bad,' he says. Stolis lives in a flat belonging to his grandfather. His parents, other family members, 'anyone who still has an income, basically', chip in to help with the €50-odd a month he lives on. 'It's frankly miserable, sometimes,' he says. 'You pay the bills. You go out with a girl you like, you can buy just one drink. No cinema. No holidays.'

If most of these young people in the worst-affected states – Greece, Spain, Italy and Portugal – are getting by, it must be at least partly thanks to some remarkably resilient, close-knit families. Many are still at home, or living – like Vasilis – in places owned by a relative, and with the help of parental handouts.

'The family,' says Andrea Pareschi, 21, a political sciences graduate from Bologna, 'has become the primary social security system.' (That's while wages, pensions and benefits hold up, of course; in Greece at least, both – certainly in the public sector – are shrinking fairly fast. Stolis's father, who works for the health service, has seen his salary slashed from €2,500 to €1,500 a month.)

One way of postponing the issue is to prolong your studies. 'As long as you're studying, you have something to do,' says Sylvia Melchiorre, 26, who graduated from Bologna, Italy's oldest university, spent 12 months as an au pair in Paris, and has come back to do two more years of languages and literature. Her boyfriend, Daniele Bitetti, also 26, will apply for a PhD in human geography unless he finds a job soon. The couple, from Puglia, pay €300 rent plus bills for their apartment – helped by their parents who send each some €600 a month.

'Studying at least makes you feel that you're not doing nothing,' says Melchiorre. 'You do three years, then a couple more, and then – my God, what next? A master's, a PhD ... and never a job at the end of it.'

Others are simply packing up and leaving: this crisis is seeing young Europeans emigrate in unprecedented numbers. More than 120,000 recently qualified doctors, engineers, IT professionals and scientists – half with second degrees – have left Greece since 2010, a University of Thessaloniki study found this year. 'It's a terrible loss for this country,' says Sofia Papadimitriou, who is applying to study bioinformatics in the Netherlands next year. 'It trains all these brains, and they all leave. The government says the future will be different; they will come back. I'm not so sure.'

In previous decades – after the Second World War, in the sixties and seventies – Italian emigrants were mainly unskilled workers, fleeing a life of poverty. Last year, emigration from Italy jumped 30 per cent. Half the leavers were aged 20 to 40, and twice as many as a decade ago had degrees. In Spain, the employment ministry estimates more than 300,000 people aged under 30 have left the country since the 2008 crash. Some 68 per cent more are seriously considering it, according to a European commission study.

Among them is Lucia Parejo-Bravo, 22, leaving Málaga University next month with a business management degree and the firm intention of finding a job in Germany, where she studied for a year. 'Most of my friends have left: to the US, UK, South America, Asia, Scandinavia, Canada,' she says. 'Staying here means fighting – I mean really fighting – to find a job. If by a miracle you do get one, it's €600 a month. Or less, if they make you work self-employed. They get away with it because there are just so many of us so desperate for work. Germany won't be easy, but at least it will be fair.'

Not all are as optimistic as Parejo-Bravo. Spain's particular problem is that of the 1.8 million Spaniards under 30 looking for a job, more than half are poorly qualified. Victims of the burst property bubble, they left school to earn €2,000 a month or more on construction sites and in building-supply firms. Those jobs have now gone, and will not return for many years. But in the meantime, says David Triguero, 27, at Málaga's crowded Playa las

Acacias with friends, 'we bought nice cars. I bought a flat. Some got married; had kids. My benefits run out in February. I don't see a future. Nothing.'

Things do not seem quite so bleak for Victor Portillo Sánchez, but he too does not see his future in Spain. At 31, about to finish his PhD (the EU-funded money has run out), he entertains no hopes of staying in a country 'that's closing research centres it opened only five years ago'. Portillo too gets by 'with the help of my parents, and on my savings. But it doesn't feel good to be spending your savings at 31.' He has failed to find part-time work teaching, and as a waiter and barman. So after defending his thesis this summer, he'll be off. 'Anywhere, it could be,' he says. 'If you'd told me three years ago I might apply for a job in Sweden, I'd have laughed. Or in Newcastle. I went there once, for a conference.'

Are they happy to leave? Three, four, maybe five years abroad, says Portillo: fine. Nice, even. But this feels more like exile. 'I don't see there being a job for me in Spain in five years' time,' he says. 'Nor in 10. Maybe not ever. And that pisses me off. My dad's not in great shape.' This is not an adventure, Portillo says: 'Sorry. It's not like a gap year. If it was my choice, then OK. If I'd fallen in love, something like that. But I'm being forced to leave, to look for food. And I may never come back. That worries me.'

They have much to worry them, these young people. Now, true, it is summer: in Thessaloniki and Bologna and Málaga the days are long, the sun is shining, the beach beckons. 'We're young, you know?' says Melchiorre in Bologna. 'We must live for the day. We have friends. Cafes. It could be worse.'

But come September, and once a few years have passed, says Vera Martinelli, 'you really don't feel so good. I know. I've been there. I'm 33. September is the time of fresh starts, new beginnings. Except for me it won't be.' Martinelli lives with her husband in a flat belonging to her grandad, a former professor. She has a degree in languages and literature, studied at the Sorbonne and in Oxford, did postgraduate work, trained as a teacher, and worked for three years with chronically ill children. Her unemployment benefit ran out in 2011. The couple live on her husband's (recently reduced) salary of €900 a month, and occasional help – 'bills, car insurance, that kind of thing' – from family. She wants to do 'something useful, that's all. For an NGO, ideally. But actually, at this stage, for anyone. I just want something to do every day.'

The worst, she says, is 'when people ask, what are you? And I have no answer. Everything seems to have blurred. I'm not a teenager any more: I'm married. I grew up with feminism; I can't say 'I'm a wife'. And I'm not a grown-up, because I don't have a job. I don't know what I am.'

What they all do know is that the world they live in has changed, completely. The kind of working lives their parents have enjoyed and are still enjoying, they understand, will not be open to these people: stable, full-time jobs, a pension. 'They could choose from lots of jobs,' says Melchiorre. 'They could take time to decide. They knew they'd have work for 40 years. Now they know they'll retire, in six or seven years' time. I have no job, and no money, now. Maybe I'll have none in 10 years. Maybe I'll never be able to retire.'

For some, this looks quite exciting. 'Every generation has its challenges,' says a bullish Stefano Onofri, 21, embarking on a master's in international management. 'This is ours. This is the world we're in. It's what we've got now. Opportunities don't die, they just change.' His friend Alessandro Calzolari, 23, midway through a masters in theoretical physics and looking at a career in nanotechnology, sees clearly that 'we will all have to be entrepreneurs, with ourselves. We will be constantly selling ourselves. It is quite exciting. Scary, but exciting.'

A few have already started. Riccardo Vastola, 28, studied marketing and communications but founded a music business in 2009, organising indie rock gigs, events, club nights in and around Bologna. It's officially an association at the moment, but next year will hopefully become a company. 'I felt I had to do this,' he says. 'I had to do something I enjoy and that let me work with other people, create like a little family in my work. That was important to me. I'm not sure I could do a 'classic' job in some big company.' For the moment, it's working: Vastola takes home a bit less than €1,000 a month, enough to live on. In Thessaloniki, the same motivation spurred Stolis to set up alterthess.gr, an alternative news website, with four friends. He's not making money. 'But it's really important to me,' Stolis says. 'We're working together. That's hope for the future. I think more and more of us will be like this, doing our own projects. People have got it now. That degree wasn't the key to prestige and security everyone said it was. And not everyone can be doctors or lawyers or engineers.'

Konstantis Sevris, a 25-year-old political science graduate in Thessaloniki, had a money-spinning idea: a youth hostel, with rented bikes, in a city with 100,000 students that doesn't have one. 'I've tried,' he says. 'The tourist office told me there was no law in Greece for youth hostels. You can have hotels, or rooms to rent. There's a lot of crazy like this in Greece.' But not everyone is ready for a brave new world. 'In Italy at least, they don't teach that mentality,' says Calzolari. 'They don't create a culture where it becomes possible. In the US, start-ups get launched right after university. Not here.'

Most said they were largely happy with the quality of university teaching. And they reject the idea of a strictly utilitarian system, tailoring courses and student numbers to available jobs. 'University has to be about developing our minds, too,' says Caterina Moruzzi, 22, a philosophy master's student at Bologna.

'People should be able to pursue what interests them. What would society be otherwise?'

But many feel universities need to do more to prepare students for a new reality. 'We're taught how to think, not how to do,' says Pareschi. 'University here is about learning, not working,' says Calzolari: 'There's very little connection with the world of work. Few internships.'

And almost all are worried about the longer-term consequences of the working environment they see being sketched out for them: Europe's social systems, they point out, are all built around stable, full-time, long-term jobs. 'So we're out there, building our own brand, for hire,' says Portillo in Malaga. 'Except nothing's set up for that. Say I go to the US, pay into a private pension fund for 10 years. Then I come back, at 41. The Spanish pension system isn't going to let me opt out. It's going to tell me I have to work 30 years, in Spain, for a pension. How's that work?'

In Bologna, Martinelli feels much the same: 'I know I'll never have a job like my mother had, teaching English all her life,' she says. 'It could be great, lots of jobs. But only if when I'm ill I'm covered, when I'm unemployed I'll be OK, when I'm 75, I'll be able to retire.' No one, Martinelli says, seems to be thinking about that. Just like no one is thinking about the implications, longer term, of her and her thirtysomething unemployed friends not having babies. Sylvia knows a couple who are putting in PhD application simply because 'that's three years' income assured. They could start a family. How wrong, as a situation, is that?'

3 JULY

For many people it's the extroverted season of strappy sandals, skimpy clothes and barbecues, but for some of us it's a sweating, miserable endurance test

LUCY MANGAN

Ecclesiastes got it wrong. It should be 'to everyone there is a season'. And mine's winter. I like duvets, cardigans, baked potatoes, not shaving my legs, shoes with socks – on me and others – thick jeans, bleak landscapes, ice, snow, hot coffee, warm whisky, warm whisky in hot coffee, a blanket on the sofa watching box sets while eating another baked potato.

Summer is for those who like salads, greenery, sleeping naked under a sheet instead of cocooned in flannelette and thermals, sleeveless dresses, pedicures and strappy sandals, iced tea and Pimms, laughing gaily in the sunshine instead of nodding sombrely indoors as another Norwegian killer is unmasked, or baking themselves on a beach as the sun beats down.

Summer makes visible all the internal and external differences between people that in kinder, gentler seasons go unnoticed, or at least unremarked. It belongs, obviously, to the outwardly gorgeous – those for whom the act of stripping down to the few clothes that are still bearable in the heat requires nothing more than a quick pass with the razor over a few small patches of unruliness, a spritz of bronzer or sunscreen and squint in the mirror to check for spinach between the teeth. Then it's off out to treat the world to the sight of their lissom frames, youthful musculature and poreless, naturally lambent skin whose glow seems to reach out and greet the sun as a cousin.

For the rest of us, it's a sweating, misery-making endurance test, a months-long battle to keep cool while keeping 90 per cent of our badly depilated, instantly-lobstered flesh covered and experimenting with different but equally futile ways of keeping our inner thighs and sockless feet unchafed.

In a further twist of the knife for pallid shut-ins, summer also belongs to the extroverts. The picnics, the barbecues, the festivals. The bloody, bloody festivals. The whole world wants company. You can't move in London for people determinedly enjoying themselves on the filthy, polluted strips of pavement outside dismal eateries that comprise England's attempt at cafe culture.

At least this year it should be mercifully brief. Soon the clouds and the temperature will lower again. Soon it will be hot drinks instead of hot weather. Soon, soon, it will be cardigans once more.

This piece was written at the beginning of the 19-day heatwave that heralded the seventh-sunniest summer since records began.

8 JULY

Andy Murray wins Wimbledon with emphatic victory over Novak Djokovic

KEVIN MITCHELL

Andy Murray shook free 77 years of unwanted history as we suspected he might, unaware of exactly how it happened and grateful for the affection of a nation that helped him beat Novak Djokovic in three pulsating, ragged sets to win Wimbledon on the sunniest of Sundays. It was one of those moments that will forever be bathed in a glow of palpable warmth, from the crowd and the skies above the opened roof of Centre Court.

That the tennis that preceded the most nerve-shredding of final moments varied hugely in quality did not matter. Murray, stretching emotions to the limit, needed four match points to break the resistance of the toughest fighter in tennis and said afterwards: 'I have no idea what happened. I don't know how long it was. Sorry.'

But he has nothing to be sorry for. All that counted in the end were the numbers and they should be etched in the national psyche alongside those that football left us: 4–2 and 1966. After just three hours and nine minutes – way quicker than nearly anyone expected – Murray beat Djokovic 6–4, 7–5, 6–4. Now we can say for a little while yet that the last British player to win the men's singles championship at Wimbledon was Andy Murray, the first one, too, in shorts. Thank you, Fred Perry, we will leave you in peace.

Murray laid that ghost with all his idiosyncrasies intact, the nerves and the grimaces, the amazing gets and the odd inexplicable blunder. There was a healthy level of good serving, with nine aces and only two double-faults, lots of running in the stifling heat and a determination to beat the world number one into the green grass.

Djokovic was as gracious as we knew he would be. 'The bottom line [is] he was the better player in decisive moments,' the Serb said. 'He was getting some incredible points on the stretch, running down the drop shots all over the court. He played fantastic tennis, no question. I believed I could come back but it wasn't my day.'

So, their 'professional friendship', as Murray said earlier, is undisturbed. As for absent friends, Rafael Nadal and Roger Federer will be emphatically reminded that their hegemony is over. They will come again, no doubt, but not with the certainty that marked their long reign at the top.

The world number one and number two players were the rightful finalists here. They may be again in New York in September and Australia after that. This is a journey worth following. Yet the match was not at all what we had expected. In their three previous grand-slam deciders they had gone to the very limits in a total of 12 sets. Here there were three. But Murray says they were every bit as draining, every bit as tough.

He had seven break points inside 20 minutes before cracking the Djokovic serve in the third game with a beautifully disguised backhand down the line. There were to be several more of those.

Dropping serve immediately after a break is a bad habit Murray looked to have kicked but he faltered to let Djokovic off the hook at 2–2 and it would set the pattern for both of them for most of the match. Murray had 17 chances to break and took seven of them. Djokovic broke Murray four times from 13 opportunities. That created the difference in the end.

The elements also played a role. Murray, who does not like wearing a cap, repeatedly caught the sun in his eyes on his ball toss to double-fault twice, aced and fought through three deuce points to hold in the eighth game.

Djokovic, who was gesturing to his box about his breathing, held serve to stay in the set as word filtered through from the umpire's office that the court temperature was 49°C with little or no breeze save that from the distant wafting of fans among the baked gathering. This was a day when the ritual brow-wiping between points was more than a muscle-memory tic.

After an hour's absorbing tennis, Murray pocketed the first set to love, serving too big and too accurately for Djokovic. There was a curious but fair symmetry to one set of numbers: Djokovic hit 17 unforced errors in the set and six winners, Murray hit six unforced errors and 17 winners.

Djokovic looked a little weary and impatient with his lapses but his frustration bloomed into grit and he was soon striking the ball fiercely again, just as Murray's consistency dipped. He dropped serve in the fourth game of the second set with the sloppiest of netted forehands. When Djokovic held without fuss to lead 4–1 after an hour and a half, he bristled with energy again. Murray clung to his towel like a security blanket between points, imploring his box to do, well, who knows what?

The net became peskier, the sun more irritating – he had finally reached for his cap – and he was relying on mistakes at the other end to help him rediscover his zest. It returned almost as quickly as it had disappeared, as Djokovic double-faulted at the end of the seventh game.

There was no clear dominance on either side of the net. What had started as an even and engaging struggle of high quality had become a lottery of missed opportunities. Then, with no challenges left, at 5–5 and 15-all on his serve, Djokovic went ballistic, a rare sight. Murray undercut a return that floated near the baseline at the Serb's feet and was called good. It enraged this normally imperturbable competitor that the chair umpire refused to overrule the call and his anger got the better of him when he belted a forehand into the tape to give Murray the serve for a two-set lead. He did it with an ace. Djokovic's error count mounted steadily in the final set, hitting 40 in the end, nearly twice as many as his tormentor. Murray was calmer but not by much.

Djokovic lost eight points in a row and Boris Becker observed of Murray: 'He can smell the roses but he's still a long way from them.' As he moved more confidently over his favourite lawn, he seemed to know exactly where he was going: the shortest route to history. It was so close. He dropped serve for the fourth time to give Djokovic a look. But the roses reappeared on the edge of the garden when, riddled again with doubt, Djokovic drilled the net from behind the baseline.

So, at 5.11 p.m., Andy Murray went up to the mark and did his duty. His brain must have been hurting as much as his every muscle. He took three championship points as if plucking them from a tree, then we watched in horror as Djokovic fought his way back, in a see-sawing end to a see-sawing match.

And then, when he could fight no longer, Djokovic drove his final shot into the net and Wimbledon went utterly bonkers for the slightly bonkers but wholly wonderful young man from Dunblane.

12 JULY

Good to meet you: Naaz Rashid

BELLA MACKIE

The *Guardian* is the paper I grew up with because my dad read it. When I asked why he read the *Guardian* he told me that he discovered it in the British Council reading room in Dhaka. He liked it for its international news coverage and, when he was posted to London in 1969, he began reading it. Our local newsagent would always keep a copy for him, describing him as 'the young liberal'.

In my teens I was interested in the women and review pages; I recall being particularly excited to find an interview with Morrissey in the early days of the Smiths. At that difficult age, it was reassuring that my dad and I could share the newspaper, even if we didn't always see eye to eye.

As I grew older and I became more interested in politics, we regularly enjoyed discussing the issues of the day. Upon retirement, my dad balked at the cost of the *Guardian*, buying it less, and catching up with news on TV instead. However, he'd often ask if I'd bought a copy and would come and pick it up from my flat.

In September 2012, my dad was diagnosed with cancer. He declined rapidly, struggling to read the papers I brought to the hospital and later the hospice. Occasionally, I would read to him but concentration was difficult for him. In the final week of his life, he still managed to ask who had won the US elections, his interest in international news remaining till the last.

Britain's royal family: cut this anti-democratic dynasty out of politics

SEUMAS MILNE

As a rule, progressive Britain prefers to ignore the monarchy. First, it's embarrassing: 364 years after we first abolished it and long after most of the rest of the world dispensed with such feudal relics, we're still lumbered with one. Second, there are always more important things to confront – from rampant corporate power and escalating inequality to incessant war and the climate crisis. And last, the media and political class form such a sycophantic ideological phalanx around the institution that dissent is treated as, at best, weird and miserabilist.

The last few days have been par for the course. As in the case of every other royal event, the birth of a son to the heir but one to the throne has been reported in tones that wouldn't be out of place in a one-party state. Newsreaders adopt regulation rictus grins. The BBC's flagship *Today* programme held a debate to mark the event between two royalists who fell over each other to laud the 'stability', 'continuity' and 'mystery' of the House of Windsor. The press is full of talk of 'fairytales' and a 'joyful nation'.

But ignoring it leaves a festering anti-democratic dynasticism at the heart of our political system. As things now stand, Britain (along with 15 other former island colonies and white settler states) has now chosen its next three heads of state – or rather, they have been selected by accident of aristocratic birth. The descendants of warlords, robber barons, invaders and German princelings – so long as they aren't Catholics – have automatic pride of place at the pinnacle of Britain's constitution.

Far from uniting the country, the monarchy's role is seen as illegitimate and offensive by millions of its citizens, and entrenches hereditary privilege at the heart of public life. While British governments preach democracy around the world, they preside over an undemocratic system at home with an unelected head of state and an appointed second chamber at the core of it.

Meanwhile celebrity culture and a relentless public relations machine have given a new lease of life to a dysfunctional family institution, as the *X Factor* meets the pre-modern. But instead of rising above class as a symbol of the nation, as its champions protest, the monarchy embodies social inequality at birth and fosters a phonily apolitical conservatism.

If the royal family were simply the decorative constitutional adornment its supporters claim, punctuating the lives of grateful subjects with pageantry and street parties, its deferential culture and invented traditions might be less corrosive. But contrary to what is routinely insisted, the monarchy retains significant unaccountable powers and influence. In extreme circumstances, they could still be decisive.

Several key crown prerogative powers, exercised by ministers without reference to parliament on behalf of the monarchy, have now been put on a statutory footing. But the monarch retains the right to appoint the prime minister and dissolve parliament. By convention, these powers are only exercised on the advice of government or party leaders. But it's not impossible to imagine, as constitutional experts concede, such conventions being overridden in a social and political crisis – for instance where parties were fracturing and alternative parliamentary majorities could be formed.

The British establishment are past masters at such constitutional sleights of hand – and the judges, police and armed forces pledge allegiance to the Crown, not parliament. The left-leaning Australian Labor leader Gough Whitlam was infamously sacked by the Queen's representative, the governor-general, in 1975. Less dramatically, the Queen in effect chose Harold Macmillan as prime minister over Rab Butler in the late fifties – and then Alec Douglas-Home over Butler in 1963.

More significant in current circumstances is the monarchy's continual covert influence on government, from the Queen's weekly audiences with the prime minister and Prince Charles's avowed 'meddling' to lesser-known arm's-length interventions.

This month the high court rejected an attempt by the *Guardian* to force the publication of Charles's 'particularly frank' letters to ministers which they feared would 'forfeit his position of political neutrality'. The evidence from the controversy around London's Chelsea barracks site development to the tax treatment of the Crown and Duchy of Lancaster estates suggests such interventions are often effective.

A striking feature of global politics in recent decades has been the resurgence of the hereditary principle across political systems: from the father and son Bush presidencies in the US and the string of family successions in south Asian parliamentary democracies to the Kim dynasty in North Korea, along with multiple other autocracies.

Some of that is driven by the kind of factors that produced hereditary systems in the first place, such as pressure to reduce conflict over political successions. But it's also a reflection of the decline of ideological and class politics.

Part of Britain's dynastic problem is that the English overthrew their monarchy in the 1640s, before the social foundations were in place for a viable republic – and the later constitutional settlement took the sting out of the issue.

But it didn't solve it, and the legacy is today's half-baked democracy. You'd never know it from the way the monarchy is treated in British public life, but polling in recent years shows between 20 per cent and 40 per cent think the country would be better off without it, and most still believe it won't last. That proportion is likely to rise when hapless Charles replaces the present Queen.

There are of course other much more powerful obstacles to social advance in Britain than the monarchy, but it remains a reactionary and anti-democratic drag. Republics have usually emerged from wars or revolutions. But there's no need for tumbrils, just elections.

It's not a very radical demand, but an elected head of state is a necessary step to democratise Britain and weaken the grip of deferential conservatism and anti-politics. People could vote for Prince William or Kate Middleton if they wanted and the royals could carry on holding garden parties and travelling around in crowns and gold coaches. The essential change is to end the constitutional role of an unelected dynasty. It might even be the saving of this week's royal baby.

25 July

The poet laureate's on holiday – can you write a poem fit for a prince?

Some poetic responses to the birth of His Royal Highness Prince George of Cambridge

Cheering crowds, waving flags, commemorative crockery – all that's missing to mark the appearance of a royal baby is a poem. So far there's no sign of an ode from the poet laureate Carol Ann Duffy. Apparently she's on holiday. So why don't we have a go instead?

Some people have already started. Here's a taste of Michael Rosen's response, 'Mind':

> *I don't mind waiting*
> *do mind being told I'm waiting*
> *don't mind good news*
> *do mind being told which news is good*

THEBLUEPELICAN, a reader of our live blog coverage, posted this poem:

> *Britain is secure.*
> *By his service, his paternity,*
> *And her maternity. English*
> *Men and women are served.*
> *Your ancestors could not be prouder.*
> *Now, it's over to you.*

CHRIS717:

> *Did i ask to be born royal?*
> *Did i ask for my own throne?*
> *I'm innocent, i'm just a baby*
> *So please leave me alone.*
> *You all seem to think it's my fault*
> *That my great granny is the Queen*
> *That my daddy is a prince no less*

Is that a reason to be so mean?
Did i ask to be born royal?
I don't know the meaning of throne
look at me i'm just a baby
Why can't you just leave me alone?

YARKER:

Wince, yet another prince.

MARKRELIAS, 'To the Boy Who Will Be King':

Admittedly, your birth is an event
That in some small way I let register
Upon my consciousness.
To see you there,
A bundle destined for a lifetime spent
In public, where both hate and sentiment
Will hold you ransom, poisoning what air
You'll feel is yours to breathe, I am aware
Despite reluctance, of a gentle bent
Towards a sympathy you do deserve.
Although your future's filled with luxury,
Involuntary sacrifices will
Prove trials I'm sure to soul and mind and nerve
Trials few of us dare judge successfully.
I wouldn't wish my child such shoes to fill.

YUGNICHGRITKIN:

U a lil baby an you not very muscly
if yuo do sum gud exrcises yuo mite get muscly

but jus in cas u dont. get sum cool tattoos
also get sum crocs an grow a goatey
spike your hair lots an buy a sik snakbord
an hide your bongs in a bin or summin.
asy

DICKTURNIP:

I was born half a mile from and ten minutes before you
And yet they named me after you
Not a week old and already I feel cheated.
Perhaps one day, George, you will sit in a cave and watch me capture
     a dragon
And I shall fly by and wave at you sitting in the dark
And be thankful I am not a king.

LEAVINGKANSAS:

Hey George, little baby, you're quite unaware
Of this media frenzy. You haven't a care.
Your mother's besotted; your father's so proud ...
And Nanny and Grandad ... and the rest of the crowd ...
We're all so delighted you're finally here,
But maybe there's one thing we ought to make clear –
While some cheer the baby that's born to be king
And the pressmen camped out by the Lindo Wing
Taking pictures of William and pictures of Kate,
Your home is a flat on the Mile Cross Estate.
You made your arrival without any fuss,
And son, you're the best thing that happened to us.

26 JULY

Online dating:
do men get ignored more
often than women?

NORTHERN LASS *(aka Jody Appleton of the* Guardian's *northern advertising department)*

A couple of weeks ago I went climbing with my friend Dan. I met Dan on an internet date last year; we got chatting because we both know how to keep bees. Up until that point, the youngest male beekeeper I had met was my stepdad, who is in his mid-sixties. So to meet a man under 40 who shared this particular common ground was great.

Over breakfast at Trove in Levenshulme, it was evident that we weren't destined to romantically chase each other around an apiary, but we clearly got on as friends. Dan expressed an interest in learning to climb, so we've been sharing our tales of internet dating and bees at Awesome Walls in Stockport once a week ever since.

This particular week Dan had a face on him like he'd been slapped with a wet flannel. After what seemed like another promising date a few days before, he was encountering 'The Silence' – that cruel tumbleweed blowing around your inbox; when a reply to your message seems to have got lost in the ether. Because no-one is rude enough to just ignore you, right? Even more so after a few messages or even a date?

After all, you read the profile, checked the pictures, sat down and typed a brilliantly composed message. You referenced something on their profile (not just looking at the pictures), complimented something in one of their pictures (in a carefully fashioned non-pervy way), said something a little cheeky (look, I can do banter!), asked some questions (proving you are genuinely interested), spell-checked twice, checked your yours and you'res – in case the recipient comes out in hives in the face of question-able spelling and grammar. Brilliant ... SEND.

The object of your desire logs on (you can see this), they read your message (you can also see this), they look at your profile (and can clearly see from your pictures that you helped build an African village on a gap year, can do dead good yoga on a beach in Goa and that you LOVE LAUGHING). How could they not reply and embark on a series of dates of going out and dancing like no-one is watching or staying in with a bottle of red and a DVD. HOW?!

But nothing, not even an acknowledgement. Just a silent rejec-tion of your efforts.

From the comments that were left under my first article ['Internet dating: Why is it so hard to find a normal, single bloke I fancy?'] it's evident that both men and women experience this silence, but from asking around my fellow internet daters and reading through the experiences of others, it seems to be more of a frequent issue for the lads than the lasses. I'm not sure how this translates when it comes to same-sex dating, or if the silence is as much of an issue, but in heterosexual dating, men seem to feel ignored more frequently (excluding those who just send penis shots. You deserve ignoring, you naughty buggers).

It sucks. I've been on the receiving end of it, like many other online daters. However in hindsight, replying to a few messages after being up all night at a Boomtown party in Bristol while typing with my fists and clearly way over the limit to operate a computer, it wasn't my finest messaging moment and I would have ignored me too.

But I guiltily hold my hands up to also not replying from time to time. When I first started online dating, I replied to every single person. Before you know it, you are juggling a fair few conversations; some that you know full well are not going to lead to a date. On asking one person I dated how they handled this situation, he simply replied: 'I just ignore them.'

After experiencing being ignored a couple of times, it kind of felt that this was just the way it was done. An unwritten code of accepted rudeness that you probably wouldn't apply in other aspects of your life – unless you were a bit of a turd.

This is where Dan was at. Post-date the text messages were not being responded to. The tumbleweed was knocking around in his phone inbox, and disappointment had set in.

In a bid to cheer Dan up – and stop him expressing his cynicism via the medium of the increasingly droopy rope he was supposed to be belaying me with – I suggested we both have a change of tack and go speed dating. Then you can't be ignored – everyone is sat there in front of your face, any awkward encounters or rejections last a maximum of three minutes. It's the dating equivalent of ripping off a plaster: when it comes to the shit bits, it's over very quickly. It would be a new experience for both of us. He agreed, so it was booked. We were off to Elite Speed Dating at Manchester's Circle club.

30 July

Too much talk for one planet: why I'm reducing my word emissions

CHARLIE BROOKER

Eagle-eyed readers may have spotted I haven't been writing this column for a while. Roughly two people noticed its absence, until the other day when a paragraph in *Private Eye* claimed I'd asked Alan Rusbridger, editor of the *Guardian*, to switch off the reader comments underneath my articles (not true), and that he'd refused to do so (also not true), so I'd quit (not entirely true). This led to an intense flurry of activity, by which I mean four people asked me about it.

Although the *Private Eye* story wasn't completely wrong – I have stopped doing this particular column for a while, for reasons I'll explain in a moment – I was all set to write to their letters page to whine in the most pompous manner imaginable, something I've always secretly wanted to do, when I figured I might as well respond here instead, for money.

Incidentally, I'm aware this is Olympic-level navel gazing, but you're a human being with free will who can stop reading any time. Here, have a full stop. And another. And another. There are exits all over this building.

Anyway, I haven't quit the newspaper, but I have, for the meantime, stopped writing weekly, partly because my overall workload was making that kind of timetable impossible, and partly because I've recently been overwhelmed by the sheer amount of jabber in the world: a vast cloud of blah I felt I was contributing to every seven days.

If a weatherman misreads the national mood and cheerfully sieg-heils on BBC Breakfast at 8.45 a.m., there'll be 86 outraged columns, 95 despairing blogs, half a million wry tweets and a rib-tickling pass-the-parcel Photoshop meme about it circulating by lunchtime. It happens every day. Every day, a billion instantly conjured words on any contemporaneous subject you can think of. Events and noise, events and noise; everything was starting to resemble nothing but events and noise. Firing more words into the middle of all that began to strike me as futile and unnecessary. I started to view myself as yet another factory mindlessly pumping carbon dioxide into a toxic sky.

This is perhaps not the ideal state of mind for someone writing a weekly column in a newspaper. Clearly it was time for a short break.

Reader comments form part of the overall wordstorm described above, and it's true I'm not a huge fan of them, but that's chiefly because I'm an elderly man from the age of steam who clings irrationally to the outmoded belief that articles and letters pages should be kept separate, just like church and state. I guess conceptually I still think I'm writing in a 'newspaper', even though the reality of what that means has changed beyond measure since I started doing it. So now I'm sitting grumpily in a spaceship with my arms folded, wearing a stovepipe hat. Ridiculous.

These days most newspaper sites are geared towards encouraging interaction with the minuscule fraction of readers who bother to interact back, which is a pity because I'm selfishly uninterested in conducting any kind of meaningful dialogue with humankind in general. I'd say Twitter's better for back-and-forth discussion anyway, if you could be arsed with it. Yelling out the window at passersby is another option.

When it comes to comments, despite not being as funny as I never was in the first place, I get an incredibly easy ride from passing wellwishers compared with any woman who dares write anything on the internet anywhere about anything at all, the ugly bitch, boo, go home bitch go home. Getting slagged off online is par for the course, and absorbing the odd bit of constructive criticism is character-building. The positive comments are more unsettling. Who needs to see typed applause accompanying an article? It's just weird. I don't get it.

But then right now I don't 'get' most forms of communication. There's just so much of it. Everybody talking at once and all over each other; everyone on the planet typing words into their computers, for ever, like I'm doing now. I fail to see the point of roughly 98 per cent of human communication at the moment, which indicates I need to stroll around somewhere quiet for a bit.

After my break, and a rethink, I'll quietly return later in the year, to write something slightly different, slightly less regularly (probably fortnightly). In other words, I'm reducing my carbon emissions. And whatever the new thing I'm writing turns out to be, it'll appear both online, still accompanied by the requisite string of comments, and in the newspaper, which is a foldable thing made of paper, containing words and pictures, which catches fire easily and is sometimes left on trains.

Now get out.

1 August

Caring for my stroke-victim husband Andrew Marr changed my life

JACKIE ASHLEY

We all have our terrors – cancer, a plane crash, being knocked off the bicycle by a speeding lorry. But so often it's the unexpected that gets you. I thought a stroke was something suffered by people who were either very old, or overweight, or heavy smokers. Yet back in January my husband, Andrew Marr, who is none of those – really, 53 is not old – suffered a very serious stroke. He went from being a super-energetic, fit, over-worker to a half-paralysed invalid. His life had totally changed, but of course, as many kind friends have pointed out, mine had too.

Six months on, after brilliant support from doctors, nurses and physiotherapists, he is back on his feet and returning to work. I have re-entered the political world, but with a different perspective on life. Since so many people have been asking me what it's like to have your life turned upside down by an unexpected illness, here are six random thoughts from my six months off.

First, although I knew a lot about disability and about caring (my father, the late Lord Jack Ashley was totally deaf and suffered from Parkinson's), I had never been a full-time carer. It is, above all, exhausting. It can also be extremely monotonous and frustrating for both the patient and the carer. Every single one of life's daily routines takes twice, if not four times, as long as it used to, from getting through the shower to putting on shoes.

Physio routines, which need practice every day, require hundreds and hundreds of small repetitive movements.

Friends would ask repeatedly why I didn't 'just get someone in to help'. I did at first. Yet, as many carers will know, it's not that simple. You book someone to help with the morning routine at seven each morning and suddenly the patient wants to get up at six. There's a physio appointment; so a complete change of clothes is necessary in the early afternoon. The times of the appointments change every day, on the day, so you never quite know when a lift will be needed ... so you either have someone in full-time attendance; or you do it yourself. Then there's the additional stress of not knowing, because all strokes are different, how long and how full the recovery will be.

I am no Florence Nightingale and there's no damn halo visible when I look in the mirror: this is just what any decent relative would do for someone who is physically disabled. One stroke victim wrote to tell me he thought that carers for stroke sufferers all experience some kind of post-traumatic stress disorder. I wouldn't go that far, but it can be tough, and carers everywhere need support and breaks.

Second, the NHS is wonderful, wonderful, wonderful. The doctors saved my husband's life, the physios have restored him to strength, and for most of them nothing has been too much trouble. But the inflexibility of the system is staggering. I've been contacted by many, many stroke victims and the general view is that hospital care is excellent, but there's very little support after that. Daily, intensive physio and occupational therapy in the hospital are suddenly replaced with a visit once a week, if you are lucky, from the community services. Given that so many stroke victims, and others who have suffered neurological injuries, would be able to get back to work and look after themselves with better rehabilitation after leaving hospital, this is surely a false economy.

Third, returning to Westminster life, I have never been so frustrated at the gap between the arguments in the House of Commons and the real issues in the NHS. I came back just as the Keogh report into failing hospitals was being debated. All I heard were politicians on both sides slagging off each other – it was all 'it's your fault', 'no, it's your fault'. For those thousands of people and their relatives currently in hospital this is the last thing we require of our MPs. There are huge issues of priorities and management and accountability to be sorted out, and rather than mudslinging, politicians should be working together to do this.

Fourth, my re-entry into the world of Twitter was an unpleasant reminder of just how nasty the public debate can be. It coincided with the 24 hours of rape threats suffered by Caroline Criado-Perez for giving a radio interview from a feminist perspective.

If you follow Twitter regularly, it's easy to believe that many of our fellow citizens are cruel, mean, misogynist and foul-mouthed. But suffering a serious illness means that you see the better side of human nature. Countless acts of kindness, messages of goodwill – including on Twitter – and examples of supreme bravery will stay with me for ever. During his rehabilitation my husband was treated for a while at the Douglas Bader wing at Queen Mary's Hospital, Roehampton. There were scores of amputees, all coping with appalling disabilities with immense fortitude and often a beaming smile. Truly, we are better than the Twitter trolls.

Fifth, from talking to the scores of people I met in hospital, and the vast postbag I have received, it's clear that for many women these urgent caring tasks for close relatives come out of the blue. Sometimes they last for years, sometimes, as is my own case, it's just a matter of months. Yet the world of work is not set up to deal with this. Too many older women lose their jobs after a few months off to care for an elderly parent, or other relative. Just as we now accept that women need to take some time out for childcare, surely we should be able to re-arrange the world of work so that 'carer's leave' becomes a normal part of all our lives, men included.

And finally, and perhaps most important, I have become aware of just how fragile life is. We walk in the sunlight, ignoring the shadows. In the blink of an eye lives can be changed utterly. Every year 150,000 people suffer a stroke, and 50,000 of them are still of working age. It can happen while leaning back in the basin at the hairdresser, or even turning your head in the car to look out of the rear window. This is not to say it's best to spend one's life worrying about what horrible illnesses or accidents may strike. But there is nothing like a near-death experience to put life's little annoyances into perspective and to learn to live each day for the day.

19 AUGUST

David Miranda, schedule 7 and the danger that all reporters now face

ALAN RUSBRIDGER

In a private viewing cinema in Soho last week I caught myself letting fly with a four-letter expletive at Bill Keller, the former executive editor of the *New York Times*. It was a confusing moment. The man who was pretending to be me – thanking Keller for 'not giving a shit' – used to be Malcolm Tucker, a foul-mouthed Scottish spin doctor who will soon be a 1,000-year-old time lord.

And Keller will correct me, but I don't remember ever swearing at him. I do remember saying something to the effect of 'we have the thumb drive, you have the first amendment'.

The fictional moment occurs at the beginning of the DreamWorks film about WikiLeaks, *The Fifth Estate*, due for release next month. Peter Capaldi is, I can report, a very plausible *Guardian* editor.

This real-life exchange with Keller happened just after we took possession of the first tranche of WikiLeaks documents in 2010. I strongly suspected that our ability to research and publish anything to do with this trove of secret material would be severely constrained in the UK. America, for all its own problems with media laws and whistleblowers, at least has press freedom enshrined in a written constitution. It is also, I hope, unthinkable that any US government would attempt prior restraint against a news organisation planning to publish material that informed an important public debate, however troublesome or embarrassing.

On Sunday morning David Miranda, the partner of *Guardian* columnist Glenn Greenwald, was detained as he was passing through Heathrow airport on his way back to Rio de Janeiro, where the couple live. Greenwald is the reporter who has broken most of the stories about state surveillance based on the leaks from the former NSA contractor Edward Snowden. Greenwald's work has undoubtedly been troublesome and embarrassing for Western governments. But, as the debate in America and Europe has shown, there is considerable public interest in what his stories have revealed about the right balance between security, civil liberties, freedom of speech and privacy. He has raised acutely disturbing questions about the oversight of intelligence; about the use of closed courts; about the cosy and secret relationship between government and vast corporations; and about the extent to which millions of citizens now routinely have their communications intercepted, collected, analysed and stored.

In this work he is regularly helped by David Miranda. Miranda is not a journalist, but he still plays a valuable role in helping his partner do his journalistic work. Greenwald has his plate full reading and analysing the Snowden material, writing, and handling media and social media requests from around the world. He can certainly use this back-up. That work is immensely complicated by the certainty that it would be highly inadvisable for Greenwald (or any other journalist) to regard any electronic means of communication as safe. The *Guardian*'s work on the Snowden story has involved many individuals taking a huge number of flights in order to have face-to-face meetings. Not good for the environment, but increasingly the only way to operate. Soon we will be back to pen and paper.

Miranda was held for nine hours under schedule 7 of the UK's terror laws, which give enormous discretion to stop, search and question people who have no connection with 'terror', as ordinarily understood. Suspects have no right to legal representation and may have their property confiscated for up to seven days. Under this measure – uniquely crafted for ports and airport transit areas – there are none of the checks and balances that apply once someone is in Britain proper. There is no need to arrest or charge anyone and there is no protection for journalists or their material. A transit lounge in Heathrow is a dangerous place to be.

Miranda's professional status – much hand-wringing about whether or not he's a proper 'journalist' – is largely irrelevant in these circumstances. Increasingly, the question about who deserves protection should be less 'is this a journalist?' than 'is the publication of this material in the public interest?'

The detention of Miranda has rightly caused international dismay because it feeds into a perception that the US and UK governments – while claiming to welcome the debate around state surveillance started by Snowden – are also intent on stemming the tide of leaks and on pursuing the whistleblower with a vengeance. That perception is right. Here follows a little background on the considerable obstacles being placed in the way of informing the public about what the intelligence agencies, governments and corporations are up to.

A little over two months ago I was contacted by a very senior government official claiming to represent the views of the prime minister. There followed two meetings in which he demanded the return or destruction of all the material we were working on. The tone was steely, if cordial, but there was an implicit threat that others within government and Whitehall favoured a far more draconian approach.

The mood toughened just over a month ago, when I received a phone call from the centre of government telling me: 'You've had your fun. Now we want the stuff back.' There followed further meetings with shadowy Whitehall figures. The demand was the same: hand the Snowden material back or destroy it. I explained that we could not research and report on this subject if we complied with this request. The man from Whitehall looked mystified. 'You've had your debate. There's no need to write any more.'

During one of these meetings I asked directly whether the government would move to close down the *Guardian*'s reporting through a legal route – by going to court to force the surrender of the material on which we were working. The official confirmed that, in the absence of handover or destruction, this was indeed the government's intention. Prior restraint, near impossible in the US, was now explicitly and imminently on the table in the UK. But my experience over WikiLeaks – the thumb drive and the first amendment – had already prepared me for this moment. I explained to the man from Whitehall about the nature of international collaborations and the way in which, these days, media organisations could take advantage of the most permissive legal environments. Bluntly, we did not have to do our reporting from London. Already most of the NSA stories were being reported and edited out of New York. And had it occurred to him that Greenwald lived in Brazil?

The man was unmoved. And so one of the more bizarre moments in the Guardian's long history occurred – with two GCHQ security experts overseeing the destruction of hard drives in the *Guardian*'s basement just to make sure there was nothing in the mangled bits of metal which could possibly be of any interest to passing Chinese agents. 'We can call off the black helicopters,' joked one as we swept up the remains of a MacBook Pro.

Whitehall was satisfied, but it felt like a peculiarly pointless piece of symbolism that understood nothing about the digital age. We will continue to do patient, painstaking reporting on the Snowden documents, we just won't do it in London. The seizure of Miranda's laptop, phones, hard drives and camera will similarly have no effect on Greenwald's work.

The state that is building such a formidable apparatus of surveillance will do its best to prevent journalists from reporting on it. Most journalists can see that. But I wonder how many have truly understood the absolute threat to journalism implicit in the idea of total surveillance, when or if it comes – and, increasingly, it looks like 'when'.

We are not there yet, but it may not be long before it will be impossible for journalists to have confidential sources. Most reporting – indeed, most human life in 2013 – leaves too much of a digital fingerprint. Those colleagues who denigrate Snowden or say reporters should trust the state to know best (many of them in the UK, oddly, on the right) may one day have a cruel awakening. One day it will be their reporting, their cause, under attack. But at least reporters now know to stay away from Heathrow transit lounges.

Alan Rusbridger has replied to several comments in the thread below the online version of this article. Here is a selection of his answers:

LIONEL said: I frankly am not clear on the extent to which suspects come into this matter. It has been indicated several times that police at Heathrow can operate without being suspicious. When exactly are they expected to operate?

ALAN RUSBRIDGER replied: You're right. In fact, the point of schedule 7 is that they are supposedly not 'suspects'. Because then the authorities would have to arrest them and they would have many rights they don't have as, er, non-suspects.

StopGMO said: Free speech must be maintained for ALL of us, not just 'reporters', so while we care about this abuse, make sure you are not just supporting 'reporters' rights, but speak up for your OWN. Do not let the greasy UN get its hands on the internet, and speak up for your rights, and the rights of reporters to furnish the truth. All two of the reporters who still bother to do that.

ALAN RUSBRIDGER replied: You're right of course: it's not just about reporters. But it would be a good start if more journalists saw what was potentially at risk here ...

AlanC said: If you meekly give into their demands without insisting that they take you to court then you've as good as admitted that they can do whatever they like as far as the UK press is concerned. Now if you had made that story a front-page feature the day after it happened then you might have a point but, as far as I can remember, there was nary a cheep.

ALAN RUSBRIDGER replied: Play out the scenario for me in which fighting this case in court would have enabled us to do a better job of reporting the Snowden documents. I'm not sure I quite see it ...

CROWFOOT said: OK Alan, There's a tide of us ordinary folks out here, shocked witless, cross, affronted by the degree to which basic democratic rights have been usurped, and fully support the *Guardian*'s David stance against Goliath. But what does one proactively do with one's anger? How can we help? How to galvanise the public's response?

ALAN RUSBRIDGER replied: Keeping reading the *Guardian* ... and I suppose you could support Snowden's defence fund.

ISKRA1903 said: Is it possible, Mr Rusbridger, for you to acknowledge that the people who held Mr Miranda may have done so with the aim of preventing their efforts to prevent a terrorist attack being compromised? They may well have transgressed their legal powers, and their actions (and the governance over those actions) does indeed need to be scrutinised. But your article only permits the conclusion that these people are acting in bad faith, and abusing their powers in an Orwellian fashion.

ALAN RUSBRIDGER replied: As the article says, there's a balancing act to be done between security, freedom of speech, privacy, etc. But it's impossible to have that debate without informed knowledge. For another point of view – in the *Guardian* – try the article by David Omand, former head of GCHQ, which defends the monitoring provided safeguards are met.

GMAN79 said: It's called a D Notice. And even if the *Guardian* had been issued with one, they wouldn't be able to tell us.

ALAN RUSBRIDGER replied: That's not quite how DA Notices operate. They are actually standing notices, available online. They did (ill-advisedly imho) circulate a reminder of them when the Snowden allegations broke. But there was no 'ban' and it didn't stop us from reporting the NSA or GCHQ stories.

DPERTH said: Why the basement and who chose to go there? It adds a nice eleement of the macabre to the story – or is that how spooks always work. (Interestingly, I have just finished reading Le Carré's *A Small Town in Germany* and that has scenes of unauthorised secretive work being carried out in a British Embassy basement).

ALAN RUSBRIDGER replied: Really smashing up computers turns out to be quite messy work ...

20 AUGUST

Egypt's cruellest week

PATRICK KINGSLEY

The police lieutenant put his boots up on the desk and casually reloaded his machine gun. 'The problem is,' he said, nodding at a television that was live-broadcasting the siege of a nearby mosque, 'these people are terrorists.' It was mid-afternoon last Saturday, and for nearly 24 hours, the lieutenant's colleagues in the police and army had surrounded the al-Fath mosque in central Cairo, inside which were hiding a few hundred supporters of ousted president Mohamed Morsi. On screen, it seemed like it was the soldiers doing the terrorising. But for the lieutenant, the terrorists were the ones on the inside. They had bombs, the policeman said: they deserved what they got. And a mob of locals agreed. 'The police and the people,' chanted a crowd that had gathered to lynch the fugitives as they exited the mosque, 'are one hand.'

It was a wretched scene – but one that has become familiar in Egypt. Here was yet another symptom of the widespread hatred of the Muslim Brotherhood, which in the space of a year has gone from being Egypt's most powerful and most popular political group to fugitives. Here, also, was brutal violence. A shortage of humanity. And above all: scant regard for the truth.

For those inside the mosque were not terrorists. An armed man may have later been filmed on top of the minaret, but the mosque's imam claimed access to it was controlled by security forces who had by that point breached parts of the building. For certain, when I visited the mosque the day before – shortly before troops surrounded it – it mainly housed doctors and corpses. After the police fired on nearby Morsi supporters – who had gathered to oppose not just the 3 July overthrow of the group's scion, Mohamed Morsi, but also the massacre of hundreds of Morsi backers last Wednesday – the mosque had been turned into a makeshift field hospital to deal with the fallout of Egypt's fourth mass killing in six weeks. 'After they finish outside, [the police] will come in here,' a doctor, Mahmoud el-Hout, said, 'and arrest all the wounded.' He wasn't far wrong, with only women and the dead later granted a safe exit.

Inside and outside the mosque, then, two parallel realities existed – much as they do across Egypt as a whole. The country is largely polarised between, on the one hand, those who believe their livelihoods and way of life were threatened under Morsi's incompetent and divisive presidency, and that his Muslim Brotherhood are violent traitors who must be destroyed and, on the other, the Brotherhood and its dwindling Islamist allies, who remained camped in Cairo's streets after Morsi's ousting to defend his democratic legitimacy.

The split is not even. Millions marched on 30 June to call for Morsi's departure, and the vast majority of the country is firmly behind the army who deposed him days later. But perhaps less than 25 per cent of Egyptians now have strong Islamist leanings, if Morsi's quarter of the vote in the first round of last year's presidential elections is anything to go by.

Here and there, activists prominent from the 2011 uprising that toppled Hosni Mubarak reject this binary division and express disgust at both the new fascistic army-backed regime and the authoritarianism of Morsi's own government. Army rule may be counter-revolutionary, they argue, accompanied as it is by a return to favour of figures, institutions and policies that buttressed the Mubarak era. But so too was Morsi, who tried to co-opt corrupt state institutions, rather than reform them and who had little interest in building consensus, reining in police brutality, or increasing social freedoms beyond those of his once-oppressed Islamist allies.

Yet few share this nuance. Most so-called liberals have thrown their lot in with the army, since the current environment has forced almost everyone into a with-or-against-us mindset. When Mohamed ElBaradei, Egypt's leading liberal politician, resigned as interim vice-president in protest at last Wednesday's massacre of Islamists, he was roundly attacked, even by former allies. Sayed Bedawy, leader of Egypt's oldest liberal party, told a breakfast show that he didn't want to call ElBaradei a traitor before strongly implying that he was. 'Mohamed ElBaradei is a son of a bitch,' summarised one woman in the mob outside the al-Fath mosque on Saturday.

Haranguing Western media's lack of support for the army's crackdown, an otherwise measured psychologist recently told me that he felt Muslim Brotherhood members – many of whom have obediently remained in the streets on the say-so of their leaders – were suffering from some sort of collective psychosis. Yet if the Brothers are delusional, then it seems only fair to apply the same rhetoric to their opponents, who seem to be under an equally debilitating spell.

Spurred on by a jingoistic and uninquiring media (some Egyptian television presenters cried with joy on air the day Morsi was overthrown) much of Egyptian society is convinced that the former president's supporters are wholly a terrorist force bent on making Egypt part of some wider Islamic state. 'We are not against any protesters but we are against terrorists. We have a war with terrorists,' says Mohamed Khamis, a spokesman for Tamarod, the grassroots campaign that successfully encouraged millions to march against Morsi in June.

Khamis said he accompanied the police last Wednesday, when security forces murdered hundreds at two six-week-old pro-Morsi campsites. 'We asked the police officers to shoot them with pistols and the police officers refused to shoot them,' Khamis counter-claimed. 'Really, that was what happened. So I am surprised people died. How come so many people died then? I think it was the Brotherhood who killed them, not the army or police.'

But while the Brotherhood is no stranger to violence – not least during clashes last December outside the presidential palace when Brotherhood members attacked anti-Morsi protesters – their recent involvement in acts of aggression, to be fair, remains unproved. Certainly, jihadi insurgents outside the Brotherhood's command – but nevertheless angered by Morsi's removal – have mounted a terrorist campaign in the lawless Sinai peninsula during the past six weeks.

Twenty-five police conscripts were murdered in cold blood by Sinai insurgents on Monday. Undeniably, Morsi sympathisers of some form have attacked dozens of police stations since Wednesday's massacre – and desecrated at least 30 Christian churches, following prolonged sectarian incitement from some Morsi supporters at Brotherhood-led sit-ins over the past month. And if the crackdown against the Brotherhood and its allies continues, it is hard to see how more extremist violence can be avoided.

But the central charges – that most Brotherhood supporters are violent, that their two huge protest camps were simply overgrown terrorist cells, and that their brutal suppression was justified and even restrained – are not supported by facts. My experience during six weeks of reporting at Rabaa al-Adawiya in Cairo suggested the vast majority of protesters there – including many women and children – were peaceful. Many may have failed to face up to Morsi's own incompetence and autocratic governance, and some may have turned too blind an eye to sectarian attacks recently completed in their name. Others have actively incited them. On the day of the coup, an imam from Minya, in southern (or 'Upper') Egypt, ominously said backstage at Rabaa: 'It's going to be a civil war and it's going to be very bad in particular for the church in Upper Egypt, because everyone knows they have spearheaded this campaign against the Islamic project.' Anti-Morsi sentiment stems from both Muslims and Christians, but some members of the Brotherhood have disgracefully scapegoated and attacked the latter.

But many Rabaa protesters have simple, sincere reasons for their anger: they are upset at the theft of their votes, and fearful of a return to the anti-Islamist oppression of the Mubarak era. 'We all voted for democracy,' housewife Aza Galal told me last week, six-year-old son Saif in tow. 'And then, because some people gathered in Tahrir Square [on 30 June], they put our votes in the rubbish bins.' Morsi's government hardly promoted the wider democratic values on which a successful democracy relies but Galal's anger is understandable: Morsi or his allies won five consecutive votes between 2011 and 2012.

'If we leave the square, it will be worse than the nineties,' added Suzanne Abdel Qadir, referring to Mubarak's treatment of Islamists. 'We're back to the days of oppression under Mubarak. If we go home, then the fight is over.'

The pro-regime propaganda comes right from the top. On Sunday, Egypt's state information service published a public memorandum to foreign correspondents in Egypt, rebuking Western media for failing to acknowledge that the 3 July coup reflected the will of the people, and for being overly sympathetic to the Brotherhood – apparently unable to distinguish between support for Morsi's disastrous and autocratic presidency, and criticism for the flagrant human rights abuses of his successors. Among many other false claims, it justified the siege of two mosques used by pro-Morsi doctors last week to house, respectively, a makeshift morgue and a field hospital on the grounds that they had, in fact, harboured terrorists.

As one journalist noted, such claims would have been amusing had they not further endangered the lives of foreign journalists in Egypt (several of whom have been either assaulted, detained, or even killed last week while trying to cover Egyptian news) and had they not flown in the face of the truth. At the Iman mosque, where hundreds of dead bodies were taken from the site of one of the massacres on Thursday, there were no insurgents – just corpses. Filling the floor of the mosque in its entirety, many of them had already begun to rot, and one was so badly burnt that it looked less like a body and more like a blackened tree stump. Doctors said it was the remains of a boy in his early teens and an old woman squatted beside it in the belief it was her lost relative. But only its sunken eye-sockets and internal organs identified the corpse as that of a human.

The next day, at the al-Fath mosque, there were again no obvious terrorists, but simply unarmed and injured protesters, many of whom were bleeding to death. One man, Mohamed Said, was carried in, barely conscious, a gunshot wound to his back, and leant against a pillar. Then his head slumped, and doctors rolled his eyelids shut.

Egypt has been awash with cruelty from the desecration of Christian churches by Islamists, to the burning of corpses at

Rabaa. But perhaps the most heartbreaking sight has been the street outside the Zeinhom morgue, Cairo's main mortuary. Due to the massacres, morgue staff, already severely stretched, struggle to deal with the unprecedented number of bodies arriving for autopsies. As a result, dozens of grieving families have clogged the street outside, their dead relatives rotting in the heat. A curfew is in place in Cairo, but families dare not leave the queue until their relatives are admitted to the morgue, decomposing though they may be. 'Curse the curfew,' said Atef Fatih, whose brother was shot dead last week. 'We don't care about it. We will wait until they let the body inside.'

Some pile the coffins high with slabs of ice to stop the rot. But the ice melts fast, leaving the ground a sludgy mess of mud, blood and corpses. To add to the injustice, many families report that the police have refused to sign off their corpses as murder. Humanity and truth are in short supply.

And nor are they the only virtues to have been sacrificed in Egypt. So too have logic and common sense. Amid the rhetoric about Islamic terrorism, few seem to recognise that most of the terrorising has in fact come from the state. The government justifies the state-sponsored violence as a necessary step towards avoiding civil war. But it does not seem to realise that its provocative brutality is the thing that makes such a horrific outcome more likely, further alienating and radicalising Islamists, and pushing some towards violence. (One commentator suggests that this may, in fact, be the state's desired outcome – a heightening of extremist violence, which gives the government more cover to increase their powers.) Similarly, few seem to have seen the irony in appointing a new cabinet whose primary objective is to fix Egypt's economy, but which has since given its full backing to the state massacres that have further frightened away the very investors on which a revived economy would depend.

With the state seemingly unwilling to rein in its violence, the Brotherhood unlikely to curtail its street presence, and unwilling or unable to prevent its allies and harder-line followers from violence, the future looks utterly bleak. Here and there, there are moments of fleeting dark humour. Egypt's leading private broadsheet, *al-Masry al-Youm*, published last week an interview with a Republican 'senator', one Maurice Bonamigo, a man very approving of Egypt's controversial new domestic direction – but one who also sadly later emerged to have never been elected to higher office.

There have also been moments of unexpected personal kindness. They range from the soldier photographed aiding a grieving woman during last Wednesday's massacres to the police lieutenant who, putting his machine gun to one side and switching off his television, handed me a carton of guava juice – bringing to an end a two-hour-long detention at the hands of both police officers and an angry mob of vigilantes. 'You are welcome in Egypt,' the lieutenant said, and smiled.

22 AUGUST

Country Diary

CHRISTINE SMITH

This morning the rock by the path that leads out of the trees is sheltered from the breeze and, with its smooth, slightly hollowed surface, it's an inviting place to sit for a while to enjoy the sunshine.

Relaxing in the warmth with face upturned and eyes closed I immediately become more aware of the sounds about me. Insect activity provides a background drone, the constant soft hum interspersed now and then with higher-pitched whinings and louder buzzings as individuals explore the plants and flowers closer to where I am sitting.

Beyond the sound of the insects there are the noises of birds too; the faint mewing of a buzzard somewhere high above, the repeated tac-tac of a wren, a willow warbler momentarily reprising its spring song.

But it's the dry rattling vibration of wings close by that causes me to start and my eyes to fly open – just in time to catch sight of the dragonfly as it darts past. It's a common hawker, making its way along the tallest of the pathside vegetation following the line of the damp ditch in a series of dashes and hovering pauses, with bright blue markings and glittering wings reflecting tiny shards of brilliant sunshine.

Now with open eyes, I become aware of the silent flyers too. Over a few minutes, a succession of green-veined white butterflies fly jauntily past. A single meadow brown flutters for a short distance above the shorter grass and then lands on the path at my feet and comes to rest with wings closed.

And just as the birds played a part in the sounds of the morning, so they have their place in this quiet too. Yet it's not the half-expected high-soaring eagle that appears when I at last look up, but a young hen harrier drifting down on soundless wings from the moorland, above to glide low over the young trees before disappearing from view.

Saturday Poem: Deer

HELEN MORT

The deer my mother swears to God we never saw,
the ones that stepped between the trees
on pound-coin-coloured hooves,
I'd bring them up each teatime in the holidays

and they were brighter every time I did;
more supple than the otters we waited for
at Ullapool, more graceful than the kingfisher
that darned the river south of Rannoch Moor.

Five years on, in that same house, I rose
for water in the middle of the night and watched
my mother at the window, looking out
to where the forest lapped the garden's edge.

From where she stood, I saw them stealing
through the pines and they must have been closer
than before, because I had no memory
of those fish-bone ribs, that ragged fur,
their eyes, like hers, that flickered back
towards whatever followed them.

From Division Street, *published by Chatto & Windus*

10 September

On the diplomatic moves
to ease the Syrian crisis

STEVE BELL

Copyright ©Steve Bell 2013 www.belltoons.co.uk/reuse

Envoi: 19 December

Christmas leftovers: turkey and ham pie with brussels sprout salad and cranberry vinaigrette recipe

FELICITY CLOAKE

The Bedside Guardian *is often chosen as a Christmas present, so I trust that readers will forgive the anachronism if I end with Felicity Cloake's tips from last December on how to turn the seasonal debris into something good and northern: a pie for 2014.*

Pies are a godsend to the harassed post-Christmas cook: the ingrates might turn up their noses at yet another platter of cold cuts post Boxing Day, but stick them under a golden halo of pastry and they'll fall upon them like ravenous wolves.

If you don't have any ham, feel free to use an extra 100g of turkey instead, or stir in a couple of chopped leeks if you're not making the accompanying salad – soften them in butter first. And a word on that salad: don't knock it until you've tried it. After all, if raw cabbage can work in a coleslaw ...

SERVES 4

For the pie:
400g roast turkey or other poultry
100g ham
25g butter

2 tbsp plain flour

150ml chicken or turkey stock, or leftover gravy

200ml milk

3 tbsp cream (either single or double, whatever you have left
over)

225g puff pastry

Flour, to dust

1 egg, beaten

For the salad:

400g raw brussels sprouts, trimmed

Handful of pecans, roughly chopped

6 tbsp olive oil

2 tbsp balsamic vinegar

3 tbsp fresh cranberry sauce

Zest of ½ orange

Tear the turkey into evenly sized pieces, and roughly chop the ham. Preheat the oven to 180°C.

Melt the butter in a medium saucepan over a low heat, and stir in the flour. Cook, stirring, for a couple of minutes, then slowly whisk in the stock or gravy and the milk to make a smooth paste. Simmer gently for about 10 minutes until thickened, then add the cream and season to taste. Add the meat, and pour into a pie dish.

Roll out the pastry on a lightly floured surface until about 5mm thick, and brush the rim of the pie dish with beaten egg. Place the pastry on top, and press down around the rim, then trim off the excess – you can use these scraps to decorate the top of the pie if you like. Poke a hole in the middle to let the steam out, and brush with beaten egg.

Bake for about 30 minutes, until the pastry is golden and well puffed up.

Meanwhile, make the salad. Shred the sprouts finely, and place in a salad bowl with the pecans. Whisk together the oil and vinegar, then stir in the cranberry sauce and orange zest. Season well, and pour over the sprouts, then toss to coat. Serve alongside the pie.

Solution to crossword on page 93

Index